Welcome to
HISTORY
★★★★★★★★★★ *of the* ★★★★★★★★★★
UNITED STATES

Though in the grand scheme of things it remains a young nation, there can be no underestimating the significance of the United States of America. Perhaps more than any other country in the last two centuries, the US has affected the world we live in profoundly, through its people, its policies, and its military power. In this bookazine we'll highlight some of the iconic leaders, fierce conflicts and unforgettable events that have come to define this great nation. From the country's revolutionary origins to its rise to superpower status, you'll find expert features here complemented by some truly stunning imagery. Read on to discover the fascinating history of the most powerful nation in the world.

HISTORY
of the
UNITED STATES

Future PLC Richmond House, 33 Richmond Hill,
Bournemouth, Dorset, BH2 6EZ

Editorial
Editor **Sarah Bankes**
Designer **Emma Birch**
Editorial Director **Jon White**
Senior Art Editor **Andy Downes**

All copyrights and trademarks are recognised and respected

Cover Images
Getty, Thinkstock

Advertising
Media packs are available on request
Commercial Director **Clare Dove**
clare.dove@futurenet.com

International
International Licensing Director **Matt Ellis**
matt.ellis@futurenet.com

Circulation
Head of Newstrade **Tim Mathers**

Production
Head of Production **Mark Constance**
Production Project Manager **Clare Scott**
Advertising Production Manager **Joanne Crosby**
Digital Editions Controller **Jason Hudson**
Production Managers **Keely Miller, Nola Cokely,
Vivienne Calvert, Fran Twentyman**

Management
Chief Operations Officer **Aaron Asadi**
Commercial Finance Director **Dan Jotcham**
Head of Art & Design **Greg Whitaker**

Printed by William Gibbons, 26 Planetary Road,
Willenhall, West Midlands, WV13 3XT

Distributed by Marketforce, 5 Churchill Place, Canary Wharf, London, E14 5HU
www.marketforce.co.uk Tel: 0203 787 9001

History of the United States Second Edition
© 2018 Future Publishing Limited

Future plc is a public   Chief executive **Zillah Byng-Thorne**
company quoted on the   Chairman **Richard Huntingford**
London Stock Exchange   Chief financial officer **Penny Ladkin-Brand**
(symbol: FUTR)
www.futureplc.com   Tel +44 (0)1225 442 244

Part of the
ALL ABOUT
HISTORY
bookazine series

CONTENTS

Founding Fathers

War & Reconstruction

22

158

The Birth of a Superpower

A New Era

State facts & figures

Do you know your state capitals and other interesting facts?

1 WASHINGTON
Date admitted to the Union: 11/11/1889
Capital: Olympia
Largest city: Seattle
Nickname: Evergreen State
State Mammal: Olympic Marmot

2 OREGON
Date admitted to the Union: 14/02/1859
Capital: Salem
Largest city: Portland
Nickname: Beaver State
State Mammal: American Beaver

3 CALIFORNIA
Date admitted to the Union: 09/09/1850
Capital: Sacramento
Largest city: Los Angeles
Nickname: Golden State
State Mammal: California Grizzly Bear

10 MONTANA
Date admitted to the Union: 08/11/1889
Capital: Helena
Largest city: Billings
Nickname: Treasure State
State Bird: Western Meadowlark

11 COLORADO
Date admitted to the Union: 01/08/1876
Capital: Denver
Largest city: Denver
Nickname: Centennial State
State Reptile: Western Painted Turtle

12 NEW MEXICO
Date admitted to the Union: 06/01/1912
Capital: Santa Fe
Largest city: Albuquerque
Nickname: The Land of Enchantment
State Mammal: Black Bear

13 NORTH DAKOTA
Date admitted to the Union: 02/11/1889
Capital: Bismarck
Largest city: Fargo
Nickname: Peace Garden State
State Fish: Northern Pike

14 SOUTH DAKOTA
Date admitted to the Union: 02/11/1889
Capital: Pierre
Largest city: Sioux Falls
Nickname: Mount Rushmore State
State Mammal: Coyote

15 NEBRASKA
Date admitted to the Union: 01/03/1867
Capital: Lincoln
Largest city: Omaha
Nickname: Cornhusker State
State Mammal: White-tailed Deer

16 KANSAS
Date admitted to the Union: 29/01/1861
Capital: Topeka
Largest city: Wichita
Nickname: Sunflower State
State Reptile: Ornate Box Turtle

17 OKLAHOMA
Date admitted to the Union: 16/11/1907
Capital: Oklahoma City
Largest city: Oklahoma City
Nickname: Sooner State
State Mammal: Bison

18 TEXAS
Date admitted to the Union: 29/12/1845
Capital: Austin
Largest city: Houston
Nickname: Lone Star State
State Mammal: Armadillo

19 MINNESOTA
Date admitted to the Union: 11/05/1858
Capital: Saint Paul
Largest city: Minneapolis
Nickname: North Star State
State Bird: Common Loon

20 IOWA
Date admitted to the Union: 28/12/1846
Capital: Des Moines
Largest city: Des Moines
Nickname: Hawkeye State
State Bird: American Goldfinch

21 MISSOURI
Date admitted to the Union: 10/08/1821
Capital: Jefferson City
Largest city: Kansas City
Nickname: Show Me State
State Mammal: Missouri Mule

22 ARKANSAS
Date admitted to the Union: 15/06/1836
Capital: Little Rock
Largest city: Little Rock
Nickname: Natural State
State Bird: Northern Mockingbird

23 LOUISIANA
Date admitted to the Union: 30/04/1812
Capital: Baton Rouge
Largest city: New Orleans
Nickname: Pelican State
State Bird: Brown Pelican

24 WISCONSIN
Date admitted to the Union: 29/05/1848
Capital: Madison
Largest city: Milwaukee
Nickname: Badger State
State Fish: Bluegill

25 ILLINOIS
Date admitted to the Union: 03/12/1818
Capital: Springfield
Largest city: Chicago
Nickname: Prairie State
State Fish: Bluegill

26 KENTUCKY
Date admitted to the Union: 01/06/1792
Capital: Frankfort
Largest city: Louisville
Nickname: Bluegrass State
State Mammal: Grey Squirrel

27 TENNESSEE
Date admitted to the Union: 01/06/1796
Capital: Nashville
Largest city: Nashville
Nickname: Volunteer State
State Mammal: Raccoon

ALASKA
Date admitted to the Union: 03/01/1959
Capital: Juneau
Largest city: Anchorage
Nickname: The Last Frontier
State Mammal: Moose

IDAHO
Date admitted to the Union: 03/07/1890
Capital: Boise
Largest city: Boise
Nickname: Gem State
State Mammal: Appaloosa Horse

NEVADA
Date admitted to the Union: 31/10/1864
Capital: Carson City
Largest city: Las Vegas
Nickname: Silver State
State Mammal: Desert Bighorn Sheep

ARIZONA
Date admitted to the Union: 14/02/1912
Capital: Phoenix
Largest city: Phoenix
Nickname: Grand Canyon State
State Mammal: Cactus Wren

UTAH
Date admitted to the Union: 04/01/1896
Capital: Salt Lake City
Largest city: Salt Lake City
Nickname: Beehive State
State Mammal: Rocky Mountain Elk

WYOMING
Date admitted to the Union: 10/07/1890
Capital: Cheyenne
Largest city: Cheyenne
Nickname: Equality State
State Mammal: Bison

WEST VIRGINIA
Date admitted to the Union: 20/06/1863
Capital: Charleston
Largest city: Charleston
Nickname: Mountain State
State Mammal: Black Bear

GEORGIA
Date admitted to the Union: 02/01/1788
Capital: Atlanta
Largest city: Atlanta
Nickname: Peach State
State Mammal: Right Whale

NEW YORK
Date admitted to the Union: 26/07/1788
Capital: Albany
Largest city: New York City
Nickname: Empire State
State Mammal: Beaver

PENNSYLVANIA
Date admitted to the Union: 12/12/1787
Capital: Harrisburg
Largest city: Philadelphia
Nickname: Keystone State
State Bird: Ruffed Grouse

MARYLAND
Date admitted to the Union: 28/04/1788
Capital: Annapolis
Largest city: Baltimore
Nickname: Old Line State
State Mammal: Calico Cat

VIRGINIA
Date admitted to the Union: 25/06/1788
Capital: Richmond
Largest city: Virginia Beach
Nickname: Old Dominion
State Mammal: American Foxhound

NORTH CAROLINA
Date admitted to the Union: 21/11/1789
Capital: Raleigh
Largest city: Charlotte
Nickname: Old North State
State Mammal: Virginia Opossum

SOUTH CAROLINA
Date admitted to the Union: 23/05/1788
Capital: Columbia
Largest city: Charleston
Nickname: Palmetto State
State Mammal: White-tailed Deer

FLORIDA
Date admitted to the Union: 03/03/1845
Capital: Tallahassee
Largest city: Jacksonville
Nickname: Sunshine State
State Mammal: Florida Panther

VERMONT
Date admitted to the Union: 04/03/1791
Capital: Montpelier
Largest city: Burlington
Nickname: Green Mountain State
State Mammal: Morgan Horse

NEW HAMPSHIRE
Date admitted to the Union: 21/06/1788
Capital: Concord
Largest city: Manchester
Nickname: Granite State
State Bird: Purple Finch

MISSISSIPPI
Date admitted to the Union: 10/12/1817
Capital: Jackson
Largest city: Jackson
Nickname: Magnolia State
State Mammal: White-tailed Deer

MICHIGAN
Date admitted to the Union: 26/01/1837
Capital: Lansing
Largest city: Detroit
Nickname: Great Lakes State
State Reptile: Painted Turtle

ALABAMA
Date admitted to the Union: 14/12/1819
Capital: Montgomery
Largest city: Birmingham
Nickname: The Heart of Dixie
State Mammal: Black Bear

MASSACHUSETTS
Date admitted to the Union: 06/02/1788
Capital: Boston
Largest city: Boston
Nickname: Bay State
State Mammal: Boston Terrier

CONNECTICUT
Date admitted to the Union: 09/01/1788
Capital: Hartford
Largest city: Bridgeport
Nickname: Constitution State
State Mammal: Sperm Whale

NEW JERSEY
Date admitted to the Union: 18/12/1787
Capital: Trenton
Largest city: Newark
Nickname: Garden State
State Mammal: Horse

HAWAII
Date admitted to the Union: 21/08/1959
Capital: Honolulu
Largest city: Honolulu
Nickname: The Aloha State
State Mammal: Hawaiian Monk Seal

INDIANA
Date admitted to the Union: 11/12/1816
Capital: Indianapolis
Largest city: Indianapolis
Nickname: Hoosier State
State Bird: Cardinal

OHIO
Date admitted to the Union: 01/03/1803
Capital: Columbus
Largest city: Columbus
Nickname: Buckeye State
State Mammal: White-tailed Deer

DELAWARE
Date admitted to the Union: 07/12/1787
Capital: Dover
Largest city: Wilmington
Nickname: First State
State Mammal: Blue Hen Chicken

MAINE
Date admitted to the Union: 15/03/1820
Capital: Augusta
Largest city: Portland
Nickname: Pine Tree State
State Mammal: Moose

RHODE ISLAND
Date admitted to the Union: 09/02/1778
Capital: Providence
Largest city: Providence
Nickname: Ocean State
State Bird: Rhode Island Red

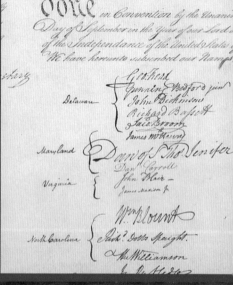

FOUNDING FATHERS

From colonisation to revolution and beyond, follow the formative years of the ascendant United States of America

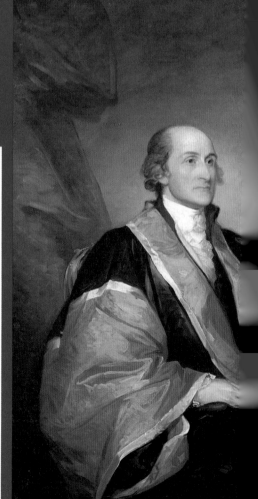

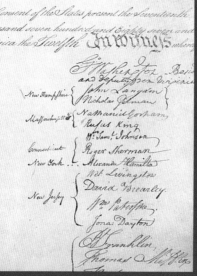

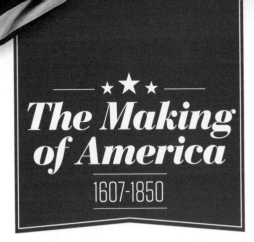

The Making of America
1607-1850

That $15 million price tag included a cancellation of debts worth $3,750,000 and and a payment of a whopping $11,250,000

30 April 1803
The Louisiana Purchase

Few events in American history hold as much significance as the deal signed between Thomas Jefferson and the kingdom of France. For $15 million dollars (that's £233 million in modern-day money), the United States government gained control of an incredibly vast and intimidating territory that had been in both Spanish and French hands for centuries. The Louisiana Purchase unified the previously divided East and West coasts with a wild frontier full of native tribes, barely reaped natural resources and endless potential.

For years, France and Spain had fought for control of the territory, and as such had done little to properly map and explore its mountains, forests, prairies and deserts. When Spain eventually signed a secret treaty to hand over control of Louisiana to the French, the Americans feared French leader Napoleon Bonaparte would use the land to stop the British from accessing the Gulf

of Mexico, ending American expansion along the Mississippi River. However, France's failure to put down a bloody coup in Haiti and its looming war with Britain forced it to approach the US government with a proposal to sell the land in its entirety.

That 828,000 square miles of land contained what would become modern-day Iowa, Nebraska, Arkansas, Kansas, Missouri and Oklahoma. It comprised territories as far north as Montana (and even included parts of Canadian provinces such as Alberta and Saskatchewan) and as far south as New Orleans. The deal finally unified the nation as a territorial whole, and proved a true turning point in American history, one that transformed the United States from the New World into a Wild West of new opportunity and danger. And for Thomas Jefferson, the third President of the United States, it would become the crowning achievement of his presidency.

> With one single deal, the United States unlocked a third of its land mass. And so the Frontier was born

Defining moments

The First Great Awakening 1730-1755
The first of four periods where the United States saw a significant rise in religious revivalism, the First Great Awakening created a schism in British America between traditional Protestants and revivalists who believed faith deserved a more personal connection to God. Evangelical by nature, the movement changed Anglicanism in America forever.

Lewis and Clark's expedition May 1804
Barely a year after the Louisiana Purchase, the United States had grown in size by almost a third. An avid scientist and explorer, president Thomas Jefferson quickly commissioned his private secretary Meriwether Lewis and former soldier William Clark to begin a two-year-long journey across the Frontier, documenting everything from local wildlife and indigenous populations to creating basic maps.

The Monroe Doctrine 2 December 1823
When James Monroe, the fifth President of the United States, addressed Congress with what would become known as the Monroe Doctrine, his words sent shockwaves across the Atlantic. The speech was an informal declaration of independence for the Americas, with Monroe stating that any further European attempts to control the continents would be, "the manifestation of an unfriendly disposition toward the United States."

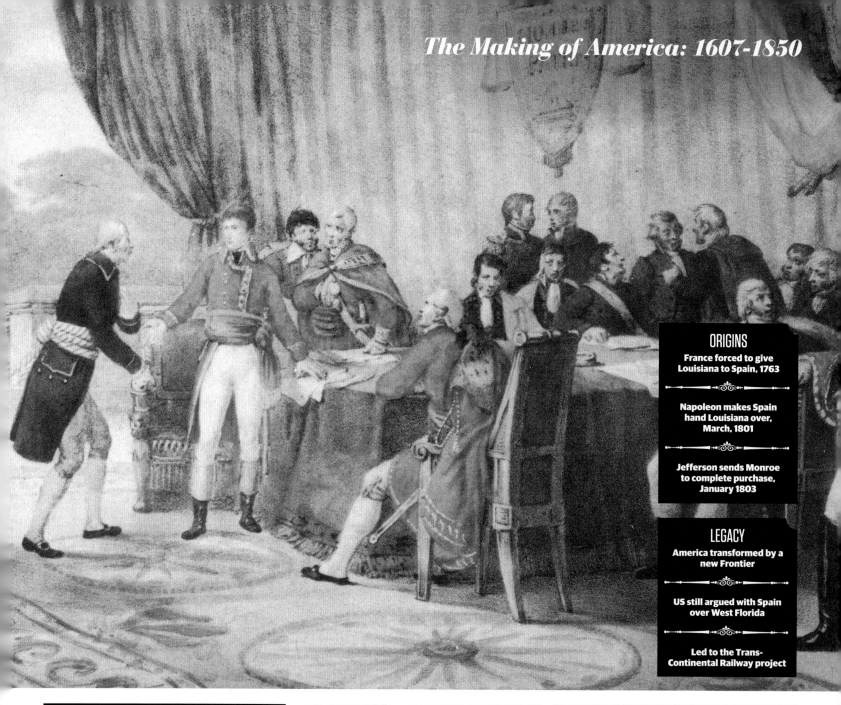

ORIGINS

France forced to give Louisiana to Spain, 1763

Napoleon makes Spain hand Louisiana over, March, 1801

Jefferson sends Monroe to complete purchase, January 1803

LEGACY

America transformed by a new Frontier

US still argued with Spain over West Florida

Led to the Trans-Continental Railway project

The Second Party System
1828-1854

By 1828, interest in voting had increased significantly enough among the American people to see two political parties rise to prominence. The Democratic Party was one, led by Andrew Jackson (future seventh president) in its earliest iteration, while their rivals formed into the Whig Party, led by Henry Clay. Clay established the Whig Party to directly oppose the Democrats, but failed to overcome his political foes.

The Panic of 1837
10 May, 1837

By the middle of 1837, the United States had slipped into a financial crisis as prices skyrocketed and unemployment along with it. Morale among the American people had dropped to a new low as banks collapsed and businesses fell into ruin across the nation. Caused mainly by imbalanced lending policies in Great Britain and a bursting land price bubble, the recession lasted for a whole seven years.

The California Gold Rush
24 January 1848

Almost half a century after the Louisiana Purchase, budding prospector James W Marshall discovered gold at Sutter's Mill in Coloma, California. His revelation sent the nation - and the rest of the world - into a frenzy as they descended on California in search of golden riches. Over 300,000 people arrived in the state, with the American economy revitalised as a result. The Gold Rush years had begun...

The Boston Tea Party was the colonial act of defiance that spurred the closing of the port of Boston

Colonisation & conflict

Centuries of British exploration and colonisation gave rise to revolution and a course toward independence among its North American colonies

European exploration and settlement in the New World were initiated for a variety of reasons: the search for a trade route to the Far East, gold fever, lust for land, and sheer adventure. By the mid-16th century, French settlements were established along the coast of present-day Canada and the Great Lakes. Spain had founded the first permanent European settlement at St Augustine, Florida, in 1565.

A curious blend of altruism, potential profit, and preservation of prestige spurred Great Britain to become involved in the colonial exercise. There were thousands of 'primitive heathens', natives who had not heard the Christian gospel, in America. It was the duty of the Christian church, some said, to convert these 'Indians'. North America's treasure and abundant resources were there to be exploited, and rival European powers were apparently on their way to establishing vast territorial empires in the New World.

For Britain, the establishment of colonies in North America might help it to fulfil its own ambitions. Spanish merchant shipping could be harassed from newly established ports, raw materials harvested to feed British industry, and surely tax revenues would increase. On 25 March

1584, Queen Elizabeth I granted a charter to Sir Walter Raleigh to colonise North America. Its intent was direct: Raleigh was to "discover, search, find out, and view such remote heathen and barbarous Lands, Countries, and territories ... to have, hold, occupy, and enjoy."

The following summer, Raleigh dispatched a group of 108 settlers to the coast of present-day North Carolina, where they established a colony on Roanoke Island, building simple shelters within the confines of a protective fort, planting crops, and exploring the vicinity. However, terrible weather – possibly even a hurricane – disease, and attacks from hostile natives doomed the attempt. Within a year the survivors of the venture returned to England.

Undaunted, Raleigh tried again in 1587, sending 118 settlers back to Roanoke under John White. A few weeks later, White returned to England to gather additional supplies. He returned to Roanoke in 1591 to find the colony completely abandoned with no sign of the inhabitants. The cryptic word 'CROATOAN', possibly a reference to another nearby island, had been scratched into a tree. The fate of the Roanoke Colony remains a mystery to this day. Although some historians surmise that the settlers were

> To date, no solid evidence has emerged to determine the ultimate fate of the settlers in the failed Roanoke Colony

© GettyImages

Rampaging Native Americans massacred settlers at Jamestown in 1622 and nearly wiped out the English settlement in Virginia

William Penn stands before King Charles II in 1680 in this painting titled the Birth of Pennsylvania by Jean Leon Gerome Ferris

assimilated into the native populations, murdered by them, or were wiped out completely by starvation and disease, no conclusive evidence has been discovered.

The Jamestown Colony was established in 1607, near present-day Williamsburg, after the Virginia Company of London was granted a charter to colonise the eastern part of North America (then known as 'Virginia') by King James I. However, the settlers were ill-prepared to deal with the privations of the wilderness. They constructed a crude fort in the midst of a swamp ridden with clouds of malaria-carrying mosquitoes, struggling to subsist on wild game and crops they planted - a number of the roughly 100 Englishmen were 'gentlemen' unaccustomed to any kind of manual labour.

The beleaguered settlers would likely have starved to death without the assistance of friendly Powhatan tribe, who assisted with agriculture and brought food to them. Even so, nearly 80 per cent of Jamestown's population perished during the harsh winter of 1609-1610, which came to be known as the 'Starving Time'. In 1612, tobacco

plants arrived from the West Indies, and the leaf developed into a viable cash crop, helping Jamestown to achieve a degree of permanence. Despite difficult relations with the local natives, which resulted in massacres and reciprocal raiding, the English gained a firm foothold in Virginia.

In 1620, Puritan religious refugees arrived in modern-day Massachusetts aboard the famed ship Mayflower. Popularly known as the 'Pilgrims', these settlers endured equally cruel starvation, hostile natives and disease. However, within a decade the population of the Massachusetts Bay colony had grown to nearly 2,000. For the next 80 years, an influx of English settlers populated the eastern coastline of the North American continent. When private ventures foundered, for example in Virginia in 1624, some territories become crown colonies.

In New Hampshire (part of Massachusetts until 1680), the first colony was founded in 1622. A Maryland colony was established in 1632, followed by others in Connecticut and Rhode Island in 1636. In 1663 Carolina, later divided north and south, was named in honour of King Charles II. Originally

settled by Dutch colonists, New Netherland was occupied by the English in 1664 and renamed New Jersey; its port city of New Amsterdam became New York, named after the Duke of York. Pennsylvania was founded by the Quaker William Penn in 1681. Delaware was granted self-government by Pennsylvania in 1682, and in 1732, the crown colony of Georgia was founded as a debtors' refuge.

With the acquiescence of the crown, the colonies elected legislative bodies. Some also

Timeline

1585

● **Misadventure at Roanoke**
Sir Walter Raleigh, commissioned by Queen Elizabeth, sends settlers to Roanoke Island off the coast of North Carolina. The venture fails twice and the fate of the settlers is unknown.
1585

● **Virginia Dare is born**
The first English child born in the Americas, Virginia Dare, arrives to parents Ananias Dare and Eleanor White. She is named after the colony of Virginia.
18 August 1587

● **Jamestown survives**
Founders of the first permanent English settlement in North America, the settlers of Jamestown battle famine and hardship to gain a foothold in the New World.
1607

Statue of Captain John Smith, a leader of the settlers at Jamestown

● **A place for Puritans**
Seeking freedom to practise their austere form of Christianity, the Puritans arrive at Plymouth in the Massachusetts Bay Colony aboard the ship Mayflower and endure hard times.
1620

● **The Navigation Acts**
To ensure that England profits from its investment in the colonies, the first in the series of Navigation Acts is implemented. Initially ignored, the acts are enforced a century later.
1650

● **War in North America**
Queen Anne's War, an 11-year extension of the European War of the Spanish Succession, erupts as Britain battles France and Spain; it gains substantial territory in North America.
1702

A soldier of the 29th Regiment of Foot, the unit involved in the Boston Massacre, stands with his musket

By 1650, a brisk trade developed between the colonies and with Britain. In distant London, Parliament passed the first of the Navigation Acts, intended to safeguard the flow of goods from the colonies and prevent trade with other nations that might impede the reaping of the nation's long-time investment in North America. Still, officials often looked the other way as smugglers and traders became wealthy while flaunting the statutes. Despite their own significant differences, new wealth, considerable freedom to govern themselves and an adventuresome spirit that compelled them to explore new frontiers fuelled within the colonists a sense of self-identity - something British but distinctly separate, perhaps even 'American'.

Throughout the 18th century, war and peace ebbed and flowed among the great powers of Europe, principally Britain, France and Spain. These

> To maximise colonial revenues, the Navigation Acts sought to prevent the colonies trading with other nations

elected governors, while the crown colonies were administered by an appointed governor and his officials. Colonists considered themselves British subjects in every respect.

Despite their common British heritage, the settlers of the 13 North American colonies were a diverse people. The continent was populated by Europeans, natives, and Negro slaves, first introduced by a Portuguese ship at Jamestown in 1619. As the colonies grew and settlement began to inexorably spread westward, the

southern colonies developed an agricultural economy as large, prosperous plantations produced cotton and tobacco for export. The middle colonies were distinctive, with many tradesmen, shippers and farmers. In New England, a budding industrial and maritime economy grew. While the colonists remained loyal to the king, a second generation, some of whom never ventured across the Atlantic, had been born and raised in North America.

Queen Anne became involved in the war to decide the Spanish succession

● **The Molasses Act**
In order to raise revenue, Parliament enacts the Molasses Act, a six pence per gallon tax on imports of molasses that did not originate in English colonies.
March 1733

● **Denouncing Parliament's tyranny**
As the Navigation Acts are enforced with renewed vigor, James Otis of Massachusetts resigns his post as the king's advocate general and calls the acts "instruments of tyranny."
1761

● **The French and Indian War ends**
The French and Indian War ends with British pre-eminence in North America. However, the coffers of the national treasury are depleted, prompting Parliament to seek new sources of revenue.
1763

Native Americans allied to the French ambush a British column

● **No westward settlement**
Veterans of the French and Indian War, promised land grants west of the Appalachians, are enraged when Parliament restricts settlement there.
1763

The Boston Massacre: ironic aftermath

At the time of the Boston Massacre, John Adams was a prominent attorney in the city. He later signed the Declaration of Independence, served as a delegate to the Continental Congress, and became the first vice president of the United States and the country's second president.

The so-called Boston Massacre was the result of a mob taunting a group of British soldiers until they feared for their lives and fired into the crowd. In its aftermath, Adams served as counsel for the defence as eight British soldiers were tried on charges of murdering five Bostonians. He was also defence co-counsel for the separate murder trial - from 24 October 1770 - of Captain Thomas Preston, commander of the troops.

The issue was whether Preston had ordered the soldiers to fire. After five days of testimony, the jury returned a verdict of not guilty. A majority of the jurors were Loyalists, and just two were actually from Boston.

A month later, the eight soldiers stood trial on five counts of murder in Massachusetts' Superior Court of Judicature. On 5 December, six were acquitted. Two, Montgomery and Kilroy, were convicted on a reduced charge of manslaughter for killing two of the demonstrators. Both were branded with the letter M for murder on the right thumb and rejoined their regiment.

No civil unrest followed the verdicts. On the third anniversary of the 'massacre', Adams wrote in his diary, "It was... one of the most gallant, generous, manly and disinterested Actions of my whole Life, and one of the best Pieces of Service I ever rendered my Country."

A fanciful engraving depicts the climactic event of the Boston Massacre, outside the Old State House on 5 March 1770

In this 1772 portrait by John Singleton Copley, revolutionary leader and propagandist Samuel Adams gestures defiantly

"A military presence in North America was still required to maintain a tenuous peace with hostile native tribes"

conflicts spread to North America as each power sought to expand its colonial empire. No fewer than four major conflicts erupted between 1689 and 1755. The most decisive of these, the French and Indian War - an extension of the Seven Years' War in Europe - ended with a British victory in 1763. Nearly 150 years of French colonisation in the New World was extinguished.

The great victory, however, had come at a tremendous price. The British Empire extended halfway around the world, and the financial burden of the prolonged wars had more than doubled the national debt. Parliament's attempts to increase taxes in Britain were met with violence in the streets of London. Predictably, the eyes of Parliament were cast across the sea to the prosperous colonies. Without question, the wars had been won with an army and navy financed by British taxpayers. A military presence in North America was still required to maintain a tenuous peace with hostile native tribes. The colonists had built a thriving economy with the tremendous

assistance of the crown and the country. Should they themselves not bear at least some of the burden, and pay for their own security and continuing prosperity?

Enacting a new policy toward the colonies, King George III, who remarked that he intended to "rule as well as reign," and Parliament sought to pacify Native American tribes with a 1763 proclamation that forbade the further settlement of lands west of the Appalachian Mountains. Strict enforcement of the existing Navigation Acts shut down previously profitable trade as seizures of property and searches of warehouses occurred without warrants. The old Molasses Act of 1733 was bolstered in 1764 with the Sugar Act, a direct threat to the lucrative rum trade carried on for years with the West Indies. In 1765, the Quartering Act asserted that 10,000 British troops would be stationed in the colonies and that the colonists themselves were responsible for their food, shelter and other needs.

That same year, the Stamp Act required any printed material in the colonies, from newspapers

The hated Stamp Act
One of numerous tax measures enacted by Parliament, the Stamp Act becomes the focus of riots in the colonies and a petition to King George III for relief from the provision.
1765

The Townshend Acts
Taxes on staples and everyday items in the colonies, including tin, tea, lead and other products, are enacted. Collectively, they bear the name of chancellor of the exchequer Charles Townshend.
1767

The Boston Massacre
Outside the Old State House, British soldiers are repeatedly harassed by an angry mob hurling snowballs, stones and insults. They fire into the crowd, killing five.
5 March 1770

A modern image of the Old State House, site of the Boston Massacre

Burning of Gaspee
After running aground while chasing the colonial packet ship Hannah, the customs schooner Gaspee is boarded and set afire by a cluster of irate Rhode Islanders in defiance of the Navigation Acts.
10 June 1772

The raiders row away from the burning hulk of the customs schooner Gaspee

to playing cards, to bear a royal stamp after the payment of a tax. In October 1765, representatives of nine colonies convened in New York to denounce the Stamp Act and organise a general boycott of goods imported from Britain. The outright defiance of the crown worked. The repeal of the Stamp Act in March 1766 was hailed as a triumph among colonists and no doubt contributed to the rising tide of separatist thought, even an American spirit rather than a 'Virginian' or 'New Yorker' perspective.

Firebrands, radicals and even-tempered statesmen alike were alarmed at the apparent tidal wave of taxation that continued even in the wake of the Stamp Act's repeal, particularly since the colonists themselves had no direct representatives in Parliament. 'No taxation without representation' became a familiar cry. In the great seaport of Boston, Massachusetts, Samuel Adams, a career politician, and John Hancock, a wealthy shipping magnate, subverted tax laws whenever possible, even assembling a group of activists called the Sons of Liberty to demonstrate, raid and otherwise harass the crown's interests in the colonies. In Virginia, the fiery and eloquent Patrick Henry railed against the excesses of the far-off government.

Nevertheless, Parliament persisted. Within months of the repeal of the Stamp Act, the Townshend Acts of 1767, named after chancellor of the exchequer Charles Townshend, imposed a litany of new taxes on a number of essential goods, including paper, tea, lead, glass and other popular commodities. Protests increased, and violence erupted. And the distance between crown and colonies grew. Then, on 5 March 1770, the same day as the horrific Boston Massacre, Parliament drew back from the brink of rebellion again, repealing all the Townshend Acts except the tax on tea.

Civil unrest continued as demonstrators in Rhode Island burned a customs schooner to the waterline, tax collectors were driven from their homes, and some were even tarred and feathered. In Boston, three ships loaded with tea rode at anchor in the harbour on the night of 16 December 1773. Massachusetts royal governor Thomas

Englishmen contemplate the word 'CROATOAN' on Roanoke Island. The disappearance of the Roanoke settlers remains a mystery

> Following the events of the Boston Tea Party, Parliament closed the port and brought in an armed occupation force

Hutchinson was determined to collect import taxes on the cargo before the ships would be allowed to sail back to England, their holds still full. That night, the Sons of Liberty boarded the vessels and tossed chest after chest of tea into the waters of the harbour. The so-called Boston Tea Party became one of the most significant events leading to the outbreak of armed revolution. In response, Parliament closed the port of Boston, enacted martial law and brought an army of occupation into the city, billeting soldiers in private homes. The colonists referred to these Parliamentary directives and others as the Intolerable Acts.

British prime minister Lord North declared, "The New England governments are in a state of rebellion... [but] four or five frigates will do business without any military force." While Parliament made plans to crush the colonial insolence, aid poured into Boston from across the colonies. The Massachusetts State House issued a call for the colonists to collectively address their myriad grievances against the crown. From 5 September through 26 October 1774, the first Continental Congress met in Philadelphia. A total of 56

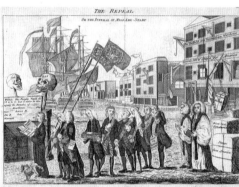

This cartoon depicts the repeal of the Stamp Act in 1766 as a funeral. Parliament backed down after protests

delegates were in attendance, and only the colony of Georgia was not represented.

Patrick Henry rose and proclaimed, "The distinctions between Virginians, Pennsylvanians, New Yorkers and New Englanders are no more. I am not a Virginian, but an American!"

The first Continental Congress adopted the Suffolk Resolves, listing the colonial disputes with Parliament and King George III and pledged to meet again in May 1775 if satisfactory remedies were not achieved. Before the second Congress convened, however, open rebellion had broken out on Lexington Green.

1775

A tea monopoly
Parliament awards a monopoly on the sale of tea to the debt-burdened East India Company. Despite some pricing benefits, colonists still resent the imposition of a tea tax.
Spring 1773

The Boston Tea Party
Raiders dressed as native tribesmen board ships in Boston harbour and toss chests of tea into the water in protest of the tea tax. In repsonse, Parliament closes the port of Boston.
16 December 1773

First Continental Congress
Delegates from 12 of the 13 British colonies in North America convene in Philadelphia to consider a response to Parliamentary oppression.
5 September 1774

Peyton Randolph of Virginia presided over the first Continental Congress

London merchants seek relief
Beleaguered by colonial boycotts, London merchants fear the outbreak of a revolution and petition King George III to initiate better relations with colonists.
1775

Lord North's conciliatory plan
Parliament approves prime minister Lord North's plan to allow colonial assemblies to levy taxes for their own maintenance and protection. Word does not reach the colonies before the revolution begins.
February 1775

Bluffer's Guide
Salem Witch Trials

MASSACHUSETTS, 1692-1693

What was it?

The Salem witch trials were a series of prosecutions of suspected witches blamed for causing a group of girls to suffer fits. Fear spread quickly, leading to the arrest and imprisonment of about 150 men, women and children. Before public opinion turned against the trials, 20 of them were executed.

When did it happen?

The first girls suffering fits were afflicted in January 1692, and by March the accusations and arrests of the 'witches' had begun. The first trials and hangings took place in June and continued throughout the summer, but by the end of the year doubts surfaced about the authenticity of the accusations. The final prisoners were freed in May 1693.

Where did it happen?

The accusations began in Salem Village, now Danvers, and quickly spread to several other communities in Massachusetts - Salem Town, Ipswich and Andover. These were settlements already under stress, threatened by attack from Native American tribes, suffering from a smallpox epidemic and ravaged by disputes and rivalry with their neighbours.

Salem's drug problem?

Some researchers explain the symptoms of the girls as being the result of eating bread infected with a fungus, which led to an LSD-like poisoning. Others think different medical conditions were to blame, and many suggested it was entirely non-medical and motivated by spite or attention seeking.

Visions and fits may have been caused by convulsions after eating bad bread

Coffin in the glass

It all began when Betty Parris and Abigail Williams broke an egg white into a glass of water to see what shape it would take, thinking it would indicate the profession of their future husbands. When the egg appeared as a coffin, Betty fell into a hysterical fit, which soon spread to others.

How to survive

Most of the 150 people who were accused avoided death. The best way to escape the hangman's noose was to confess to witchcraft. Many also tried to help themselves by accusing others, fuelling more arrests. Interrogators often chose easy targets who they thought would confess. Torture was used if they did not.

A sinister motive

Many of the accused had crossed Salem resident Thomas Putnam over previous years. This has led to suggestions that the trials were abused by him to settle old scores and grudges. Of the 21 accusation records that survive, 15 were signed by at least one member of the Putnam family.

More weight

Five men were among the 19 who were hanged, while Giles Corey was pressed to death because he refused to enter a plea. Heavier and heavier rocks were placed on his chest until his ribs cracked and he could not breathe. According to tradition, his last words were "more weight."

Why were they believed?

Belief that the devil gave witches the power to harm others was widespread in Puritan New England. Much of the proof used was spectral evidence, where accusers said they had a vision of the person who was afflicting them. When spectral evidence was deemed inadmissible, the trials came to an abrupt end.

William Stoughton, chief justice and prosecutor, was the driving force behind the trials

The Crucible

Playwright Arthur Miller saw parallels between the Salem witch trials and life in 1950s America. He wrote *The Crucible* as a critical allegory of McCarthyism. He fictionalised many aspects of the witch trials, especially the invention of a love story between Abigail Williams and John Proctor - in real life, she was 11 and he was 60.

Key figures

Tituba
Unknown-unknown
A Native American slave, Tituba was the first to confess to using witchcraft after being beaten by her owner.

Cotton Mather
1663-1728
A Puritan minister and vigorous supporter of the trials, Mather was influential in the creation of the courts for the trials.

William Stoughton
1631-1701
Chief justice of the court, Stoughton was in charge of the trials and a firm believer in the use of spectral evidence.

Rebecca Nurse
1621-1692
Initially cleared of witchcraft, Nurse was executed after Stoughton urged the jury to reconsider its verdict.

William Phips
1651-1695
Governor of Massachusetts, Phips established the court and later disbanded it, perhaps because his wife was accused.

Key events

The hysteria begins
20 January 1692
Two girls begin to suffer fits that are quickly deemed to be the result of witchcraft.

The authorities become involved
29 February 1692
Thomas and Edward Putnam file a complaint to magistrates and the first arrest warrants for witches are issued.

The first victim
10 June 1692
Bridget Bishop is the first to be hanged for witchcraft, two days after her trial.

The deadliest day
22 September 1692
Eight people are hanged but critics of the hysteria are becoming more vocal.

Beginning of the end
6 December 1692
A new court is created to deal with witch trials and spectral evidence is banned.

GEORGE WASHINGTON
1732-1799

Brief Bio

Hailed by many as the greatest US president of all time, George Washington served as commander in chief of the US Continental Army during the American Revolution. He then went on to become the first US president, serving from 1789 to 1797. Today Washington remains an icon of liberty and freedom, and is one of the most recognisable faces in the world.

In his final will Washington freed all his slaves

THE FIRST PRESIDENT

WASHINGTON

Today George Washington is hailed as the father of the USA, but his journey to legendary hero was a perilous and difficult one

Long Island was supposed to be a success. The enemy was stronger and greater in number but the rebels had got there first. The commander had prepared everything for his foe's arrival in New York, strengthening his batteries and placing his generals perfectly. But the British had broken through. First Sullivan fell, then Stirling, and the commander could only watch as the lives of his brave men were brutally wiped away. Knowing all was lost he ordered his men to retreat before the carnage could reach them. As relentless rain pelted down he used the cover of darkness to

help conceal his soldiers as they climbed into every available boat he could get his hands on. He waited until the last man was on board before he boarded himself. As the boat drew away the commander looked back through the thick fog that had descended over the bay. The mist had concealed them from the British, his men were safe, but Brooklyn had been lost.

This is not the story of a failed general, forgotten by the history books, but instead that of the most glorified and worshipped president in US history - George Washington. Just as his men were hidden by the fog that grim morning

in Brooklyn, today Washington himself is cloaked and obscured by layers of myths and legends. He has become an almost messianic figure in the United States, a legend of justice and freedom, a brilliant commander who led his underdog army to the greatest victory in US history. But as with most legends, the stories are not always true. Far from being a brilliant military strategist, Washington actually lost more battles than he won. He was no Alexander or Caesar, but an entirely different kind of hero altogether - one who persevered in the face of devastating failure for his men and country.

MAKING HISTORY

Three reasons why Washington is considered the USA's greatest leader

1 **VIRTUE**
Washington twice gave up the chance of ultimate power. First at the end of the Revolutionary War when he surrendered his role as commander in chief, and again when he refused to rule as president for a third term. When George III was presented with the idea of Washington doing this, he said, "If he does that he will be the greatest man in the world."

2 **COMMITMENT TO COUNTRY**
Washington did not become involved in the hostile arguments and squabbling of political debates, but instead acted as a peacekeeper between the groups. A true non-partisan, his primary aim was always the betterment of the country, rather than any personal gain.

3 **PERSISTENCE**
Washington was not the most gifted military leader; he suffered multiple losses and personal humiliations, but his determination to persevere in spite of repeated setbacks inspired his soldiers to do the same, which resulted in him creating one of the most celebrated underdog success stories in world history.

inspiring nature to try to persuade the French to remove themselves from land claimed by Britain. When they refused, Washington returned with a small force and attacked the French post at Fort Duquesne, killing the commander and nine men and taking the others as prisoners, all in 15 minutes. The event had huge international implications, and Great Britain and France began to pump forces into North America - The French and Indian War had begun. In a matter of minutes the name Washington became synonymous with three things - bravery, daring and recklessness.

Washington was rewarded for his quick thinking by being appointed commander in chief and colonel of the Virginia Regiment, the first full-time American military unit. With command of a thousand soldiers, Washington was tasked with defending Virginia's frontier, and he demonstrated his resolve and forthright approach as his unit engaged in 20 battles over 12 months. But his reckless attitude and inexperience was demonstrated when his unit exchanged friendly fire with another British force, killing 14 men.

His time commanding an army had taught Washington many things - how to bring the best out of his men, the importance of stamina and bravery, as well as discipline and training. It had also given him valuable insight into the British military tactics, and his struggles in dealing with government officials convinced him that a national government was the only way forward. However, when Washington retired from service in 1758, as far as he was concerned his time on the battlefield was over.

In 1759 Washington married the intelligent and wealthy Martha Dandridge Custis and together with her two children they moved to the

> ## "He was no Alexander or Caesar, but an entirely different kind of hero altogether"

plantation of Mount Vernon. Enjoying the newly inherited wealth from his marriage, Washington was now one of Virginia's wealthiest men and he concentrated on expanding and making the most out of his plantation. Little did he know that revolution was bubbling, and soon he would find himself back on the battlefield in what would become the most famous war in American history.

Washington wasn't the most likely of revolutionary leaders; although he opposed the controversial Stamp Act of 1765, during the early stirrings of revolution he was actually opposed to the colonies declaring independence. It wasn't until the passing of the Townshend acts of 1767 that he took an active role in the resistance. In an act of rebellion he encouraged the people of Virginia to boycott English goods until the acts were repealed. However, when the Intolerable acts were passed in 1774, Washington decided that more forthright action needed to be taken.

Passionate and charismatic, Washington was an obvious choice to attend the First Continental Congress. Although the delegates appealed to the crown to revoke the intolerable acts, they didn't even make a dink in the steely British armour, and a Second Continental Congress was called the following year.

A lot had changed in a year, and Washington too had undergone something of a transformation. The battles at Lexington and Concord had shown the colonies that they were capable of taking on the might of the British, and when Washington arrived in Pennsylvania for the state meeting dressed head to toe in military gear, it sent a strong message: he was prepared for war. So was Congress. It formed the Continental Army on 14 June 1775 and it needed a leader. Reluctant and somewhat modest,

Born on 22 February 1732, George Washington was the son of a slave-owning tobacco planter. George received a mixed education from a variety of tutors, and plans for him to join the British Royal Navy were cut short when his mother objected. Fate instead led Washington to become a surveyor, and he travelled for two years surveying land in the Culpeper, Frederick and Augusta counties. This position began a lifelong interest in landholdings, and he purchased his first piece of land as soon as his sizable income filled his pockets. And when his older brother died in 1752, Washington inherited not only his father's vast lands, but also the position of major in the Virginia militia.

It would not be long until Washington's natural leadership and drive would send him straight into the heat of battle. At a staggering 188 centimetres (6'2") tall, the young man towered above his contemporaries, and Virginia's Lieutenant General Robert Dinwiddie saw fit to use his imposing but

THE MARCH TO EVOLUTION
Follow the path leading to the greatest war in American history

1754-1763

French and Indian War
The French and Indian War was part of a much longer conflict between Great Britain and France, known as the Seven Years War. The war was fought in the north of North America between the colonies of the two powers, ending with France losing its territory in North America. However, funding the war created a huge national debt in Britain and gave France a good reason to support American independence.

1765

Stamp Act
The resulting national debt of the Seven Years War in Britain had reached £130 million by 1764. Britain also needed a way to pay for its army in North America and decided the colonies should subsidise it. The Stamp Act forced citizens to pay taxes on documents and paper goods and was immediately unpopular as it was carried out without any consent. The outrage soon turned violent and the tax was never collected.

1767-1770

Townshend Acts
The Townshend Acts were a series of acts passed by the British Parliament upon the colonies in North America. These acts placed duties on vital, high-volume imported items such as glass, paints, paper and tea, among other things. The money raised was intended to pay to keep governors and judges loyal, and also to set a general precedent that the British had the right to tax the American colonies.

1770

Boston Massacre
This incident occurred when a heckling crowd gathered around a British guard, who was quickly joined by eight more British soldiers. The soldiers fired at the crowd, killing three people and wounding multiple others. Two more later died of their wounds. The soldiers were arrested for manslaughter but were released without charge. This event helped to create an immensely anti-British sentiment in the colonies.

Washington's ability to evacuate his army from Long Island without any loss of life or supplies stunned the British

Washington was very fond of dogs and gave them unusual names such as Tarter, True Love and Sweet Lips

George Washington fought with the British in the assault on the French-held Fort Duquesne

An illustration of Washington's home in Mount Vernon

1773

Boston Tea Party
In an effort to force the colonies to accept the Townshend duty on Tea, Britain passed the Tea Act, allowing the East India Company to ship its tea to North America. In defiance, protestors boarded the ships and threw chests full of tea into Boston Harbour. Parliament responded harshly, by passing the Intolerable Acts, which took away the rights of the state of Massachusetts to govern itself.

1774

First Continental Congress
Delegates from 12 of the 13 British colonies in America met at Carpenters' Hall in Philadelphia to discuss ways to halt the Intolerable Acts. They made plans to refuse to import British goods until their grievances were met. When these efforts proved unsuccessful, a Second Continental Congress was held the next year to prepare the country for the impending American Revolutionary War.

1775

The Battles of Lexington and Concord
When American intelligence learned that British troops planned to march on Concord, they were quick to assemble their forces and take up arms against them. However only 77 militiamen faced 700 British at Lexington and were quickly defeated. The British continued to Concord to search for arms, but they were forced back by 500 militiamen, winning the colonies their first war victory.

1775

Battle of Bunker Hill
Set during the Siege of Boston, this battle saw the British mount an attack against the colonial troops stationed in Bunker Hill and Breed's Hill. Although the British were victorious, the heavy losses suffered by the redcoats led it to be a hollow victory, and it proved the Americans could hold their own against their foes in battle. Shortly after the conflict, King George III officially declared the colonies to be in a state of rebellion.

Washington did not see himself as a leader capable of leading such a vitally important force, but for those around him there was no other choice. With proven military experience, a devoted patriot and a strong, commanding presence, Washington was appointed commander in chief of the force that would take on the mightiest nation on Earth.

It did not take very long for the new commander to prove just what he was worth. In early-March 1776, Washington turned the Siege of Boston around by placing artillery on Dorchester Heights, low hills with a good view of Boston and its harbour. The perfectly placed, powerful cannons forced the British to retreat from the city, and the American commander moved his army into New York City. Even the critical British papers couldn't deny the skills of the captivating and exciting new leader who seemed capable of repelling their great empire with ease.

Victory and gossip aside, in truth Washington was out of his depth. He had commanded men before, but only a force of a thousand soldiers - far from the tens of thousands at his disposal now. He had only fought in frontier warfare, far removed from the open-field battles he now faced. He had never commanded legions of cavalry or artillery - he was constantly learning on the job. Washington had to rely on his own intelligence and courage

to have any hope of snatching victory from his seasoned, experienced rivals.

This inexperience manifested itself in the crippling defeat the commander suffered during the Battle of Long Island. In an effort to seize New York, the British general William Howe unleashed a devastating campaign that Washington failed to subdue. So great was the British attack that Washington was forced to retreat his entire army across the East River under cover of darkness. Although this feat itself was remarkable, for the self-critical leader it was a swift and brutal reminder of his own inadequacies as a general, and he quickly realised this war would not be easily won.

But the British had a crippling weakness, too. They were simply too sure they were going to win. Howe so fatally underestimated the will of the American troops and their reckless leader that he left his Hessian soldiers at Trenton, confident the war would be won in the next few months. Washington, on the other hand, was acutely aware of the morale of his soldiers. After the defeat in New York and the humiliating retreat, they needed something positive to inspire them, and Trenton was right there for the taking.

The plan was one only Washington could have thought up - bold, gutsy and downright dangerous, he led his soldiers across the perilous and icy Delaware River on a freezing Boxing Day in 1776. Only 2,400 of his men were able to make it across without turning back, but it was enough.

REBELS

Organisation

There were 35,000 continentals in the United States with 44,500 militia. Their French allies increased their numbers with 12,000 French soldiers in America and 63,000 at Gibraltar. They also had 53 ships in service throughout the war. George Washington was commander in chief and Nathanael Greene served as major general.

Weapons

When the war began the colonies did not have a professional standing army of any kind, with many colonies only able to supply minutemen who were required to equip themselves - with most carrying rifles. The army's weapon of choice was the flintlock musket and they also carried bayonets.

Resources

The Continental Army suffered from massive supply issues. Supplies were repeatedly seized by British patrols. They also had to combat a primitive road system, which resulted in regular shortages of food, clothing, ammunition, tents and a host of essential military equipment, constantly pitching the odds against them.

Morale

The rebels' greatest weapon was the belief in their grand cause - fighting for their liberty from the oppressive British Crown. It was this strong morale belief in their cause that encouraged American leaders, who knew they were facing a well equipped and disciplined foe, to push on despite multiple crippling defeats.

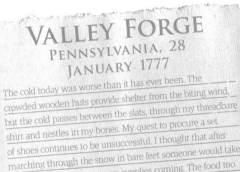

VALLEY FORGE
PENNSYLVANIA, 28 JANUARY 1777

The cold today was worse than it has ever been. The crowded wooden huts provide shelter from the biting wind, but the cold passes between the slats, through my threadbare shirt and nestles in my bones. My quest to procure a set of shoes continues to be unsuccessful. I thought that after marching through the snow in bare feet someone would take pity on me - but there are no supplies coming. The food too is running low. For the past week I have only eaten firecake - a sticky, bland abomination of water and flour that fills my stomach but leaves the soul ravenous.

I shouldn't complain - I am one of the lucky few untouched by the diseases that ravage the camp. So many men have been plagued by itchy rashes and blisters or fevers that refuse to calm. The only relief here are the brave few women who wash and mend our uniforms, or sometimes simply provide a shoulder to men who have no will to go on.

Washington and his men crossing the Delaware River

Adjusted for inflation, Washington was the wealthiest US president of all time

REDCOATS

Organisation

There were 56,000 British redcoats in North America along with a combined force of 52,000 loyalists, freed slaves and natives. They also had 78 Royal Navy ships at their service. William Howe served as commander in chief, but there were many decorated generals and officers such as Thomas Gage and Henry Clinton.

Weapons

The British army depended on the .75-calibre flintlock musket popularly known as "Brown Bess." They also carried bayonets and, occasionally, short-barrel muskets. The redcoats also used cannons to great effect, to the degree that if an American unit was without cannon, they would not face a cannon-supported British troop.

Resources

Although British soldiers were better equipped than their American counterparts, they were fighting away from home, and supplies could take months to reach their destinations. Many British had to rely on loyal locals supplying them with food and praying the vital supplies would survive the 4,800km (3,000mi) trip across the ocean.

Morale

The British believed they could easily steamroll the rebels and this underestimation of their foe cost them dearly. The war was also expensive, and support at home was mixed at best. For many soldiers struggling in terrible conditions away from home, there was little motivation to fight.

Completely unprepared for the attack, the Hessians at Trenton were overwhelmed and swiftly defeated by Washington and his men. A few days later the commander led a counter-attack on a British force sent to attack his army at Princeton, achieving another small - but essential - American victory.

Meanwhile, the British redcoats still believed the rebellion could be stopped like a cork in a bottle. Howe thought that by taking control of key colonial cities, the river of rebellion would turn into a drought and the population would surrender to British rule. When Howe set his sights on the revolutionary hub of Philadelphia, Washington rode out to meet him, but, perhaps with his previous victories clouding his judgement, the commander was outmatched and Philadelphia fell to the British. However, the colonists' cause received a major boon when British General Burgoyne was forced to surrender his entire army of 6,300 men at the Battle of Saratoga. It seemed that major world players were finally beginning to believe the Americans had a chance of besting the mighty British Empire, and France openly allied itself with the rebels.

While General Howe concentrated on capturing key cities, Washington had a revelation. Although individual battles were important, the key to victory was not military success, but instead his ability to keep the heart of the resistance alive and pumping.

> "When Washington retired from service in 1758, as far as he was concerned, his time on the battlefield was over"

This was something out of British hands and solely in his own.

This spirit of rebellion faced its most challenging obstacle yet over the long winter of 1977. For six long months the soldiers at the military camp of Valley Forge suffered thousands of disease-ridden deaths. With starvation rife and supplies low, many feared the horrendous conditions would force the desperate army to mutiny. Washington himself faced immense criticism from the American public and Congress, who urged him to hurry the war effort, while behind the scenes anti-Washington movements gained ground. Washington simply replied: "Whenever the public gets dissatisfied with my service [...] I shall quit the helm [...] and retire to a private life." The critics soon fell silent.

Although the conditions had been testing, to put it mildly, the soldiers emerged from the

winter in good spirits. Washington demonstrated that his sting was stronger than ever when his forces attacked the British flank attempting to leave Monmouth Courthouse. Although the battle ultimately ended in a stalemate, Washington had finally achieved what he set out to do since the beginning of the war - hold his own in a pitched battle. This was massive for the Americans; it proved the growing Continental Army was developing its skills at an alarming speed, and if the horrendous winter they had emerged from had not crushed them, what chance did the British have? The French seemed to share this attitude. On 5 September 1781, 24 French ships emerged victorious against 19 British vessels at the Battle of Chesapeake. The success prevented the British from reinforcing the troops of Lord Cornwallis, who was blockaded in Yorktown, Virginia, and allowed crucial French troops to pour into the Continental Army, bringing vast supplies of artillery with them. This was exactly the opportunity Washington needed, and he didn't plan to let it go to waste.

With the British army trapped and exposed, and his own swelling in size, Washington led his men out of Williamsburg and surrounded Yorktown. From late-September the Continental Army moved steadily closer to the redcoats, forcing them to pull back from their outer defences, which left them

open for the Americans and French to use. As the colonists began to set up artilleries, the British pelted them with steady fire. In spite of this and at some great risk to himself, Washington continued to visit and motivate his men on the front line, and by 5 October the commander was ready to make his move.

As a vicious storm raged, Washington grasped his pickaxe in his hand and struck several blows into the dirt that would become the new trench the Americans would use to bombard the British. By 5pm on 9 October, the Americans were pelting the British with a relentless stream of cannon fire. The British ships were sunk and soldiers deserted en masse. More American trenches were dug as they gained land, and when Washington's men rushed toward the British redoubt, they overwhelmed the surprised redcoats. As Washington rained artillery fire down on the town, Cornwallis's attempts at escape across the York River were unsuccessful and he finally surrendered.

Little did Washington know that the victory he had secured at Yorktown would lead to the ultimate surrender of British hostilities, the end of the war and ultimately American freedom. On 3 September 1783 the Treaty of Paris was signed between representatives of both countries, which proclaimed that Britain recognised the independence of

The Capitol in Washington, DC, under construction

SIEGE OF YORKTOWN

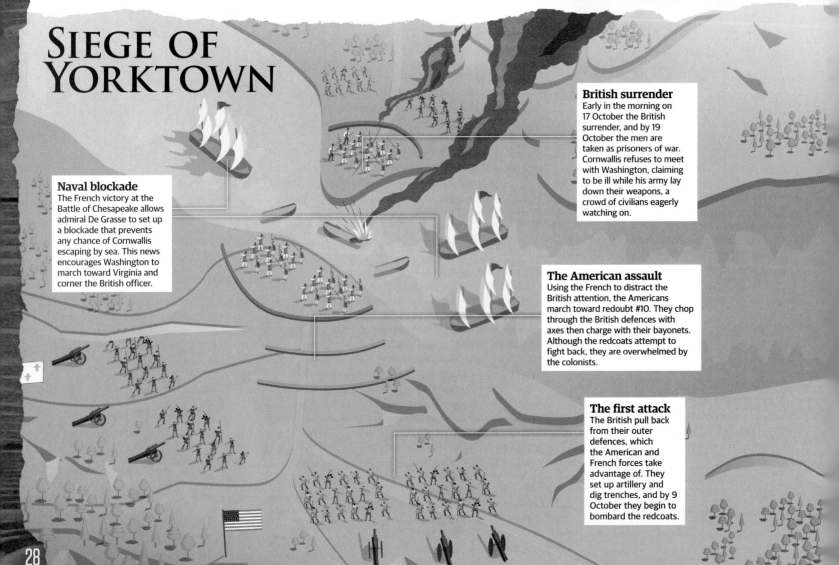

Naval blockade
The French victory at the Battle of Chesapeake allows admiral De Grasse to set up a blockade that prevents any chance of Cornwallis escaping by sea. This news encourages Washington to march toward Virginia and corner the British officer.

British surrender
Early in the morning on 17 October the British surrender, and by 19 October the men are taken as prisoners of war. Cornwallis refuses to meet with Washington, claiming to be ill while his army lay down their weapons, a crowd of civilians eagerly watching on.

The American assault
Using the French to distract the British attention, the Americans march toward redoubt #10. They chop through the British defences with axes then charge with their bayonets. Although the redcoats attempt to fight back, they are overwhelmed by the colonists.

The first attack
The British pull back from their outer defences, which the American and French forces take advantage of. They set up artillery and dig trenches, and by 9 October they begin to bombard the redcoats.

A depiction of Washington's entry into New York in 1759

Washington has been immortalised on Mount Rushmore along with Thomas Jefferson, Theodore Roosevelt and Abraham Lincoln

WASHINGTON MYTHS CUT DOWN

We get an expert opinion on the myths surrounding this legendary man

Stephen Brumwell is a freelance writer and independent historian living in Amsterdam. His book, *George Washington: Gentleman Warrior*, won the 2013 George Washington Book Prize.

He had wooden teeth

George Washington was plagued with dental problems from his twenties, and by 1789, had just one of his own teeth remaining. He owned several sets of false teeth, but none was crafted from wood. Instead, Washington's dentures incorporated a variety of materials – bone, 'sea-horse', or hippopotamus ivory, and human teeth – fixed by lead, gold and metal wire. The belief that Washington's false teeth were wooden probably originated in the brown-stained appearance of surviving examples – apparently owing to his fondness for port wine.

Washington was one of the tallest and biggest presidents at 1.88m (6'2") and 90kg (200lb)

He cut down a cherry tree and confessed to his father

Perhaps the best known of all the legends spun around Washington, the 'cherry tree story' first surfaced in a biography written after his death by Mason Locke Weems. Concerned with portraying Washington as an exemplary role model for his countrymen, 'Parson Weems' concocted the fable of the six-year-old hatcheting his father's prized cherry tree, and then deflecting parental wrath by frankly confessing to the deed with the words "I can't tell a lie, Pa."

Washington was a moonshiner

While there's no proof that Washington set up illicit liquor stills to make moonshine, he was certainly in the forefront of American whiskey production. On the advice of his Scottish farm manager, James Anderson, he established a whiskey distillery at Mount Vernon in 1797. By the year of Washington's death, 1799, this was producing almost 41,640l (11,000gal) of rye and corn whiskey, making it the largest US distillery of its day.

He threw a silver dollar across the Potomac River

Standing 188cm (6'2") tall, and with a well-muscled physique, young George Washington was renowned for his strength. Yet even Washington in his prime would have struggled to hurl a silver dollar across the Potomac River, which is more than 1.6km (1mi) wide opposite his Virginian home at Mount Vernon. Also, silver dollars were only introduced in 1794, when Washington was already in his sixties.

He wore a wig

Although wigs were fashionable during Washington's lifetime, he never wore one, preferring to keep his own hair, which was reddish-brown, long and tied back in a tight queue, or 'pigtail'. However, Washington regularly used the white hair powder that was customary among men of his wealthy social class, especially for formal occasions, and this gave the impression of a wig, apparent in many of his portraits.

---

the United States. With victory declared, Washington disbanded his army and wished farewell to the men who had valued him not only as a leader, but also a fellow soldier. On 23 December 1783, in an action that would define him in the history books, he resigned as commander in chief of the army and humbly returned to his home in Mount Vernon.

However, without him his country was struggling. With nobody to unite them the states fought and squabbled among themselves over boundaries and inflicted harsh taxes on their own citizens. The ex-commander watched from afar as the land he had led to freedom struggled to support itself. He was dismayed, but hesitant to act. It wasn't until an armed uprising known as Shays' Rebellion took place in Massachusetts that Washington was finally persuaded to step into the limelight once more.

Washington quietly attended the Constitution Convention held in Philadelphia in 1787. There

> "Washington did not see himself as a leader capable of leading such a vitally important force"

he sat and listened silently to the proceedings, speaking only once. However, his prestige spoke volumes and those gathered there agreed the national government needed more authority - it needed a figure strong and commanding enough to maintain control. Washington was unanimously chosen to fulfil this role. He became president of the convention in 1787, and by 1789 he was unanimously elected once more, but this time as the first-ever president of the United States - the only one in history to receive 100 per cent of the votes. He would serve two terms as president from 1789 to 1797 until he would yet again relinquish the power he could so easily have exploited. In the spring of 1797, he finally returned to his precious Mount Vernon, realising, perhaps more so than any one of the many people who supported him, that ultimate power in the land of the free could not lay solely in one man's hands indefinitely.

Building a nation

Finding common ground in government presented a major challenge as the colonies emerged from revolution and set about building a nation

The Founding Fathers of the United States, those men who led the American Revolution and then worked to establish a framework for the government of their new country, realised that simply declaring independence from Great Britain and achieving that independence through insurrection would not lead to long-term stability or serve as the firm footing for the colonies to survive as one nation.

In the midst of the War for Independence, a committee appointed by the Second Continental Congress convened in Philadelphia to draft a document that might bind the colonies together while preserving the rights of individual states in the context of a central government. The committee convened on 12 July 1776, just eight days after the signing of the Declaration of Independence. Sixteen months later, on 15 November 1777, a draft was presented to the colonies for ratification. Still, it took more than three years for all 13 to agree to the principles of the Articles of Confederation, which became effective on 1 March 1781.

The Articles created a Congress with specific powers, such as the conduct of foreign relations, making war and peace, settling boundary disputes, and establishing a common currency. However, those powers not expressly given to this relatively weak body in a so-called "league of friendship" were reserved for each state to "retain its sovereignty, freedom and independence, and every power, jurisdiction and right." Congress was not vested with the authority to levy or collect taxes or impose its decisions on the states. There was no provision for a chief executive or a judicial branch of government.

The Articles of Confederation were, by design, intended to curb the authority of a central government. After all, the current revolution was intended to throw off the yoke of an oppressive 'despot'. However, issues emerged soon enough that indicated the necessity of establishing a national government that would serve a nation of diverse beliefs, economic conditions and world views, a nation that was growing and whose inhabitants already numbered more than four million people.

The immediate catalyst for the discourse that resulted in the drafting of the Constitution of the United States occurred in the summer of 1786 when Daniel Shays led a group of disgruntled

> Towards the end of the revolution came the need to form a stable system of government for the fledgling nation

After much deliberation and debate, the signing of the US Constitution took place in Philadelphia on 17 September 1787

"They determined that a new, stronger national government was a prerequisite to stability and future prosperity"

Massachusetts farmers in an uprising against creditors and others who they believed had made them the victims of exploitation. Shays's Rebellion lasted until June 1787, when the Massachusetts state militia put down the revolt. The national government had no authority to intervene, call up troops, or otherwise act to restore order. The message was clear. Another such threat might result in the total collapse of the national government, such as it was. Each state would then be left to its own devices, even to the extent that its neighbours were in peril of foreign intervention, annexation, or a descent into chaos.

At this critical moment in the life of the fledgling country, a core group of statesmen, including Alexander Hamilton, John Adams, John Jay, James Madison, Thomas Jefferson, Benjamin Franklin, George Washington and others, determined that a new, stronger national government was a prerequisite to stability and future prosperity. Collectively, these men, along with numerous others, had already left their mark on the new nation. Jefferson authored the Declaration of

Independence but did not attend the coming constitutional convention. The aging Franklin served on the committee of five that assisted in its final draft and served as ambassador to France during a critical period of the revolution. Hamilton, Jay and Madison authored the Federalist Papers that lucidly set out the tenets of the proposed Constitution. Hamilton, in fact, is rightly considered the father of the Federalist party and the architect of the nation's financial system. Madison shied away from the sobriquet 'Father of the Constitution', but his tremendous knowledge of history and varied forms of government, along with his interest in balancing states' rights with the need for a strong central administration, brought an immeasurable contribution.

By early 1787, Washington had spent some time in retirement at Mount Vernon, his sprawling estate in Virginia. Called from repose to preside over the constitutional convention that would assemble in Philadelphia to determine a new form of national government, he offered his leadership to the country once again. "We are either a united people

under one head, for Federal purposes, or we are 13 independent sovereignties, eternally counteracting each other."

In the spring of that year, after 74 delegates had been chosen, the framing of the Constitution of the United States began. Recalcitrant Rhode Island refused to participate. Although their differences sometimes seemed insurmountable, the delegates agreed to a man that only a republic, its power to govern derived from the people, could accurately perpetuate the high principles for which the revolution had been fought. Heated debate swirled around the structure of the new government. Delegates from small states feared that the large states would dominate future deliberations if representatives to the proposed congress were elected only on the basis of population. Two gentlemen from Connecticut, Roger Sherman and Oliver Ellsworth, proposed a compromise, a bicameral legislature with a House of Representatives elected from each state according to population and a Senate with each state seating two representatives elected by the members of the House. It was genius.

In addition, the delegates established the office of president as the executive branch of government and specified that it would be occupied by one man rather than a committee. They established a judicial branch of government as well. Each branch eventually achieved the

The words 'We the People...' open the preamble to the Constitution. The original document resides in the US National Archives

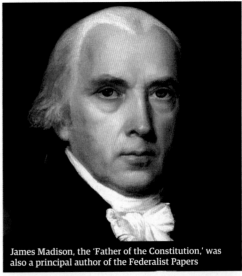

James Madison, the 'Father of the Constitution,' was also a principal author of the Federalist Papers

John Jay, one of three authors of the Federalist Papers, was the first Chief Justice of the US Supreme Court

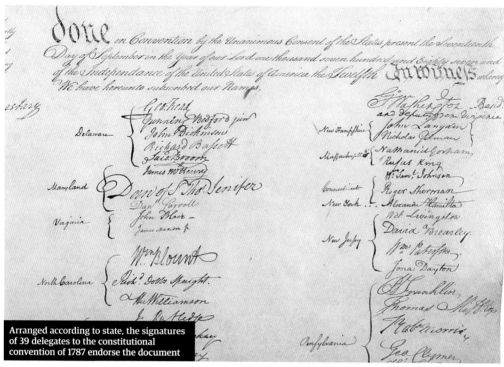

Arranged according to state, the signatures of 39 delegates to the constitutional convention of 1787 endorse the document

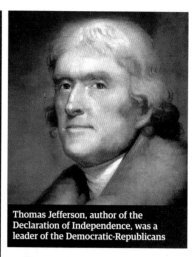

Thomas Jefferson, author of the Declaration of Independence, was a leader of the Democratic-Republicans

standing required to provide a system of "checks and balances" so that no single branch might dominate the others. This system survives today. While other issues were left unresolved, there were discussions regarding the institution of slavery, trade, foreign relations and other important topics. Finally, the Constitution's opening phrase, "We the people..." was intended to acknowledge the source of the government's authority.

Ultimately, 55 delegates attended the constitutional convention at various times, and 39 signed the document. On 21 June 1788, the Constitution was ratified and became the law of the land. Still there were those who were wary of its implications. Virginian Patrick Henry, whose pamphlet Common Sense and impassioned "Give me liberty, or give me death!" speech had stoked the revolutionary flame, was solidly against the proposal, noting that he "smelled a rat!"

At a critical moment when the Constitution appeared destined for defeat, Madison prevailed on the divided Virginia delegation, particularly Edmund Randolph, to drop their anti-Federalist objections and support ratification. He assured other doubters that in exchange for their 'yea' votes he would sponsor the drafting and adoption of a 'bill of rights' intended to limit the powers of the central government.

Opponents of the Constitution argued forcefully that it did little to protect the rights of the individual. While the Federalists were generally convinced that it went far enough, Jefferson and others weren't convinced. The ratification of the Constitution without a bill of rights was incomplete. He reasoned, "A bill of rights is what the people are entitled to against every government on Earth."

Although he personally considered the drafting of the Bill of Rights a "nauseous project," Madison came to realise that it had to be accomplished. The Constitution specified that the process of amendment required approval of three-quarters of the state legislatures.

There were modifications; some measures were dropped. Twelve of an original 17 proposed amendments survived the House and Senate and went to the state legislatures. Ten of these were ratified swiftly, and on 15 December 1791, the Virginia legislature was the last to approve the Bill of Rights.

The ten amendments of the Bill of Rights entrenched basic individual liberties in the theory and practice of the United States government. The first amendment, for example, protected freedom of religion and freedom of speech, the third harkened back to the despised Quartering Act of 1765 and prohibited the billeting of soldiers in private homes during peacetime without the owner's consent. The fourth amendment barred unlawful search and seizure.

Despite their differences, the Founding Fathers had provided the American people with a remarkable document intended to preserve, protect and defend liberty. The amendment process, in itself, alludes to the fact that they realised the Constitution was not perfect and that changing times might require its alteration. It was, however, the basis for a noble experiment in government - the likes of which had not been seen on Earth since Ancient Greece. Still, stern tests lay ahead.

> Comprising the first ten ratified amendments, the Bill of Rights safeguarded basic individual liberties

The two-party system

The two-party system that characterises American politics was born of sectionalism and differing ideological visions

The Founding Fathers initially criticised the idea of political parties. John Adams, for one, believed that party factions were "the greatest of political evils." Thomas Jefferson once said, "If I could not go to Heaven but with a party, I would not go there at all."

Still, within a few years of the ratification of the US Constitution, two major political parties, the Federalists and the Democratic-Republicans, had emerged. The genesis of these parties lay in the Federalist assertion for a strong central government, which seemed to contradict the notion of states' and individual rights, which were the main tenets of the Democratic-Republicans.

Sectionalism played a role in their development as well. On 30 April 1789, George Washington was inaugurated as the first president. Subsequently, the Federalist Party began to take shape with the approval of its chief executive, Alexander Hamilton, the first Secretary of the Treasury. While Hamilton shaped early American fiscal processes and policy, his Federalist ideals were embraced primarily by the wealthy, landed merchants and businessmen of the Northeast. The Federalists also emphasised the growth of American industry.

Meanwhile, subsistence farmers, planters and those tied to agricultural livelihoods perceived the preponderance of 'nobly born and wealthy' individuals in government as a threat to their prosperity. Many also decried the new government's neutrality during the French Revolution. These somewhat disaffected citizens found champions for their cause in Jefferson and, somewhat surprisingly, Madison, whose views on states' rights moderated later in his life.

Unintentionally, the two-party system had evolved from differing political and social points of view. US political parties have continued to rise, fall away and revive.

Washington burning

How plundering, sabotage and a series of atrocities set the War of 1812 alight

The British force slogging its way towards Washington, the capital city of the still infant United States of America, was hot, tired and in an ugly mood after costly fighting in scorching temperatures.

Having scattered the disorganised American defenders at Bladensburg, the advanced units of the British column, which had borne the brunt of the fighting, sat down to recover. Casualties had been heavy, with perhaps as many as 180 men dying in order to secure the route to the capital, and hundreds more had been wounded. The final push to Washington would be undertaken by fresh troops, who had played no part in the fighting.

Arriving in the capital in the fading light of 24 August 1814, the British, led by Major General Robert Ross and Rear Admiral George Cockburn, made their way to the White House and found it completely deserted. The table being laid for a generous meal for 40, the British officers took advantage and enjoyed a fine dinner to cap off a hard but productive day's work.

But the pleasant diversion could not last for long. Ross and Cockburn had not come to the White House to dine out - in fact they had come to burn it to the ground.

On to Canada

After the end of the War of Independence, it would be more than a century before Britain and America forged their 'special relationship', and early interactions between the two nations were marked by suspicion and lingering enmity. This finally boiled over in the War of 1812, which stubbornly held onto its name despite almost all of the important events happening in later years.

Trouble had been brewing for some time. British and French high-handedness in their dealings with the young United States had injured American pride. Prickly in their attitude to the British, who

they had so recently ousted as their colonial masters, Americans were aware that they were still a minor country, liable to be pushed around by the major powers.

Grievances steadily built up, most notably caused by Britain's insistence that it had the right to stop and search neutral ships during its war with Napoleon, and impress any British sailors thus discovered. The 'Order in Council' of 1807 went further, insisting all neutral vessels must first call in at a British port and pay duties before continuing to their destination, wherever that may be.

The United States also had territorial ambitions and had an eye on Canada, still controlled by the British. The war in Europe offered an opportunity - perhaps while the British had their hands full fighting Napoleon across the Atlantic, the US could take control of its northern neighbour.

Distrust between Britain and the US ran so deep that there were suspicions the British were trying to convince the New England states to secede from the Union, while Spanish territories in Texas and the Floridas offered the British (on good terms with Spain thanks to Wellington's army in the Iberian peninsula) an easy route into the US.

'War hawks' like Henry Clay were prominent in stirring up patriotic fervour and, despite having an army of just 4,000 men, war was declared on Britain in 1812. Ironically, it was declared at almost the exact moment that Britain repealed its unpopular 1807 Order in Council, one of the main causes of American unrest.

The five theatres

Despite limited resources, the Americans opted for a bold plan, launching three campaigns against Canada in two theatres: the north-west and the Niagara Frontier. Further fighting would take place on the Saint Lawrence and Lake Champlain Front, the Chesapeake Bay and in the south west,

"Despite their limited resources, the Americans opted for a bold plan, launching three campaigns against Canada in two theatres"

meaning that American forces were committed in no fewer than five theatres.

In their favour was the fact that Britain really could not spare much in the way of manpower or naval forces. The start of the war offered the Americans a chance to make rapid gains while Britain's attention was focused elsewhere.

It was in Canada that the fiercest fighting took place - and it was here that the seeds for the destruction of Washington were sown.

Henry Clay had famously remarked that the militia of Kentucky could conquer Canada on its own. When it came time to actually invade, however, problems quickly presented themselves.

Quebec was the obvious target, and had been the goal of an American invasion in 1775, before the colonies had even declared their independence. It had proved too tough a nut to crack then and

was considered too formidable in 1812, having the strongest British garrison.

A thrust on Montreal was planned instead, alongside a two-pronged invasion of the territory known as 'Upper Canada', one from Detroit and one across the Niagara Frontier.

Questionable planning and faulty leadership blighted all three of the American offensives and in each case elements of the state militia refused to cross the border into Canada - a decided impediment for an invasion.

Brigadier General William Hull's offensive from Detroit was a disaster, leading to the loss of two forts and then Detroit itself. William Henry Harrison took command and suffered a serious defeat when an 850-strong scouting party was routed by a combined British/Indian force. With the murder of surrendered men marking the end of

the fighting, animosity between the two sides was quickly growing.

On the Niagara Frontier there was further trouble for the Americans, with 300 casualties (as well as close to 1,000 prisoners) taken during an attack on Queenston Heights, while the move on Montreal also miscarried.

It had been an inauspicious start to the war, but USS Constitution had won glory by battering HMS Guerriere in August, earning the nickname, 'Old Ironsides' in the process. Despite this signal success, American plans needed to be revised for the next campaign. The war was about to ignite.

A capital burns

Having learned their lesson the previous year, just one American offensive was planned into Canada for 1813 - across the Niagara Frontier. A move towards Lake Ontario was intended to lay the foundations for a later assault on Montreal, but General Henry Dearborn, the commanding officer, had serious doubts.

Initially ordered to take Forts George and Erie, as well as attacking Kingston, Ontario, he felt more comfortable limiting himself to one objective and

The fourth President of the United States, James Madison, The War of 1812 was often referred to as 'Madison's War'

Above: The flag situated at Fort McHenry when a British attack was successfully repulsed in September 1814

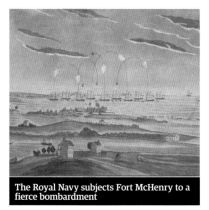

The Royal Navy subjects Fort McHenry to a fierce bombardment

The star-spangled banner

As well as helping to create an atmosphere of national unity, the War of 1812 also gave the United States its national anthem – although it took more than a century for it to be adopted as such.

The British assault on Baltimore, in which Major General Robert Ross lost his life, featured a heavy naval bombardment of Fort McHenry, which resisted all attempts to subdue it. On the morning of 14 September 1814, a Washington lawyer called Francis Scott Key saw the Stars and Stripes still defiantly flying above Fort McHenry and scribbled some song lyrics on the back of a letter he happened to have in his pocket.

British naval might had been resisted, and the Congreve rockets used in the bombardment had served only to provide the 'rockets' red glare' that had illuminated the flag throughout the night. The poetic lyrics (it was always intended to be a song, and Key suggested it should be sung to the tune of To Anacreon In Heaven), were renamed The Star-Spangled Banner, having originally been titled The Defence Of Fort M'Henry. Though notoriously difficult to sing, it was officially adopted as the nation's anthem in 1931.

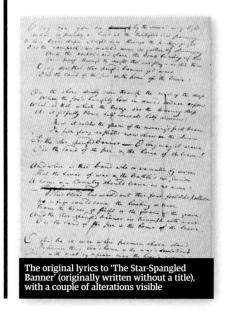

The original lyrics to 'The Star-Spangled Banner' (originally written without a title), with a couple of alterations visible

opted instead for York, the capital of Upper Canada. Despite being the capital, however, York was strategically unimportant and its capture would achieve little practical advantage aside from a little positive propaganda.

Nevertheless, on 27 April, Dearborn launched his attack. Landing his forces from Lake Ontario, the offensive almost came unstuck immediately as the first wave was nearly overwhelmed. Managing to hang on until the second wave landed, the Americans were able to press home their numerical advantage (their 1,500-strong force outnumbered the British and their Native American allies by 2:1).

Once the American landing was secure, in fact, the British regulars recognised the hopelessness of their situation and withdrew from York entirely, leaving Canadian militia to continue the defence. Their principal action was the detonation of a large powder magazine, which sent a vast amount of earth and boulders into the air. One of the boulders landed on the American officer commanding the landing, the extravagantly named Zebulon Pike, who was mortally wounded.

Prior to the attack, Pike had warned his men against mistreating the civilian population of the town. The Canadians, according to Pike, were unwilling participants in the war, having been forced to take part by the British. Whether or not Pike's death influenced American actions, looting of civilian properties soon started and Parliament buildings were put to the torch. Unwilling to stop his troops actions and perhaps supporting their actions, Dearborn ordered the destruction of the remaining military structures and the Government House the next day.

Dearborn would draw criticism for letting the British regulars escape to fight another day, but there was no word of censure for the destruction of York. It would recover, of course, and eventually became better known as Toronto.

Britain's response

As far as the British were concerned, the early years of the war were very much a case of making do with what was at hand. Canada, under the overall

From slaves to soldiers

Britain's diversionary raids on the American east coast, designed to take the pressure off the defensive forces in Canada, provided an opportunity for slaves in the area to escape and build new lives.

The view of slaves at the time was that they were docile and happy enough in their state of captivity. While it is true that the Maryland and Virginia slaves were on the whole better treated than their southern counterparts, the idea that they were happy being slaves was obviously mistaken and this was placed beyond doubt when British forces started to arrive in the region in early 1813.

Although incitement of the slave population was firmly prohibited by orders from home, the British commanders, Admiral John Borlase Warren and Colonel Sir Thomas Sydney Beckwith, did have permission to offer protection to slaves who were willing to help, whether by offering labour or giving information on the local territory. This protection extended to taking the slaves, as free men, to British territories (known as 'emigration'), or allowing the slaves to join the British army or navy.

American slave owners soon began to fear that almost all of their 'property' would take advantage of this generous offer whenever a British ship appeared. Some of the slaves were taken to the West Indies or Nova Scotia, while many served as labourers or scouts.

As well as the valuable work done by the freed slaves, the white population of America had a dread of their former property turning against them, making the defection of slaves a major propaganda tool.

By 1814, under the command of Admiral Cochrane, British policy had expanded to the point where emigration was acively encouraged. They were, in Cochrane's own words, "more terrific to the Americans than any troops that can be brought forward."

As well as large numbers leaving their former masters, around 200 slaves enlisted in a 'Corps of Colonial Marines', which saw service at Bladensburg on the approach to Washington and drew praise for the steadiness and bravery of its troops. The unit also performed well as skirmishers in the ill-fated approach to Baltimore.

Gabriel Hall, who migrated from the United States to Nova Scotia during the War of 1812

The Shawnee Chief Tecumseh is shot and killed by Richard Johnson during the Battle of the Thames

command of Sir George Prevost, could not look for any serious reinforcements while the Napoleonic War raged in Europe.

British policy became one of hanging on to Canada while mounting limited naval raids on the East Coast of America, more to divert attention from Canada than anything else. The disorganised nature of American operations helped, but the fighting in Canada and along the border became increasingly bitter.

The Americans abandoned Fort George and set fire to the village of Newark. Later, the British forces attacked and burned Buffalo (following the Battle of Buffalo or Battle of Black Rock). In turn, United States forces destroyed Port Dover.

American fortunes appeared to have turned with a naval victory on Lake Erie, followed by success at the Battle of the Thames on 5 October 1813, in which the charismatic Native American leader Tecumseh, who had dreamed of building an Indian confederacy, was killed.

A costly British assault on Fort Erie continued the seesaw nature of the conflict; the assault was repulsed, but the Americans then destroyed the fort and withdrew from Canada. Their dream of an easy conquest had come to nothing.

In contrast to the inconclusive fighting in Canada, however, a very decisive battle was fought that year in Europe, at Leipzig, from 16-19 October. Napoleon was defeated and was soon to be exiled. Britain could finally devote some serious attention to its little war across the Atlantic.

By the summer of 1814, 10,000 British regulars, many of them veterans of Wellington's Peninsula campaign, were heading for America. Meanwhile, the British naval blockade, with the benefit of extra ships now they were not needed to blockade French ports, was starting to bite. Extended across the entire eastern seaboard, it suffocated American commerce; exports were at just ten per cent of

their pre-war levels in 1814. Raids had also proved effective - 25 American ships had been destroyed in an operation on the Connecticut River.

It was the sort of warfare that only a select few had championed during the War of Independence. There had been no appetite for punitive coastal raids then, with reconciliation the primary goal of the British war effort. Now, with the intention of putting the young nation in its place and enforcing peace terms favourable to the British, there were no such qualms.

The raid on Washington

Although it is easy to see the operation against Washington as retaliation for the burning of York, Newark and Dover Port, the reality was not quite so clear-cut. Certainly temperatures on both sides had been raised by acts of destruction, but neither side could claim the moral high ground.

Prevost in Canada did ask for retaliatory raids against the Americans, but the British had been raiding coastal towns even before news of the destruction of York reached home. The decision to attack Washington was also not as obvious as might seem today. The capital city of America was not as important to the nation as, for instance, Paris or London were to their respective nations. The various states were still very loosely bound and, as the British had discovered when occupation of the capital in 1777 (Philadelphia) had brought no strategic advantage, there was little tangible benefit in taking the capital in 1814. Britain, of course, did not intend to actually occupy the capital this time.

It may have been a Royal Navy captain, Joseph Nourse, who planted the idea for the raid on Washington - not because it would be payback for York, but simply because it would be so easy to accomplish. The Americans were in no fit state to offer serious resistance.

British troops retain remarkable discipline in this sanitized depiction of the burning of Washington.

The local commander, General William Winder, was a political appointment lacking any real military nous. As the nephew of Maryland governor Levin Winder, it was expected that he would be able to mobilise state militia in order to offer resistance to any British landing. In the event, only 250 Maryland militia had been forthcoming when the critical moment came.

Making matters worse for Winder, there was doubt about where the British would strike. British Vice Admiral Sir Alexander Forester Inglis Cochrane had deployed ships to several areas to disguise intentions. When General Ross's brigade of 4,000 men landed on 19 August, there was nobody to meet them and over the next two days, they marched unopposed, covering 32 kilometres despite the fierce summer heat.

The American response was so lackadaisical that the British were able to get through two potential crisis points uninterrupted. First, Ross and Cockburn could not decide which route to take to Washington and halted their march for the best part of two days to ponder the matter.

Having finally decided to loop around and attack from the north east, they started marching again on 23 August, only to receive a recall order from Admiral Cochrane. Ross and Cockburn, as joint army and navy commanders, now debated on whether or not Cochrane's order could or should be ignored. The following morning, they came to the conclusion that they were so far committed to the attack that it could no longer be called off, and they set off once more. Bladensburg, where a bridge offered a convenient crossing of the Potomac, was their interim destination.

The Battle of Bladensburg

American resistance may have been disorganised, but it finally took solid form on the opposite side of the bridge at Bladensburg. General Winder had been in position at the Washington Navy Yard, fearing a strike there, when firm news came of the British movements. He arrived at Bladensburg in time to witness a fierce struggle.

The British assault included the use of Congreve rockets, which added a banshee-like mayhem to the battlefield, and the first two American lines were soon broken. A third, boosted by a strong artillery component, promised to stand firm until Winder ordered it to retreat as well. The British had paid a price, but the road to Washington was clear.

The Capitol Building was the first to burn, before Ross and his fellow officers took advantage of President Madison's hospitality in the dining room of the White House. Actually called either the 'President's House' or the 'Executive Mansion' at the time, the building was impressive but incomplete when it received its uninvited visitors. It was, however, already painted white, as several historical references confirm. The story that it was painted white to cover the scorch marks of the 1814 burning is, sadly, a myth.

As well as furniture and clothing, Madison's library was destroyed in the fire, set by Cockburn's sailors rather than Ross's soldiers, and the damage was estimated at around $12,000. Famously, a portrait of George Washington had been removed from the house at the last moment, supposedly by the fleeing staff, and preserved.

The Treasury Building was next, but the British did not consider private property a target, although a dwelling was burned after shots were fired from its windows, one of which downed Ross's horse.

However, the fires in Washington were dwarfed by the one at the Navy Yard, set by the Americans themselves so that it would not fall into British hands. The following day, an increasingly exhausted British force set fire to the buildings of the State and War Departments, and the printing presses of the National Intelligencer were wrecked.

A severely outnumbered American force, commanded by future president Andrew Jackson, defeats the British at New Orleans

Built to take on and overpower enemy frigates, USS Constitution was designed by Joshua Humphreys

As if to put a stop to the unsavoury activities, a severe thunderstorm then erupted, which has been interpreted as both the wrath of God at British brutality and also a final punishment on the town itself - it destroyed many private dwellings and the British beat a hasty retreat. The raid on Washington was over.

The aftermath

There were many ways of looking at the burning of Washington. It was a demonstration of British power - especially in relation to its fleet, which could land men anywhere it chose - and a warning to the Americans to respect their former masters. It was perhaps a fitting retaliation for similar acts by American forces during the war, although exactly where such tit-for-tat actions began or ended could be debated endlessly.

It was, as the naval captain Joseph Nourse had suggested, something that just seemed too easy to ignore, and the civilian population was not targeted in any case. Still, there were many who saw it as an act of barbarism and there were shocked reactions on both sides of the Atlantic.

Unsurprisingly, the president himself objected strongly, but in London there were cutting remarks in the press to the effect that even the Cossacks had been more merciful to Paris.

Most incredible, however, was the ease with which the whole feat had been accomplished. After more than two years of war, the summer weather was the strongest opponent the British had to contend with in a straight march to the heart of their enemy's capital. America had once dreamed of adding all of Canada to its territory, but it had eventually proven unable to protect even its own seat of government.

Flushed with their success, the British attempted another raid, this time on Baltimore, which promised far greater spoils if they could repeat their feats at Washington. Ross once more led his men into battle, but paid the ultimate price when he was killed by American sharpshooters on the approach to the city. The Royal Navy was then stymied in its assault on Fort McHenry, guarding Baltimore's fine harbour, and the attack was called off.

The War of 1812 has been called a 'silly little war', full of bad decisions and blundering leadership, but it provided a wake-up call for the United States and helped set it on a course for greater unity and enormous expansion. The lack of complete harmony between the states would erupt in far more bloody fashion a couple of generations later, but as the war wound down, it had served to bring the states a little closer together.

Fittingly, for a war that had started despite the British repealing the very act that had, in large part, provoked it, the greatest American victory of the war came after it had ended. Peace had already been agreed before Andrew Jackson won his famous victory at New Orleans on 8 January 1815.

Both sides were able to put their worst experiences of the War of 1812 behind them rapidly. The Americans may have greeted the Treaty of Ghent with a sigh of relief rather than a shout of triumph, as the historian George Dangerfield noted, but soon they were remembering fondly their victories at New Orleans, on Lake Erie and on the high seas where the USS Constitution had immortalised herself.

The British, meanwhile, soon had a major victory to savour after putting the cork back into Napoleon's bottle at Waterloo. The events of the 'silly little war', even the burning of Washington itself, paled into insignificance in comparison.

THE INDIAN REMOVAL ACT

President Andrew Jackson's controversial legislation removed tens of thousands of Native Americans from their own land. The exodus became known as the Trail of Tears

By 1830, the number of white settlers desiring to move into Indian-occupied territory, and the clamour of their demands, prompted the US government to take drastic action in favour of its electorate. The 'solution' arrived at under the presidency of Andrew Jackson was the Indian Removal Act, which would uproot the "Five Civilised Tribes" (Choctaw, Seminole, Muscogee/Creek, Chickasaw and Cherokee) from their lands in the Deep South of America and displace them hundreds of miles to new territories further west.

Prior to the act, the five tribes had been assured of their right to remain east of the Mississippi as long as they toed certain lines of European society, such as adopting Anglo-European cultural behaviours and practices and converting to Christianity. Jackson, however, called an end to this era in his State of the Union speech in 1829, arguing that nobody can stand in the way of "progress", and that relocation was the only way to prevent the Indians' otherwise inevitable annihilation. According to his proposal, Indians could only observe self-rule in federally designated reservations west of the Mississippi, and would be forcibly escorted to those lands.

The act was passed in the senate on 28 May 1830, after much acrimonious debate; although in the end, only the maverick congressman Davy Crockett voted against it. Over the course of the subsequent 20 years, the Five Tribes were "escorted" on foot to their new destination in Oklahoma by local militia forces. Many resisted, leading to scrappy wars before the Indians could be subdued and marched on their way again. Disease was rife, environmental conditions were severe, and the Indians were subject to constant attacks en route, meaning that thousands died without seeing the end point of their arduous and unjust journey. The European Americans inherited 25 million acres of land, little caring about the appalling price.

President Andrew Jackson, painted in 1824 by Thomas Sully. Jackson was incumbent in office for almost the entire Removal period

THE CHOCTAW

George W Harkins replaced his uncle Greenwood LeFlore as Choctaw chief in 1830

The Choctaw were the earliest of the Five Civilised Tribes to be evicted from their lands in Alabama, Arkansas, Mississippi and Louisiana, following the Indian Removal Act. Their relocation was managed in three stages between 1831 and 1833 - although some Choctaw refused to leave and their uprooting continued throughout the rest of the 19th century and well into the 20th.

The Choctaw nation had come together in the 17th century from the remnants of other tribes that had occupied lands in the Deep South of America for many thousands of years. A lot of Choctaw had fought for George Washington's army during the American Revolutionary War, and in the politically fraught times that followed, the Choctaw generally sided with the nascent United States Government (or at least, never took up arms against it; they even fought with the US against the Creek Indians in 1813). This spirit of cooperation, however, didn't garner them any special treatment or privileges. Jackson visited them in 1820 as a commissioner representing the United States in a treaty negotiating the boundaries of Choctaw lands. He decided to resort to blackmail, bribery and threats to get his way.

The 1820 Treaty of Doak's Stand saw the Choctaw ceding half their land to the US Government, and agreeing to work towards US citizenship, which would only be granted once they were deemed "civilised and enlightened". But a decade later with Jackson now in office, those remaining rights were lost, and the final 11 million acres of traditional Choctaw land exchanged for 15 million in what's now Oklahoma in the Treaty of Dancing Rabbit Creek. It was the Choctaw's final significant land cession treaty, and the first under the Removal Act. Chief Greenwood LeFlore was almost immediately deposed by the Choctaw for signing the treaty, and succeeded by his nephew, George W Harkins.

Following the treaty, the Choctaw divided into two distinct groups: the Choctaw Nation who undertook the trek to Oklahoma, and the Choctaw Tribe, who stayed behind in Mississippi. Those 5,000 or so who held out were granted US citizenship, but endured legal conflict, harassment, intimidation and violence at the hands of the European Americans who wanted them gone (by 1930 only about 1,600 were still there). The 15,000 who left, meanwhile, had to contend with the brutal winter of 1830-31 and a cholera epidemic in 1832. About 6,000 Choctaw died on the journey.

In the years that followed, most Choctaw supported the Confederacy during the American Civil War, largely due to the promise of a state under Indian control. In World War I, the Choctaw were the first of the US Army's famous codetalkers (their language, as far as the enemy was concerned, an unbreakable code). Today they are the third largest of the remaining Native American tribes.

Two Choctaw tribes are descended from the relocated Choctaw bands: the Jena Band and the Mississippi Band

US Marines search for Seminole warriors in the Everglades during the Second Seminole War

Seminole Chief Osceola

General Ethan Allen Hitchcock denounced the treatment of the Seminole by his own government and troops in 1835

THE
SEMINOLE

The Seminole had settled in the Florida area in the early 18th century. As a people they were a culture made up of offshoots of the Creek, Choctaw and other tribes. Their name is derived from the Spanish 'cimarrón', meaning 'wild' or even 'runaway'. Under the Indian Removal Act they were to be settled in Creek territory west of the Mississippi and be folded back into the Creek tribe. They put up fierce resistance to this, however, fearing that the Creek – who considered them deserters – would take it upon themselves to be aggressively unwelcoming to the Seminole people.

They had fought Andrew Jackson's initial incursions into Florida in a prolonged conflict between 1816 and 1819. However, the Removal Act sparked the Second Seminole War, which raged from 1835 until 1842.

The specific treaty detailing the proposed removal of the Seminole was the Treaty of Payne's Landing. The seven chiefs of the Seminole had travelled to the new Oklahoma reservation and reportedly signed documents agreeing that it was acceptable.

But on returning to Florida the chiefs retracted their apparent consent, saying they had been coerced and bullied into compliance. Even some US Army officers supported this claim. Nevertheless, the Treaty was ratified in April 1834, giving the Seminole three years to vacate the land. When the Seminole refused to recognise the treaty, Florida prepared for conflict.

The 28th of December 1835 saw the Dade Massacre, where 110 American soldiers under the command of Major Francis Dade were ambushed and killed by Seminole Warriors. US Major Ethan Allen Hitchcock, who found the bodies, wrote that it was a wholly avoidable tragedy brought about by "the tyranny of our government". Further skirmishes took place in the subsequent months at Fort Brooke, Fort Barnwell, Camp Cooper, Fort Alabama and Fort Drane, none of which resulted in the defeat of the Seminole: several of the forts even had to be abandoned by the American troops. It eventually took a force of 9,000 US marines, navy and militia,

under the command of Major General Thomas Jesup, to subdue an Indian resistance that had never numbered more than 1,400 warriors. A truce was reached following the Battle of Hatchee-Lustee in January 1837. Hundreds of Seminole surrendered at this point, but those few who did not kept the conflict going until August 1842.

The last act of the war was the capture of Chief Tiger Tail (one of the Seminole leaders during the Dade Massacre) and the killing of his small band of holdouts. Tiger Tail died in New Orleans before he could be transported to Oklahoma. Most of the Seminole resigned themselves to removal, although a hundred or so remained in the Florida Everglades and were left alone on an-ad-hoc reservation of their own. To date, they remain the only tribe never to relinquish their sovereignty or sign a peace treaty with the US.

THE CREEK

Indigenous to the Southeastern Woodlands of the United States, the Creek had been the first Native Americans to be classed as "civilised": they were the first of the Five Civilised Tribes. That's perhaps surprising given their history of resistance and conflict with the US. They had seen their lands ceded to the US by the British following the American Revolution, and had fought alongside the Cherokee against the white settlers of Tennessee during the Cherokee-American Wars of the late 1700s.

The outbreak of the Creek War in 1813 was a series of conflicts between the Creek's Red Stick faction and American militias. There were several Red Stick attacks on American forts, including a famous massacre at Fort Mims, Alabama in August. Creek men, women and children were slaughtered in retaliation for an atrocity at Tallushatchee in November of the same year. General Andrew Jackson finally put down the rebellion at the Battle of Horseshoe Bend in March 1814. The Creek signed the Treaty of Fort Jackson in August, ceding 23 million acres of land in Georgia and Alabama to the US Government. The war effectively undid all the work of previous Creek generations who had attempted to coexist peacefully with the European-American settlers. The antipathy Jackson developed for the Creek during the conflict would be carried into his presidency.

By the time of the Indian Removal Act, there were still about 20,000 Creek in Alabama. Their lands had been divided into individual allotments, and the terms of 1832's Treaty of Cusseta actually gave them the choice of remaining in situ (and submitting to state laws) or relocating to Oklahoma with financial compensation for doing so. In practice, however, staying in place was never really an option. Illegal occupation of Creek lands by settlers was widespread, with US authorities largely turning a blind eye. The increasingly impoverished and desperate Creek resorted once again to attacking the interlopers, leading to the short-lived Second Creek War of 1836. It ended with the forced removal of the Creek by troops under the command of General Winfield Scott. In mid-1837 about 15,000 Creek were first rounded up into internment camps and then driven from their land for the final time. About a quarter of them died on the arduous journey west to Oklahoma.

Subsequently the Creek were divided in their loyalties during the American Civil War, with some supporting the Confederacy and others siding with the Union. President Abraham Lincoln initially rewarded the loyalists with increased government aid, but the actions of the rebels meant a new treaty was required in 1866. Under its terms the Creek lost further territory, with part of the Creek reservation given over to recently emancipated slaves.

Members of the Creek Nation, photographed in 1877

Chief Red Eagle surrenders to Andrew Jackson following the Battle of Horseshoe Bend in 1814

THE CHICKASAW

The Chickasaw are closely related to the Choctaw. Their oral history recalls their settling in Mississippi in prehistoric times, and the two peoples separated into distinct tribes sometime in the 17th century. Their first contact with Europeans was when the Spanish explorer Hernando de Soto encountered them in 1540. After several disagreements they attacked his entourage and he swiftly moved on. They allied with the British in 1670 (a period that often brought them into conflict with the Choctaw), and with the newly formed United States in the Revolutionary War. Subsequently they tended always to side with the US and its government, even as their rights and lands were eroded.

The treaty securing their removal west was that of Pontotoc Creek in 1832. A previous attempt had failed in 1830, when the Chickasaw had baulked at the poor quality of the land they were being offered in Oklahoma. But two years later, with the encroachment of the European-American settlers onto their valuable Mississippi territories, and an epidemic of whiskey addiction, they began to feel their culture was being overwhelmed and on the point of being wiped out. An indication of their desperation at this point is that they ended up ceding their Mississippi lands to the government on merely the promise of new land being found for them. Uniquely among the Five Civilised Tribes, they were also persuaded to pay for their own migration. They used the financial compensation they received for their Mississippi lands to buy a part of the Choctaw tribe's new Oklahoma territory. The American Senate ratified the agreement between the Chickasaw and the Choctaw in the 1837 Treaty of Doaksville – unusual for an internal matter between Native Americans.

The Chickasaw's migration west began in 1837 and continued into the following year. Just under 5,000 Chickasaw made the journey, which was accomplished relatively successfully compared to the trails of tears the other four tribes endured. Instead, their privations began on arrival, when most Chickasaw, rather than gaining their own new district on former Choctaw land as arranged, were interned in temporary camps in Choctaw towns and government supply depots. Poverty, addiction, internal political disputes and attacks from other tribes were rife, and it would be another 15 years before they were finally settled in a dedicated Chickasaw territory.

The Chickasaw formally separated from the Choctaw, emerging as a new Chickasaw Nation in 1856. In the Civil War they joined the Confederacy. By 1907, following the defeat of the Five Tribes' petition for statehood, the Chickasaw were a powerless minority in their own lands. The 20th century saw a revival in their fortunes, however. They were officially recognised as a Nation again in 1983.

The Chickasaw Holmes Colbert represented the tribe politically after the Civil War

An unknown Chickasaw warrior, photographed in the 1880s

A rising of the Chickasaw people, angry at mistreatment, is suppressed by the United States Cavalry

The Cherokee are pictured here removing to the West

President Martin Van Buren succeeded Andrew Jackson and enforced the Cherokee Removal

Elizabeth Brown Stephens was one of thousands of Cherokee on the Trail of Tears. This photograph was taken in 1903 when she was 82

THE CHEROKEE

Incursion on Indian land by European-American settlers had always been due to its particular desirability, whether for perfect farming conditions, mineral deposits, or both. In the case of the Cherokee's land in Georgia, however, there was a very specific reason: gold. The Georgia Gold Rush, in which thousands of prospectors descended on Cherokee land in search of their fortune, began in 1829, preceding the more famous California Gold Rush by 20 years. The Cherokee, who had inhabited the land since prehistoric times, were quickly overwhelmed. The State of Georgia, far from supporting its indigenous people, was desperate to get them out of the way.

Even by the previous standards of the Indian Removal Act, the treaty that uprooted the Cherokee was dubious in its morality and legality. The Treaty of New Echota was accepted neither by the tribal leaders nor the majority of the Cherokee people, but was nevertheless enforced in 1838 by Andrew Jackson's successor, Martin Van Buren. Sadly a new president didn't mean a change in Native American fortunes. Having refused to recognise the terms of the deal, the Cherokee were first herded into internment camps for several months, before being forcibly marched from their lands by militia troops. Twelve wagon trains, each comprising about a thousand Cherokee, began the arduous trek in the winter of 1838. Their various routes encompassed trails through Kentucky, Illinois, Tennessee,

Mississippi, Arkansas and Missouri. Most of the Cherokee travelled barefoot.

Malnutrition, disease, pneumonia and exposure were rife on the journey. The summer in the camps had been one of blistering heat and severe drought, and the winter of that year was freakishly cold, making progress brutally slow (the 96 kilometres between the Ohio and Mississippi rivers alone took three months). The risk of the Cherokee bringing sickness to populations meant their journey was made even longer than it might have been, since they were forbidden from passing through towns or settlements and had to go around them. When they reached the Ohio river they were charged a dollar a head by the ferryman who usually only charged 12 cents. On the long wait to cross the river, many Cherokee died from exhaustion and starvation. Some were even murdered by locals.

The Cherokee finally reached their destination in Oklahoma in the early months of 1839. Between the internment camps and the journey itself, the estimated death toll was between 4,000 and 6,000.

Today, the Cherokee are the largest Native American group in the US, but the shameful ethnic cleansing of them and the other Civilised Tribes has not been forgotten. The 3,540-kilometre Trail of Tears National Historic Trail was opened in commemoration in 1987. The Five Tribes finally received a formal apology from the US Government in 2008.

Bluffer's Guide
The Texas Revolution

MEXICO, 2 OCTOBER 1835 - 21 APRIL 1836

Did you know?

The modern city of Houston, Texas, was named after General Sam Houston following his leadership at the Battle of San Jacinto

Timeline

2 OCTOBER 1835

COME AND TAKE IT

Though little more than a skirmish, the Battle of Gonzales marks the first official conflict of the revolution, ending in a Texian victory.

23 OCTOBER 1835

After months of manoeuvring, the Constitution of 1824 is overturned, and in December the Siete Leyes are enacted, underlining the validity of the Texian cause.

6 MARCH 1836

After holding out for 13 days against vastly superior numbers, Texian forces are overrun and slaughtered at the Battle of the Alamo.

27 MARCH 1836

On the orders of Santa Anna, hundreds of Texian prisoners are massacred at Goliad following their surrender at the Battle of Coleto Creek.

The Texas Revolution

? What was it?

In protest at legislative changes made by the federal government, residents of the Mexican province of Texas took up arms in late 1835 and expelled the region's federal troops. Shortly after, the Consultation (a provisional Texian government) was assembled to oversee the burgeoning revolution, and determine its goals - a return to the Mexican Constitution of 1824 or independence.

Angered by the rebellion, President Antonio López de Santa Anna opted to personally lead a military force to retake Texas, entering the province in early 1836. The cruelty shown by the Mexican army caused swathes of civilians to flee before them, an exodus known as the Runaway Scrape, and ultimately won more sympathy for the revolutionaries' cause. The decisive conflict came at the Battle of San Jacinto, where Santa Anna was captured following a surprise attack. The Texian army emerged victorious after just 18 minutes.

The revolution left Texas as an independent republic, though Mexico refused to recognise it as such. This state of affairs, which would exist for almost a decade, culminated in annexation by the United States and the outbreak of the Mexican-American War.

? Why did it happen?

There were a number of factors that contributed to the outbreak of the Texas Revolution, but chief among them was a cultural and political disconnect between the Anglo-American population of the region, and the Mexican government. After winning independence in 1821, Mexico relaxed regulations on colonists or 'empresarios', which allowed thousands of settlers to move to Texas from the southern United States. The end result was a region where Anglo-American Texians outnumbered the Spanish and Mexican Tejanos.

The final straw came with the introduction of the 'Siete Leyes' (Seven Laws) in 1835. This legislation radically changed the governmental structure of Mexico, but their most salient consequence was the further centralisation of political power under Santa Anna. Reaction to these changes in Texas was overwhelmingly negative, and effectively lit the revolutionary touch paper, though it's safe to say that revolution had already become a case of 'when' and not 'if'.

? Who was involved?

Antonio López de Santa Anna
21 February 1794 - 21 June 1876
President of Mexico, Santa Anna personally led the Mexican Army during the revolution and was ultimately captured at San Jacinto.

Sam Houston
2 March 1793 - 26 July 1863
Leader of the Texian army, Houston successfully led his forces in the Battle of San Jacinto to clinch victory for the revolutionaries.

Davy Crockett
17 August 1786 - 6 March 1836
A famed American frontiersman and politician, Crockett passed into folklore thanks to his heroic death at the Battle of the Alamo.

21 APRIL 1836

Texian forces rout the Mexican army in the decisive Battle of San Jacinto, the final major armed conflict of the Texas Revolution. Santa Anna is taken prisoner.

14 MAY 1836

The Treaties of Velasco are signed by the captured Santa Anna, ending hostilities, though they are not officially ratified by the Mexican government.

The Mexican-American War

America's Manifest Destiny is a concept that is taught in schools across the globe, but it wasn't something that happened easily

M anifest Destiny - the phrase and its sentiment would soon grow strong in the fledgling United States of America after shrugging off its colonial shackles. However, it wasn't enough for this newborn country to thrive on its hard-fought freedoms while still clutching to the east coast of the continent - its booming populations and pioneer spirit demanded more.

By the time James K Polk was sworn in as the 11th president, all eyes were already fixed on the west and the riches it could yield. "Our Union is a confederation of independent States, whose policy is peace with each other and all the world," he declared in his address. "To enlarge its limits is to extend the dominions of peace over additional territories and increasing millions. The world has nothing to fear from military ambition in our Government." However, just one year later in 1846,

the US would be at war and American blood would be shed on foreign soil for the first time.

After fighting hard to break from the grip of their respective European parents, the US and Mexico was each seeking to define itself on the North American continent. However, the former Spanish dependency immediately struggled to control the vast swathes of land it had inherited in 1821, stretching from the state of Coahuila y Tejas in the north-east, to California in the north-west and all the way down to the Yucatan in the south. The population of Texas (a part of the Coahuila y Tejas state) in particular proved a problem for the Mexican government, as it was mainly populated by American immigrants fresh with the notions of freedom, democracy and equality. Though there was willingness to join the newly created nation of Mexico, as more and more Mexican immigrants travelled the state it became increasingly clear that an American-majority could prove troublesome.

By 1835, tensions reached a crescendo. Through desperate attempts to maintain control over its outlying state, the Mexican government had stopped all legal American immigration into Texas. Worse, under the new dictatorship of Antonio López de Santa Anna, an increased centralisation of power was dashing the hopes of a free democracy in the state and the country. In the meantime Texas had grown rich, with its exports of cotton and animal skins amounting to some half a million dollars. This made it a prize worth keeping or, for the American government, one well worth acquiring. It wasn't long before tensions boiled over into outright hostilities, with the Mexican government seeking to tighten its grip on Texas. The military presence in Texas was stepped up dramatically, and when Mexican troops under Francisco de Castaneda were sent to confiscate a cannon belonging to the colonists of Gonzales, the Texians refused. The ensuing skirmish sparked the Texas Revolution, which

1836-1845

UNITED STATES

Arkansas R.

Claimed Territory

TEXAS

Rio Grande

Washington

S. Antonio

MEXICO

Nueces River

The Mexican-American war saw the beginning of the Manifest Destiny. It saw Texas take independence from Mexico

KEY FIGURES

General Antonio López de Santa Anna

Dubbed the Napoleon of the West, Santa Anna's ambitions both as a general and president of Mexico are unsurpassed in the country's history. He offered to lead the Mexican forces defending the invasion by the US, shortly before announcing himself president.

President James K Polk

After running on a ticket supporting widespread expansion of US borders, Polk was sworn in as the 11th President of the USA just as tensions with Mexico were coming to a head. He served only one term in office, before retiring soon after the end of the ensuing war.

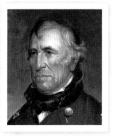

General Zachary Taylor

A seasoned veteran, Taylor had fought in the War of 1812, as well as against the Black Crow and Seminole Native American tribes. During the Mexican-American War his experience helped win many battles. He was elected the 12th President of the US after President Polk's death in 1849.

John C Frémont

Frémont was involved in numerous missions into the West, searching for potential routes to the Pacific. While operating in California he came into conflict with Mexican populations, who saw his mission as hostile. He was actively involved in armed uprisings, and became the first Senator of California in 1850.

General Mariano Arista

Serving in the New Spanish army before joining the revolutionary cause, Arista fought during the Texas Revolution. Soon after the Mexican-American War he succeeded de Herrera as president.

José Joaquín de Herrera

At times serving as the President of Mexico, Herrera's willingness to compromise with American officials in the sale of territory cost him his office. He served as a general during the war.

The Mexican General Santa Anna surrenders to Texan Sam Houston after a battle that lasted just 18 minutes

"The Manifest Destiny, it would seem, was not something that would happen of its own accord"

would prove to be brief, but bloody. The Battle of the Alamo stands as its most-iconic moment, where just under 200 Texians, defending their position against nearly ten times as many Mexicans, were slaughtered ruthlessly by Santa Anna's men. The battle, more aptly described as a massacre, only served to inspire further resistance against Mexican rule and is even to this day inscribed in the folklore of the Lone Star State. The Alamo, as well as Goliad where hundreds of Texian prisoners were executed, quickly became rallying cries for the Revolution and united the colonists. After the embarrassing but decisive defeat by an inferior Texian force at the Battle of San Jacinto, Santa Anna was forced

to surrender. It had taken just a few months for the small uprising to bring the Mexican state to its knees. Even before the election of President Polk, the US was working to strengthen its presence in California, Oregon and the disputed lands west of Texas. The Manifest Destiny, it would seem, was not something that would happen of its own accord. Shortly after Texas' successful revolution, talk of its annexation by the US was rife. The many American colonists in Texas were in favour of the idea, but it wasn't until 1845 that a bill was successfully passed through congress to officially form the 28th State of the USA. All the while John C Frémont, a lieutenant in the Topographical

Engineers of the US Army, had been tasked with finding a route from the Mississippi River to the Pacific, acting almost as the spearhead of further American expansionist ambitions. In January 1846, during his latest exploration of California, Frémont took with him an armed group of around 60. Like Texas, California was a contentious territory and was desired by Mexico, the US and even Great Britain for its potential riches, as well as its access to the Pacific Ocean.

Whether or not Frémont's presence was intended to galvanise the pro-independence American settlers in California or not, shortly after his arrival the Bear Flag Revolution sprang up to gain the province's own freedom from the Mexican state. This was yet another thorn in the side of the Mexican government, who now saw the American grip on the western territories tightening. In the meantime yet another of President Polk's agents, John Slidell, had been sent to Mexico City to meet with President José

Timeline

1821

● **Mexico wins independence**
After over 11 years of fighting the Spanish crown, revolutionary forces of former New Spain, or the Mexican Empire, declare independence from the colonial power.
28 September 1821

● **Texas Revolution begins**
Responding to an increased centralising of power and military aggression by the Mexican government, many Texans revolt in a bid to win independence for the state.
21 October 1835

● **Battle of the Alamo**
General Santa Anna's army of around 1,600 surrounds a small Texan garrison at the Alamo. After a short siege, the Mexican army massacres almost the entire garrison.
6 March 1836

● **Battle of San Jacinto**
Taking Santa Anna's force entirely by surprise, a smaller force of Texans under Sam Houston defeats the Mexican army in a battle that lasts just 18 minutes. Texas independence is declared.
21 April 1836

● **Battle of Salado Creek**
After re-election as President of Mexico, Santa Anna attempts to retake the former province of Texas. His army under Adrián Woll is defeated by the Texians.
17 September 1842

Joaquín de Herrera. His supposed intention was discussing peace terms over Texas, which wasn't yet recognised as a US State by Mexico. Secretly, however, Slidell had been sent with a mandate to offer over $20,000,000 in exchange for the territories of New Mexico and California. When the Mexican press heard of the deal they were outraged and Herrera was branded as a traitor to his country - there was no way a Mexican president could even entertain the notion of making deals with the Americans. Slidell was forced to leave empty-handed - methods of diplomacy and even commerce had failed to settle the situation, so now it seemed a slip into war was inevitable. With all the pieces in place, only the slightest of confrontations was needed to set the coming war into motion. In January 1846 President Polk directed General Zachary Taylor, which he had previously positioned at Corpus Christi in the south of the state, towards the Rio Grande river. This was seen as an act of aggression and is in fact the natural border between the two countries even today.

On the evening of 24 April Captain Seth Barton Thornton, part of Taylor's contingent, set off with around 70 dragoons to patrol an area near La Rosia, nearer the Rio Grande. They cautiously scouted out the area after sunrise on the 25 April to discover if and where the Mexican force had crossed the Rio Grande. They would find out soon enough.

While investigating a plantation, Thornton and his men became trapped by a vastly

During the Battle of Alamo the Mexican army massacred almost all of the Texan garrison

superior Mexican force commanded by General Torrejon. Without setting any guards or taking any precautions to stay alert of the enemy, the Americans had been taken completely by surprise by thousands Mexican troops already encamped in the area. 16 of the dragoons were killed and the rest taken by Torrejon's force, including Captain Thornton and his officers.

News of the Thornton Affair, as it would later become known, reached Washington in May and gave President Polk his casus belli. He stood before Congress on 11 May and declared Mexico had "invaded our territory and shed American blood upon American soil. She has proclaimed that hostilities have commenced, and that the two nations are now at war". There was no question of whether Congress would vote for the war, which was officially declared on 13 May.

From the fires of revolution, both Mexico and the United States had finally collided and the following conflict would decide the shape of the continent for future generations.

The Manifest Destiny, the self-fulfilling prophecy of the USA's dominance in North America, was to be fought for on the battlefields of Palo Alto, Tabasco and many others. Soon Mexico City itself fell to the American forces and the Mexican government was bitterly forced to concede defeat.

A small band of Texans took the Mexican army by surprise during the Battle of San Jacinto in an 18-minute battle

CALIFORNIA REPUBLIC

The first official state flag of the state of California. It was first raised in the 1846 revolt

● Polk elected president
After winning the presidency on a ticket promising further expansion into the west, James Polk takes office amid heightened tensions between the US, Mexico and Great Britain.
4 March 1845

● U.S.A. annexes Texas
After negotiations between the Republic of Texas and the USA, the bill to incorporate Texas as a US State is passed by Congress. Texas becomes a state by the end of the year.
29 December 1845

● de Herrera deposed
After Polk sends an agent with an offer to buy the territories of California and New Mexico for $20m, President José Joaquín de Herrera is deposed for even considering the possibility.
December 1845

● Thornton Affair
With General Zachary Taylor encamped north of the Rio Grande river, a small contingent of dragoons under Captain Seth Thornton is attacked and captured by a superior Mexican force.
25 April 1846

● War declared
After receiving news of the Thornton Affair, President Polk addresses congress and presents his case for war with Mexico. The vote passes with a large majority and war is declared.
13 May 1846

WAR & RECONSTRUCTION

Civil war and an immigration boom transformed the United States through the 19th and early 20th centuries

The Making of America
1850-1930

31 December 1879
Edison's light bulb moment

It was a cold, bitter evening in Menlo Park, New Jersey when a large group of New Year's Eve revellers gathered to see the latest invention from Thomas Alva Edison. His creation, a new type of incandescent light bulb, was the talk of the town and the Pennsylvania Railroad Company had been running a special train route all day so it could ferry excited citizens to the dimly lit park.

The 'Wizard of Menlo Park' had already made a huge impact on the progress of American technology with the invention of the phonograph (an early form of the gramophone), but his next project would change every street, road and avenue in America — and the world beyond. With the single flick of a switch, the gathered crowds outside his laboratories at Menlo Park were suddenly bathed in light as Edison unveiled a brand new form of incandescent light bulb — one which would be long-lasting and affordable.

Edison is often credited as the sole inventor of the light bulb, but older, cruder versions of the gaslight alternative had been humming with life in select American homes for the better part of four decades. The light bulb was more of a group effort, a social cabal of brilliant minds that co-operated, borrowed and outright stole ideas along the way to that evening in New Jersey. Edison's version was a true game-changer — he'd worked for years, testing over 600 materials from across the world, endlessly experimenting until he found one that could potentially conduct light for over 1,000 hours.

Edison had patented his design, which used a form of carbonised threat, the month before and it went on to transform America and the world in the years to come. Not only was his incandescent light bulb small and simple to use, but it was cheap. By making an affordable light source, Edison helped take the world out of partial darkness and into a new one of bright lights and illumination.

> While light bulbs already existed in American in the 19th century, Edison was the man to make them affordable

It was here, in Edison's laboratory in New Jersey that he debuted his affordable take on the incandescent light bulb in 1879

Defining moments

Statue of Liberty is dedicated
28 October 1886
Originally conceived as a monument gift from France to the United States to celebrate the centennial of the Declaration of Independence, the Statue of Liberty proved to be a costly and difficult project for both nations. It wasn't until 1886, a full decade after its planned completion date, that then president Grover Cleveland was able to dedicate it properly.

The Panic of 1893
February 1893
One of many economic crises suffered by the United States in the 19th and 20th centuries, the Panic of 1893 lasted for four years before financial stability was somewhat restored. The recession was caused by poor crop yields (leading to a collapse of wheat prices), European investments pulling out and domestic issues such as the bankruptcy of the Philadelphia and Reading Railroad in February 1893.

Assassination of William McKinley
6 September 1901
While attending the Pan-American Exposition in Buffalo, New York, 25th president William McKinley was shot by a disgruntled anarchist, Leon Czolgosz. Czolgosz had lost is livelihood in the Panic of 1893 and blamed McKinley for his misfortune. McKinley died eight days later. Czolgosz was executed by electric chair on 29 October 1901.

ORIGINS

Humphry Davy demonstrates first electric lamp, 1809

Arc-lighting used for lighting in Paris, 1841

Alexander Lodygin patents his incandescent light bulb, 1874

LEGACY

Edison produces 1,500 hour light bulb

Street lighting becomes more common

Electric lighting completely replaces gaslight

• San Francisco earthquake
18 April 1906

In the early hours of a Wednesday morning, San Francisco suffered one of the worst natural disasters in the history of the United States. The city was rocked by an earthquake that registered 7.9 on the Richter scale. The initial quake and its aftershocks killed over 3,000 people and levelled 80 per cent of the city's buildings and dwellings.

• First ever jazz album recorded
26 February 1917

Jazz, in its earliest forms, had been developing in New Orleans throughout the 19th century before the first jazz (or 'jass' as it was known among some grassroots musicians) was recorded in 1917. The record, 'Livery Stable Blues', was made by the all-white Original Dixieland Jass Band and proved a breakout success for jazz music outside the 'Big Easy'.

• US enters World War I
6 April 1917

For years, the United States had done its best to remain neutral in the steadily worsening conflict in Europe. While it wasn't officially part of the Allies (taking part as an independent nation), the US was eventually prompted to join when British intelligence intercepted an encoded message from Germany urging Mexico to form a military alliance. The US's involvement, especially its supply of resources, helped turn the tide of the war.

A land of hope built on suffering

For millions of people, the American Dream had a horrendous flip side: the living nightmare of slavery

Slavery looms large in the history of the United States. But there should be little surprise that slavery was practised - first in the British colonies and then, after the War of Independence - in the new United States of America, for slavery has been a universal human institution, carried out throughout history and in pretty well every civilisation. What is unusual about slavery in America was that it eventually became the great political, moral and religious issue of its day, finally dragging the country into the bloodiest war in its history. In the end, America baptised itself in blood over a principle: that no man might own another.

The first African slaves were landed in the British colony of Virginia in 1619. They were brought there by Dutch traders who had captured a Spanish slave ship. However, the Spaniards had already baptised the Africans so, according to English common law, they were treated as indentured servants, a condition shared by many of the poor white colonists who could not afford to pay their own passage across the Atlantic. As indentured servants, they were bound to an employer for a fixed period, but after that time had

expired they were entitled to their freedom. But over the next century the distinction between black and white, and the institution of slavery, was gradually put into law, with Massachusetts the first state to authorise slavery in law. In 1662, in response to a case where a mixed-race woman, Elizabeth Key Grinstead, had successfully won her freedom and that of her son on the grounds that she was a Christian and the daughter of an Englishman, Virginia changed its statutes so that children took their status from their mother, not their father. This meant that the child of a slave woman would be born into slavery and it also freed male white slave owners from the responsibility of raising children fathered on slave women. Although slavery existed throughout the colonies, by the 18th century there was a significant difference in how slaves were employed, with those in the north usually working as servants, craftsmen and labourers in cities, while those in the south largely worked the land, on crops such as tobacco and rice. For such labour-intensive work, southern plantation owners invested heavily in slaves. However, voices were already being raised against slavery throughout the

> The hotly contested issue of slavery would eventually be one of the major factors that led to the Civil War in 1861

John Brown going to his execution. On the morning of his death he wrote: "I, John Brown, am now quite certain that the crimes of this guilty land will never be purged away but with blood. I had, as I now think, vainly flattered myself that without very much bloodshed it might be done"

Nat Turner's rebellion

A Virginian slave, Nat Turner had learned to read and write when he was very young and had immersed himself in the Bible, seeing visions and hearing messages that convinced him that God had appointed to him a great mission. These visions had coalesced into the belief that, "I should arise and prepare myself, and slay my enemies with their own weapons";

He would lead a great slave uprising against the white masters. The signs from heaven throughout the year of 1831 – including an annular solar eclipse – had convinced him the time had come. Now, standing in front of a small group of men gathered in the woods of Southampton County, Turner told them what they had to do. In the depths of that night they would rise and "kill all the white people". This would be no gentle revolt but one born of decades of cruel treatment.

The first to die were Turner's owners. In the early hours of 22 August, the seven men made their way to the Travis farmstead. Turner had become the property of Joseph Travis when the widow of his previous owner had married Travis. Turner climbed into the house through an open window and let the other rebels in, before they filed silently into the room where Travis lay sleeping. Turner struck the first blow but it served only to wake Travis, who rose, yelling for his wife. Another slave killed Travis with an axe, before turning the weapon on Travis's wife, her nine-year-old son, and a farmworker. It was only after they left the house that they realised they had left one family alive: the baby. Two men went back and killed him in his cradle.

Gathering men as they went, the rebels attacked other farmsteads, killing everyone they found, but soon the alarm was spread, church bells ringing through the district and the white militia arming itself against its worst fears. In two days, the rebels killed 60 men, women and children, before the group was overwhelmed, although Turner managed to escape, hiding out in the woods for two months before he was finally discovered. He was tried on 5 November and executed on 11 November 1831, his body flayed and beheaded. The bloodiest slave rebellion in US history was over – but not forgotten.

On Sunday 30 October 1831, farmer Benjamin Phipps, armed with a loaded gun, spotted some out-of-place fence rails and discovered Nat Turner after he had eluded searchers for two months

> "By 1804, every northern state had outlawed slavery, while the economy of the southern states was becoming tied ever more closely to slavery, in particular following the invention of the cotton gin"

British Empire and the North American colonies. Individual colonies, and later states, would outlaw slavery outright during the United States' fledgling years of independence, but the trans-Atlantic slave trade would not formally be prohibited until the passing of a federal act in 1807. Conditions for slaves in the British colonies were comparatively better than elsewhere in the New World, and the population of slaves expanded rapidly.

During the American War of Independence, both British loyalists and American patriots promised freedom to slaves who fought on their side but despite the Revolutionary army being between one fifth and one quarter black, the new Constitution of the United States required free states to return escaped slaves to slave states. Already, the divide between the northern 'free' and the southern 'slave' states was deepening. By 1804, every northern

> Vermont abolished slavery in 1777, while it was still an independent republic; it joined the Union in 1791

state had outlawed slavery, while the economy of the southern states was becoming tied ever more closely to slavery, in particular following the invention of the cotton gin. Tobacco growing exhausts the soil but when Eli Whitney invented the cotton gin in 1793, making it much easier to remove the seeds from cotton fibre, the southern states quickly moved to growing cotton to supply the rapidly growing demand for cotton from the newly mechanised textile industry in England. Slavery, which might have declined, was reinforced and although Congress outlawed the importation of African slaves in 1807, the domestic population expanded rapidly, reaching nearly four million by 1860.

Slaves in the south were not allowed to learn to read and write. In order to control a population that amounted to a third of the populace, slave owners pursued a policy of creating a hierarchy among their slaves, with the more privileged house slaves lording it over agricultural workers. While slaves did marry, these marriages had no legal basis and slave owners could sell off children and split husbands from wives. Punishments for misbehavious were severe and when rebellions did occur, they were dealt with savagely.

In the face of what southerners came to call their 'peculiar institution', a growing abolitionist movement spread in the northern states. Quakers were prominent early opponents of slavery, and they formed the core of the first abolitionist society, the Society for the Relief of Free Negroes Unlawfully Held in Bondage, founded in 1775 and renamed the Pennsylvania Abolition Society in 1784. No less a figure than Benjamin Franklin became its president.

However, political power in Congress was evenly split between 'free' and 'slave' states, with 11 states in each camp. But as the United States spread westward, and new territories petitioned to be admitted to the union, the question of whether these new states would be 'free' or 'slave' states became ever more pressing. When Missouri asked to join the union as a slave state, a compromise was effected whereby Maine simultaneously became part of the United States as a free state, maintaining the uneasy balance. But the Missouri Compromise also stipulated that any future states north of the line of latitude at 36 degrees and 30 minutes would be free states, while those south of it would be slave states, extending slavery westwards with the same north/south divide.

A further effort at a solution was made in 1854 when the Kansas-Nebraska Act stipulated that whether new states should be free or slave should be decided by a popular vote. Many politicians,

seeing this as an effort by the slavery-supporting Democratic Party to expand the 'peculiar institution', left the party to join the new anti-slavery party, the Republicans. When Kansas came to vote on whether it should be free or slave, many natives of Missouri came across the border to vote for slavery, skewing the results and leading to growing anger among Kansas abolitionists. The conflict grew increasingly nasty, with a rash of murders and lynchings committed by both sides, leading to the new state being given the nickname 'bleeding Kansas'.

Some abolitionists became increasingly impatient at the slow pace of reform, chief among these being John Brown. He had come to see the conflict in apocalyptic terms, and slavery as so heinous a sin that it could only be redeemed by a great blood sacrifice. To that end he led an attack at the armoury at Harper's Ferry in West Virginia with the aim of raising a general slave revolt. The attack failed, and Brown and most of his followers were either killed or executed, but the incident further inflamed the tensions between free and slave states.

In 1852, Harriet Beecher Stowe published Uncle Tom's Cabin, an anti-slavery novel that became the bestseller of the 19th century, further convincing the northern free states of the immorality of slavery. In response, outraged southerners produced a stream of anti-Tom novels, attempting to show how slavery was a necessary institution for a race that was unable to look after itself.

A slave auction block at Green Hill Plantation, Campbell County, Virginia

Dred Scott was an African-American slave whose plea for emancipation was rejected by the Supreme Court

Then, in 1857, the Supreme Court made its infamous Dred Scott decision, which declared that the descendants of Africans imported into the US as a slave could not be American citizens and that the federal government had no power to outlaw slavery in the new territories being acquired with westward expansion. Thinking to end the political debate over slavery by making it a matter of settled law, the Supreme Court's decision had the opposite effect, enraging northern opposition to slavery and splitting the Democratic Party into two. In 1860, Abraham Lincoln, of the new abolitionist political party, the Republicans, took advantage of the split among the Democrats and was elected president. In response, the southern slave states withdrew from the Union, forming the Confederate States of America on 4 February 1861. There would be no more talking. The great moral question of America's founding would be answered in blood.

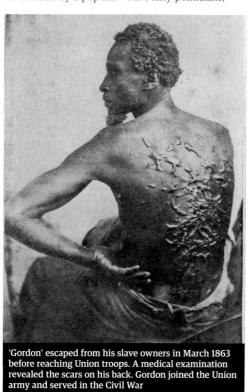

'Gordon' escaped from his slave owners in March 1863 before reaching Union troops. A medical examination revealed the scars on his back. Gordon joined the Union army and served in the Civil War

Slaves planting sweet potatoes. The majority of southern slaves worked the land

LINCOLN'S CIVIL WAR

Politically, the president of a country waging war on itself ought to have failed, yet Abraham Lincoln is revered for his leadership when American fought American

The bombardment began at 4.30am. Cannon batteries stationed around the harbour at Charleston in South Carolina launched salvo after salvo upon a small island fort. By 11am, a fifth of its buildings were on fire. Soon after midday, the fort's flagpole was struck, and 'Old Glory', the national flag of the United States, fell. For the structure under fire was Fort Sumter, a stronghold of the Federal Government in the first state to secede from the Union. The commander of the fort, Major Robert Anderson, had refused to surrender it to General PGT Beauregard of the Confederate army, and the cannons were lit. It was 12 April 1861. The American Civil War had begun.

The besieged fort remained under fire for 34 hours before Anderson surrendered. Somehow, no one perished in the actual attack. Yet, unmistakably, the forces of the Confederate States of America had opened fire on the forces of the United States of America. The nation was divided and at war with itself. How had it come to this?

Perhaps it was inevitable given the contradiction between the words in the 1776 Declaration of Independence and the morality of those who wrote them. The Declaration stated that it was a "self-evident" truth that "all men are created equal." Yet its guiding author, Thomas Jefferson, and many other signatories were slave owners. Indeed, the Constitution of 1787 permitted slavery. As many as eight presidents owned slaves while in office and many others in government were slaveholders.

However, opposition to slavery was growing on moral, political and religious grounds. Many of the Northern States had abolished it by 1800. It was soon to be outlawed by the British Empire, too. As the abolition movement grew, inhabitants of the Southern States took to defending slavery as a 'paternalistic' institution, and a 'positive good', even using biblical references in their arguments. In reality, slavery in the South was the driving

> "WE ALL DECLARE FOR LIBERTY, BUT IN USING THE SAME WORD WE DO NOT ALL MEAN THE SAME THING"
> **Address to Baltimore, 1864**

force of the region's economy. Plantation owners, particularly in the cotton fields, relied heavily upon slave labour. It wasn't going to be given up easily.

After the war with Mexico ended in 1848, the borders of the American Republic became finalised. Expansion into the new territories to the west began, but disputes about whether they should become free or slave states were fierce, and at times violent. Various compromises and short-term fixes gave some stability, but the ultimate problem was crystallised by a speech on 16 June 1858 in Springfield, Illinois. It was given by the newly

formed Republican Party's candidate for the Illinois Senate seat. He argued: "A house divided against itself cannot stand. I believe this government cannot endure permanently, half slave and half free. I do not expect the Union to be dissolved. I do not expect this house to fall. But I do expect it will cease to be divided." The candidate's name was Abraham Lincoln.

Born in 1809 to a poor Kentucky farming family, Lincoln was raised in a single-room log cabin. With minimal formal education, he virtually taught himself, later earning a living through various manual jobs. After the family moved to Illinois, he applied his mind to learning the law, eventually passing the bar exam in 1836. Lincoln made a success of his profession to earn a good living. He married Mary Todd, the daughter of a wealthy Kentucky slaveholder, in 1846 and later served a single term in the House of Representatives as a Whig party member. The Whigs, though, were a waning political force. A new grouping, the Republicans, which opposed the extension of slavery to the newer states, appealed to Lincoln. He joined them in 1856. Within two years, he was selected as the Republican Party's Illinois nomination for the US Senate.

Lincoln's opponent was the sitting US senator of the Democrat Party Stephen Douglas. The pair contested seven debates, which were extensively reported in newspapers across the country. Lincoln's closely argued proposition of prohibiting

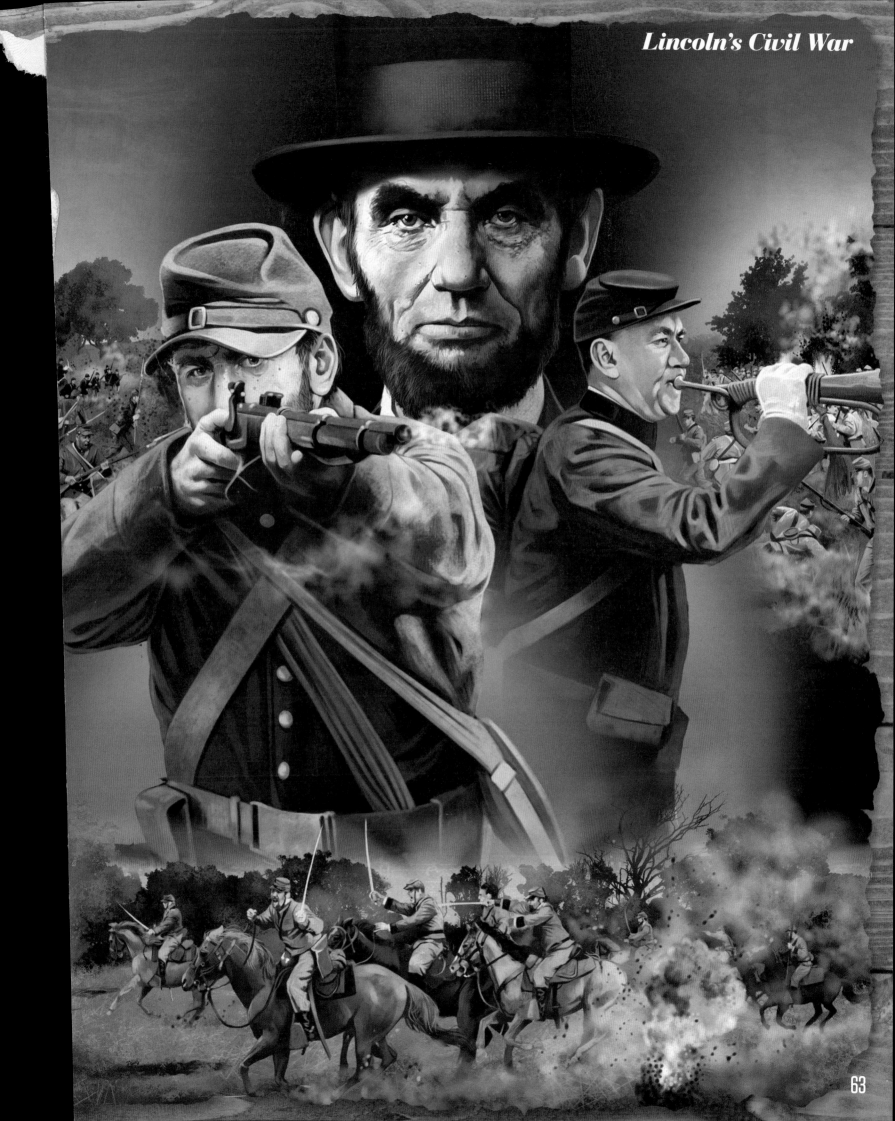

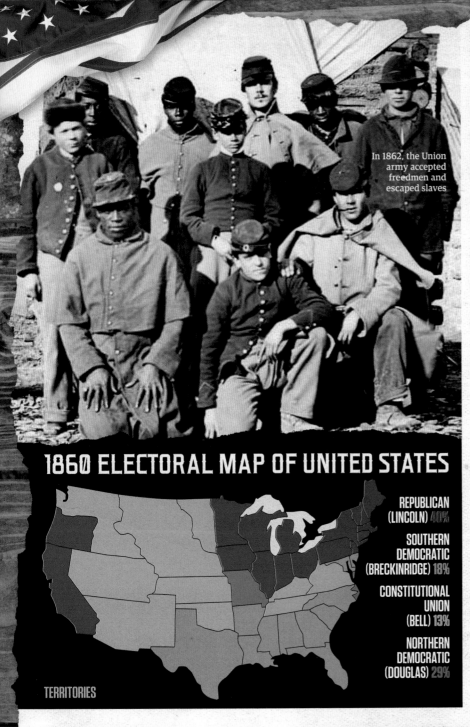

In 1862, the Union army accepted freedmen and escaped slaves

1860 ELECTORAL MAP OF UNITED STATES

REPUBLICAN (LINCOLN) 40%

SOUTHERN DEMOCRATIC (BRECKINRIDGE) 18%

CONSTITUTIONAL UNION (BELL) 13%

NORTHERN DEMOCRATIC (DOUGLAS) 29%

TERRITORIES

The 54th Massachusetts Infantry Regiment at the Second Battle of Fort Wagner

the extension of slavery in the new territories frequently forced Douglas on to the back foot. Despite that, Douglas prevailed when the state legislature (which at that time elected US senators) voted 54-46 in the Democrat's favour. However, the positions Douglas had adopted in countering Lincoln's arguments angered his party's members in the Southern States, which later proved costly.

In contrast, despite losing the Senate race, Lincoln won widespread acclaim as an eloquent debater for Republican values. When his party sought a candidate to run for president in 1860, it turned to the poor farmer's boy from Kentucky.

The belief was that as a moderate candidate, Lincoln could win in Pennsylvania and the Mid-west States. He was not an abolitionist, like some more radical members of his party, and he pledged not to interfere with slavery in the Southern States. Indeed, he felt the Constitution prohibited any attempt to do so. Yet he had always been against slavery, labelling it wrong both morally and politically. His fervent hope was that it would

"WHEN I HEAR ANYONE ARGUING FOR SLAVERY, I FEEL A STRONG IMPULSE TO SEE IT TRIED ON HIM PERSONALLY"

Statement to an Indiana regiment passing through Washington, 1865

become extinct over time as states moved to reject it. Crucially, however, he was firm in his opposition to allowing it to spread to the new territories.

Meanwhile, as if seeking to test the view that 'a house divided cannot stand', the Democrats split into North and South when choosing a presidential candidate. Those in the North championed Lincoln's Senate adversary Stephen Douglas. Democrats in the South, though, remained hostile to him. Hardening their position, they selected then current vice-president John Breckinridge, a staunch pro-slavery man, to also stand.

With slightly less than 40 per cent of the national vote, Lincoln garnered enough state electoral votes to become the Union's 16th president. Yet in the Southern States, where his name often didn't even appear on the ballot paper, hardly anyone voted

for him. Fuelled by a sense of unfairness, within days of Lincoln's victory South Carolina organised a secession convention. On 20 December 1860, the state left the Union.

Before the new president's inauguration on 4 March 1861, the states Mississippi, Florida, Alabama, Georgia, Louisiana and Texas also seceded. The seven declared themselves a new nation called The Confederate States of America. It even had a president in place, Jefferson Davis, before Lincoln had actually taken office.

Yet when he did, the 16th president's inauguration speech set out very clearly what was at stake. "In your hands, my dissatisfied fellow countrymen, and not in mine, is the momentous issue of civil war," he cautioned. Lincoln stated unequivocally that his government would not

FREDERICK DOUGLASS AND THE ABOLITIONIST MOVEMENT

orchestrate an invasion of the Confederacy, but if Union outposts in it came under attack, he was duty bound as president to act in their defence. "You can have no conflict," the speech continued, "without yourselves being the aggressors." And so they proved to be at Fort Sumter. Perhaps inevitably, then, war it was.

Four more states - Virginia, Arkansas, North Carolina and Tennessee - quickly joined the other rebels, making it 11 against the Union's 23. The act of firing upon the flag was seen as treasonous, even by Lincoln's Democrat adversaries like Douglas, and after the fall of Old Glory at Fort Sumter, the North now had a reason to go to war. Its aim was to put an end to secession and save the Union. The South's objective was far simpler: it merely needed to survive.

The Confederacy was suffering from a much smaller population and was massively weaker in terms of industrial power and financial resources. Taken together, these factors pointed to a war that was going to be a long struggle. Both sides needed

to call on large numbers of volunteers to form their armies. Leading them were officers from the pre-war US Army Military Academy at West Point. A significant number of the more able were from the South, and many resigned their commissions in order to fight for the Confederate cause.

This presented Lincoln with a problem. His general-in-chief, Winfield Scott, was a 75-year-old veteran on the verge of retirement, and there was no obvious successor. One contender was Brigadier General Irwin McDowell, who led the Union army in the war's earliest major clash, the First Battle of Bull Run in Virginia. To begin with, this confusing conflict between two virtually new armies of limited training appeared to be going McDowell's way, but stubborn Confederate resistance turned it into a humiliating Union defeat.

With McDowell's star waning, General George McClellan was promoted to general-in-chief when Scott retired. Arrogant and ambitious, McClellan clashed with his political superiors in Washington, and while he trained the army well through

Born into slavery in 1818, Frederick Douglass escaped to become a leading campaigner to end the practice and a significant African-American leader of the 19th century.

The son of a slave woman and an unknown white man, Frederick took the surname Douglass after a second, and this time successful, escape from bondage. Living in New Bedford, Massachusetts, he married and became involved in the abolitionist movement, delivering moving lectures on the brutality of his upbringing.

Encouraged to write his autobiography, a powerful indictment of slavery, the book revealed he was a fugitive slave, forcing him to flee to England. Supporters 'purchased' his freedom, allowing Douglass to return in 1847. He quickly set up an anti-slavery newspaper, which continued under various names until 1863.

During the civil war, Douglass lobbied for African-Americans to be allowed to fight. After the Emancipation Proclamation, he recruited for the 54th Massachusetts Infantry, the first regiment of black soldiers. At war's end, he turned to campaigning for black rights, going on to hold several government posts before his death in 1895.

the winter, he didn't deliver decisive battlefield victories. McClellan's tactical caution was in stark contrast to the aggressive instincts of Confederate commanders like Robert E Lee. When the pair clashed at the Battle of Antietam in September 1862, McClellan's force outnumbered Lee's by almost two to one. In ferocious combat - in terms of casualties, it was the costliest day of fighting in American history - the Confederates were driven back to Virginia, but Lincoln was left frustrated that the retreating army was not vigorously pursued. He sacked McClellan two months later.

Conflicts with his generals were a feature of Lincoln's early years in the White House. With war imminent, he had read up voraciously on military theory. He sought to be an involved commander-in-chief, going far beyond visits to troops and military hospitals to raise the moral - which he did many times - to advocating strategy on how the war should be fought. Initially, this came in the form of his Memorandum on Military Policy, which he wrote in the wake of the First Battle of

Bull Run debacle. By January 1862, the president was articulating how the land war could be won: by using the Union's superior numbers to attack simultaneously across a broad number of fronts, forcing breakthroughs when the enemy moved forces to secure pressure points, and at the same time engaging and defeating the enemy armies wherever possible rather than trying to occupy or capture specific places. Lincoln's difficulty was in finding generals who thought like he did.

Still, Antietam was claimed as a Union victory, and following it, Lincoln seized the opportunity to confront the issue of slavery. At war's onset, he had maintained its purpose was to save the Union and pledged to leave the institution of slavery unaffected in the Southern States. Lincoln believed he wasn't able to challenge state-sanctioned servitude under the Constitution, which kept the important border slave states of Missouri, Kentucky, Maryland and Delaware loyal to the Union.

However, as the war unfolded, slavery's effects couldn't be ignored, as they were damaging the

Union campaign. Slaves were used to construct defences for the Confederate armies, while slave work on farms and plantations kept the South's economy going, allowing more of the white population to fight. Determined to affect the balance of the war, Lincoln issued the Preliminary Emancipation Proclamation in September 1862.

The timing had to be right. Lincoln himself had already been forced to quash military decree emancipations made by several Union generals, because he believed only the president, through constitutionally sanctioned war powers, could enforce emancipation. He was also anxious about public opinion, fearing that if he moved too soon, not enough people in the North would support him, or that he might lose those important border states. It was knife-edge politics, but Lincoln judged that, just five days after the Union victory at Antietam, the time was right to press home the advantage and further undermine the Confederate war effort with the Proclamation.

The document offered terms for the rebel states to return to the Union provided they agreed to begin arrangements to end slavery, but if they failed to do so by 1 January 1863, all slaves in those states would be set free forever. As such a move would harm the Confederacy, the president argued it was a legitimate war measure that was both necessary and just. When, as anticipated, the rebel states ignored the Preliminary Proclamation, Lincoln was

"IN GIVING FREEDOM TO THE SLAVE, WE ASSURE FREEDOM TO THE FREE"

Message to Congress, 1862

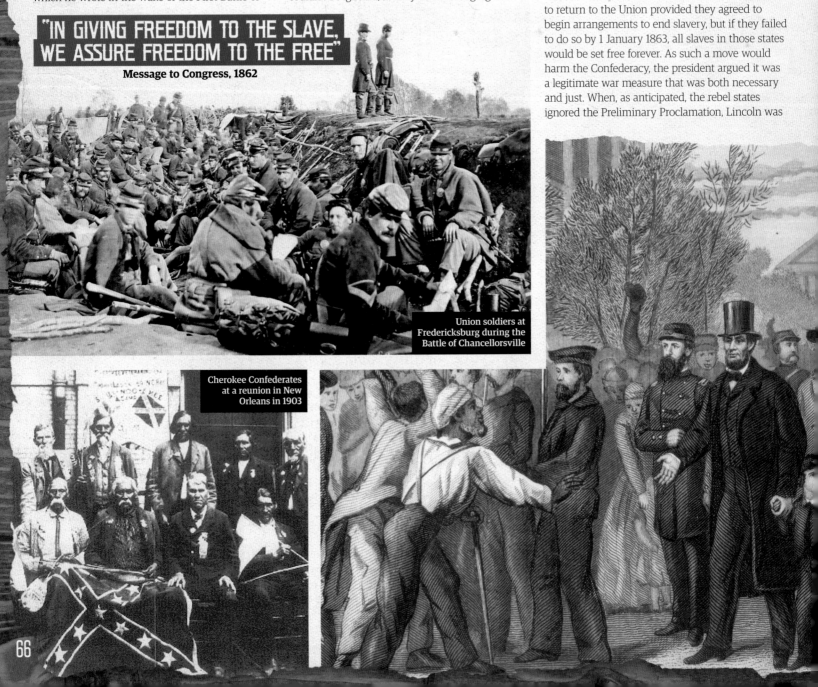

Union soldiers at Fredericksburg during the Battle of Chancellorsville

Cherokee Confederates at a reunion in New Orleans in 1903

able to issue the Final Proclamation on the first day of 1863. "I never in my life felt more certain that I am doing right than I do in signing this paper," he said on putting his name to the document. He was sure, and there was considerable hope in the Union that it would hasten the end of the conflict.

The Emancipation Proclamation also had two other important effects. First, it brought a moral dimension to the war. Always an opponent of slavery on grounds of morality, Lincoln had now shifted the aim of the war from being not just about preserving the Union, but to setting people free. While personally important to Lincoln, this was also vital internationally, as the Confederacy had hoped to secure support from Europe. Yet France and the British Empire, where slavery had been outlawed since 1833, could not legitimately be seen to support a slave-holding republic against a nation embarked on setting slaves free.

Second, the Proclamation allowed for freedmen to enlist in the Union army. This, coupled with a surge of African-American volunteers already free in the North, offered a timely and welcome boost in manpower. It paved the way for the United States Colored Troops, which became a significant component of the Union armies.

However, the Proclamation only freed slaves in the states still outside the Union. To go further, Lincoln needed the affirmation of a second election victory, but in the first half of 1864, that didn't

Lincoln and son Tad in the Confederate capital Richmond after its capture. Days later, Lincoln was assassinated

★ UNION GENERALS ★

Identifying the right man to command Union forces on the ground and fight the campaign he envisaged proved challenging and frustrating for the president

ULYSSES S GRANT
HIGHEST RANK: GENERAL-IN-CHIEF OF UNION ARMIES
APPOINTED: MARCH 1864
★★★★★

After successful raids on forts in Tennessee, Grant was promoted to major general. He was almost routed at Shiloh but retrieved the situation, then further distinguished himself at Vicksburg. He took charge of all Union forces, confronting and finally defeating Lee in Virginia.

WILLIAM SHERMAN
HIGHEST RANK: MAJOR GENERAL, OVERSEEING THE UNION'S WESTERN ARMIES
APPOINTED: MARCH 1864
★★★★☆

Sherman was promoted to brigadier general after the First Battle of Bull Run, but he suffered a nervous breakdown. After being reinstated, he then led the capture of Atlanta. He waged 'total war' through Georgia and the Carolinas.

GEORGE MEADE
HIGHEST RANK: MAJOR GENERAL, ARMY OF THE POTOMAC
APPOINTED: AUGUST 1864
★★★☆☆

Despite taking command only days before, Meade defeated Lee at Gettysburg, yet he was heavily criticised for not pursuing the retreating force. Guided by Grant, he led the Army of the Potomac successfully in later campaigns, later earning the rank of major general.

WINFIELD SCOTT
HIGHEST RANK: GENERAL-IN-CHIEF OF UNION ARMIES
APPOINTED: FEBRUARY 1855, RETIRED NOVEMBER 1861
★★★☆☆

Aged 75 as the conflict began, Scott was unable to take field command, nevertheless he devised the strategy of blockading the South's ports and raiding down the Mississippi. Although rejected, the North triumphed using similar tactics.

JOSEPH HOOKER
HIGHEST RANK: MAJOR GENERAL, ARMY OF THE POTOMAC
APPOINTED: JANUARY 1863
★★★☆☆

Hooker revitalised the army, restoring morale. However, after successes prior to his appointment when he was dubbed 'Fighting Joe', he endured a chequered career in battle afterwards, and never fully recovered from heavy defeat and retreat at Chancellorsville.

AMBROSE BURNSIDE
HIGHEST RANK: MAJOR GENERAL, ARMY OF THE POTOMAC
APPOINTED: NOVEMBER 1862
★★☆☆☆

When he finally replaced McClellan, Burnside attacked but lost expensively at Fredericksburg. Relieved of command, he resurfaced to outwit General Longstreet in Tennessee, but failed badly again at the Battle of Crater.

GEORGE McCLELLAN
HIGHEST RANK: GENERAL-IN-CHIEF OF UNION ARMIES
APPOINTED: NOVEMBER 1861
★☆☆☆☆

Although he reorganised the Union army, turning volunteers into an efficient force, McClellan was cripplingly cautious on the battlefield. Failure to exploit advantages frustrated Lincoln, who lost patience and relieved him of command in November 1862.

And one that got away...
ROBERT E LEE
HIGHEST RANK: GENERAL-IN-CHIEF OF CONFEDERATE ARMIES
APPOINTED: FEBRUARY 1865
★★★★★

Lee declined the command of Union forces in April 1861, claiming he was unable to fight fellow Virginians. Becoming a Confederate General. Lee commanded the Army of North Virginia, and later all Confederate forces.

Civil War Performance					
	Superb	Effective	Mixed	Disappointing	Poor

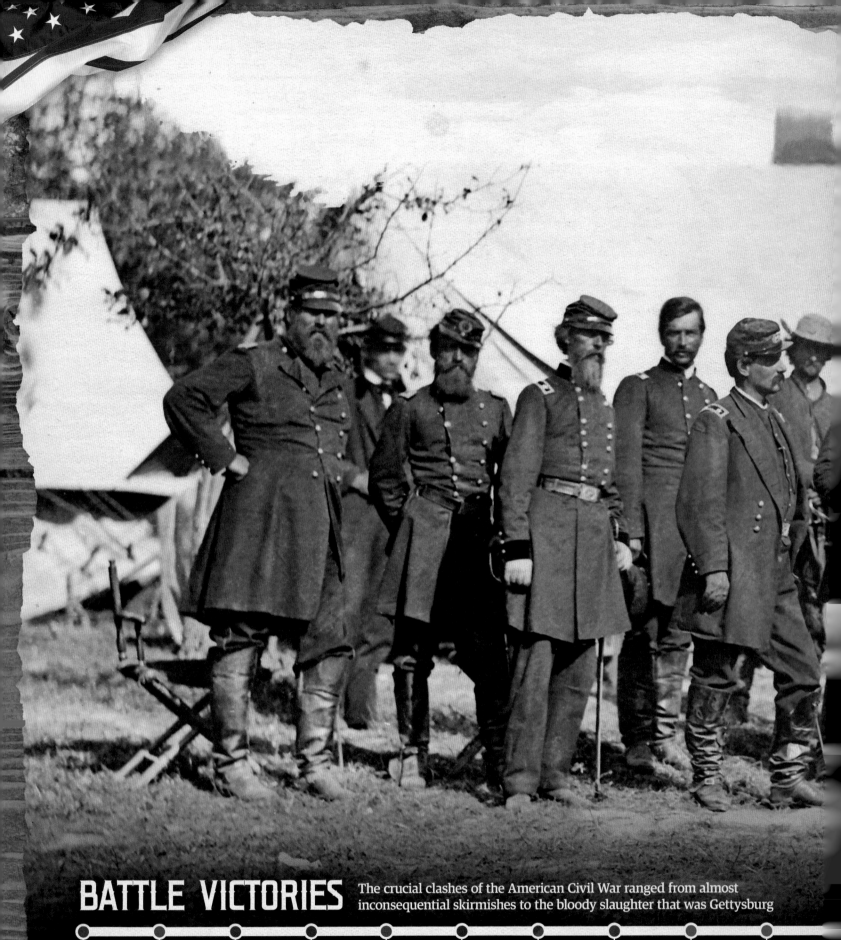

BATTLE VICTORIES

The crucial clashes of the American Civil War ranged from almost inconsequential skirmishes to the bloody slaughter that was Gettysburg

First Battle of Bull Run

21 JULY 1861

Shiloh

6-7 APRIL 1862

The Seven Days Battles

25 JUNE – 1 JULY 1862

Second Battle of Bull Run

29-30 AUGUST 1862

Antietam

17 SEPTEMBER 1862

Fredericksburg

13 DECEMBER 1862

Stones River

31 DECEMBER 1862 – 2 JANUARY 1863

Chancellorsville

1 MAY – 5 MAY 1863

Siege at Vicksburg

18 MAY – 4 JULY 1863

Gettysburg

1-3 JULY 1863

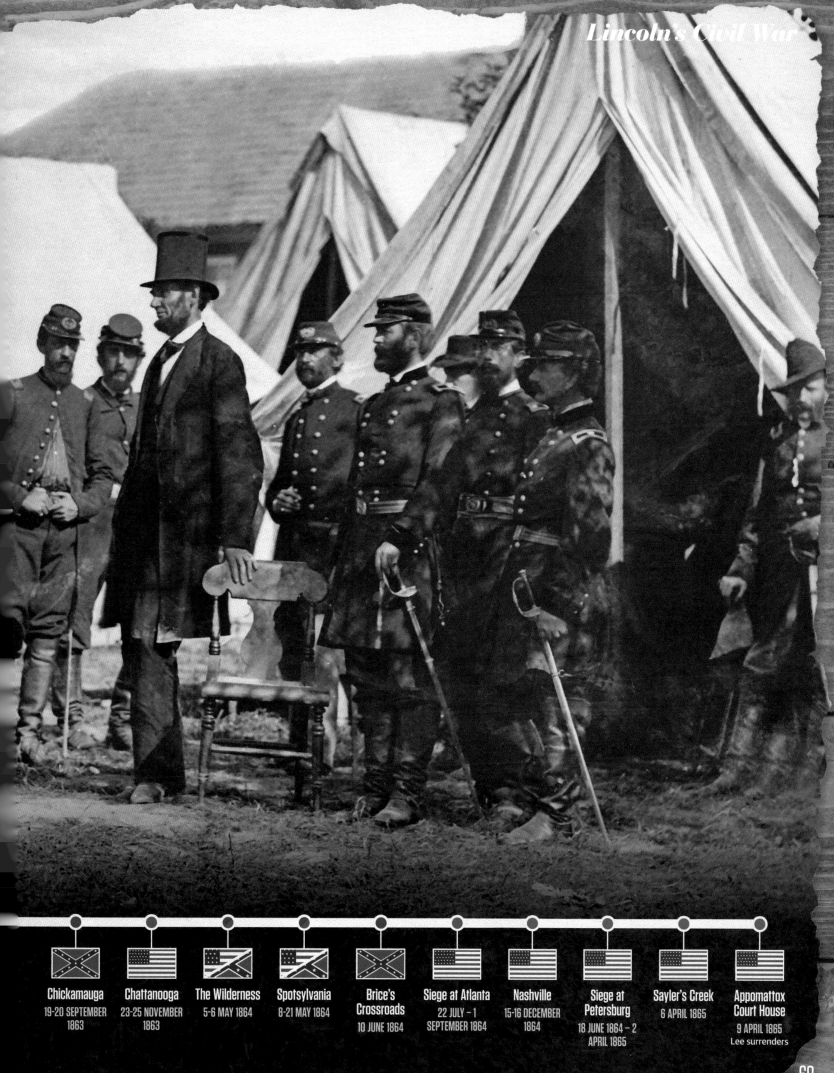

Chickamauga
19-20 SEPTEMBER 1863

Chattanooga
23-25 NOVEMBER 1863

The Wilderness
5-6 MAY 1864

Spotsylvania
8-21 MAY 1864

Brice's Crossroads
10 JUNE 1864

Siege at Atlanta
22 JULY – 1 SEPTEMBER 1864

Nashville
15-16 DECEMBER 1864

Siege at Petersburg
18 JUNE 1864 – 2 APRIL 1865

Sayler's Creek
6 APRIL 1865

Appomattox Court House
9 APRIL 1865
Lee surrenders

seem likely. The war was costing so many lives on both sides that Republican radicals felt the president had mismanaged the conflict and were lobbying for a different candidate, while rebel state armies were proving stubbornly resistant. A small Confederate force led by General Jubal Early even launched an audacious attack on Washington, DC in July. They got close and caused panic in the capital. Lincoln sought to quell it by being a visible presence, facing down the crisis with visits to fortifications on the edge of the city. Observing some skirmishing from the parapet of Fort Stevens, he came under sniper fire until extolled to climb down, in the process earning the distinction of the only wartime commander-in-chief to be directly shot at by the enemy.

By that time, though, Lincoln had a general-in-chief he could rely on after he appointed Ulysses S Grant earlier in the year. Union strength finally began to show with crucial battlefield successes in August and September, turning the election tide in Lincoln's favour. He faced his sacked general, McClellan, for the Democrats, who were still split between those wanting a swift peace and pro-war moderates like McClellan himself. Lincoln triumphed emphatically.

A major policy plank of the Republican Party's re-election campaign was to amend the Constitution to permanently ban slavery across the country. Vindicated by his election victory, Lincoln moved swiftly to bring the Thirteenth Amendment into being. It took skilled political manoeuvring but Lincoln convinced the outgoing 38th Congress to give it bipartisan support, and the amendment was passed on 31 January 1865.

Unquestionably, however, Lincoln also wrestled with the issue of what effect freeing millions of black people would have on race relations in the nation. Part of his Preliminary Proclamation referred to voluntary colonisation abroad for those set free. This was dropped from the Final Proclamation, and Lincoln never spoke publicly about the issue again, leaving historians to debate his motives. Some suggest coupling freeing slaves with colonisation was a ploy to help sell emancipation to doubters. Others argue that, given Union ranks were set to be swelled by black recruits, he changed his view on the issue.

Both opinions essentially give the president a pass on the colonisation policy, but recent evidence has come to light suggesting he never fully abandoned it. In *Colonisation After*

Emancipation: Lincoln And The Movement For Black Resettlement, authors Phillip Magness and Sebastian Page have discovered evidence that the president was still attempting to make colonisation arrangements long after the Final Proclamation. Their research reveals that in addition to the colonies he hoped to set up in Panama, Haiti and Liberia, the president was in extensive secretive discussions with the British government to find further suitable lands in the West Indies. The authors suggest that Lincoln was actively pursuing the policy far longer than has previously been acknowledged, potentially into 1865.

The idea of voluntary colonisation took shape in 1816 with the formation of the American Colonisation Society. Bluntly, the view was that as slaves had been stolen from abroad, once emancipated they should be humanely returned abroad. One of the society's founders was Henry Clay, leader of the Whig party and a political hero of Lincoln's. Clay's views profoundly influenced the president's ideas, apparently to the extent that on the issue of colonisation, he appears never to have fully revised them.

In his defence, even the best of men are not immune from alighting upon the wrong answer, and nobody knew what a post-civil war, post-slavery USA would look like. Lincoln, seeking to avoid extensive racial disharmony and searching for a way forward, thought consented colonisation might offer a solution. While a miscalculated, impractical and embarrassingly paternalistic solution in hindsight, everything else we know about him tells us he wouldn't have suggested it through malice.

As events transpired, Lincoln never got to see post-civil war USA himself. Grant's tactics of attacking across a wide front created advances deep into Confederate territory. Once Atlanta fell to General Sherman in September 1864, he pushed on to the coast, slicing Georgia in two. The following April, after a nine-month campaign, Grant's army pierced Lee's resistance at Petersburg. The Confederate capital of Richmond fell soon after. His troops exhausted and heavily outnumbered, Lee had no option but to surrender on 9 April 1865. Five nights later, Lincoln visited Ford Theatre in Washington, where Confederate sympathiser John Wilkes Booth assassinated him with a single bullet to the head. By June, the last unit of Confederate troops had lain down their arms. The civil war was over, though the president who felt compelled to fight it was not alive to construct its peace.

Private Edwin Francis Jemison came to represent child soldiers of the war

"THE PROBABILITY THAT WE MAY FAIL IN THE STRUGGLE OUGHT NOT TO DETER US FROM US FROM THE SUPPORT OF A CAUSE WE BELIEVE TO BE JUST; IT SHALL NOT DETER ME"

Speech to sub-committee, 1839

MEN OF COLOR
To Arms! To Arms!
NOW OR NEVER
THREE YEARS' SERVICE!
AND JOIN IN FIGHTING THE
BATTLES OF LIBERTY AND THE UNION

FAIL NOW, & OUR RACE IS DOOMED

SILENCE THE TONGUE OF CALUMNY
VALOR AND HEROISM
OUR BROTHERS DISPLAYED AT
PORT HUDSON AND MILLIKEN'S BEND,

ARE FREEMEN LESS BRAVE THAN SLAVES

OUR LAST OPPORTUNITY HAS COME
MEN OF COLOR, BROTHERS AND FATHERS!
WE APPEAL TO YOU!
STRIKE NOW!

Lincoln finally found the general he wanted in Ulysses S Grant, who later became president himself

A depiction of the confused fighting at the First Battle of Bull Run, the first large-scale confrontation of the war

WAS LINCOLN THE GREATEST US PRESIDENT EVER?

Louis P Masur is a distinguished professor of American studies and history at Rutgers University and the author of numerous books including *Lincoln's Last Speech: Wartime Reconstruction And The Crisis Of Reunion*, *Lincoln's Hundred Days: The Emancipation Proclamation And The War For Union*, and *The Civil War: A Concise History*.

Washington and Lincoln. One made the nation and the other saved it. For me, Lincoln is the greatest president not only for what he did – defend democracy, preserve the Union, issue the Emancipation Proclamation and lay the foundations for a modernising, industrial USA – but also for the qualities of leadership he exhibited. Lincoln was patient, deliberate, a shrewd judge of character, and most important of all willing to change his mind over time. "The dogmas of the quiet past are inadequate to the stormy present," he declared. With actions and words that continue to inspire, he led the nation through war to peace and set the framework for a "new birth of freedom." 150 years after his death, his legacy continues to bear fruit.

FROM THE ASHES

After the bloodshed of the Civil War, the United States tried to piece itself back together in the Reconstruction Era

◆

Lincoln's assassination just after the Civil War had a marked effect on the reconstruction of the country and the new civil liberties afforded to freed slaves. Although the provisional Southern governments that were established were all white, conditions did seem to improve for the newly free black communities – with universities and schools springing up all through the South. This would be tempered by the fact that, although many former slaves felt that they had been promised land after the Civil War, confiscated Confederate land was given back to its original owners. In reality the agricultural landscape of the South barely changed from what it was before the Civil War.

The Civil Rights Bill of 1866 established that anyone born in the USA was automatically a citizen and, in theory, all had equal rights in the eyes of the law, regardless of race. After this the 14th and 15th amendments cemented these rights and gave black people the right to vote. This period, know as 'radical reconstruction' saw the national government become the 'custodian of freedom', allowing a great number of its citizens equal rights – in theory at least.

All of these improvements were publicly funded, which meant that Republican governments were becoming unpopular due to the rising tax levels. Many white Southerners wanted things to return to how they had been before the Civil War. Intimidation, violence and murder carried out by racist organisations such as the Ku Klux Klan saw a marked drop in the number of black voters, allowing white democrats to seize power.

The Bargain of 1877 saw reconstruction end in the South, and as Federal troops and jurisdiction were removed, the Democratic Party was free to clamp down on black people's freedoms once again. What followed were the passing of the infamous 'Jim Crow' laws, which enforced segregated public services for blacks and whites, with the black services always suffering from lower quality and chronic underfunding. For a few brief years, freed black people had had more rights than ever before, but these were systematically erased under the democratic South and many continued to endure until the Civil Rights Movement of the 1960s.

5364 MULBERRY STREET, NEW YORK

Mulberry Street in Manhattan's Lower East Side was the centre of the 'Little Italy' that formed in the city in the wake of Italian immigration

American Dreamers

Millions of people gave up everything to cross the ocean and start again. This is their story

The United States of America was built on people. Blessed with the resources of a continent and, for the newcomers, a blank page of history, what the country would become would be determined by the people who came there.

The founding population of the 13 colonies that went on to declare their independence of Britain in 1776 were mainly from England, with half again being Scots-Irish Protestants. The largest immigrant group from outside the British Isles were Germans, who were nearly as numerous as the Scots-Irish, and there were significant minorities from Scandinavia and Holland. Many of these settlers arrived in the New World in order to be able to practise their own particular brands of religion without persecution, establishing a pattern of land ownership that produced largely self-sufficient and self-governing communities. Although these settlers brought much from their native lands, one institution notable for its absence was the aristocracy: there were no lords and ladies in the New World.

Passage across the Atlantic Ocean was expensive. Many, possibly as much as half, of the people who emigrated to America from Europe did so as indentured servants. That is, they sold their liberty for a fixed period of time, tying themselves to an employer, in return for his payment of passage. Britain, spreading its convict population around the world, also transported criminals to the colonies.

The other significant early population had even less wish to be in the New World than the transported convicts. These were the black Africans shipped across the Atlantic by the slave trade. For more about this, see the piece on slavery in the United States (page 58).

The population of the 13 colonies grew quickly, largely because the birth rate greatly exceeded the death rate (the cold winters of New England killed off mosquitoes and other pathogens, resulting in the greatest increase in population taking place there). Following the American War of Independence, and decades of disruption caused by the Napoleonic Wars in Europe, immigration to the newly formed United States tailed off, only to resume its growth from 1830 onwards.

The 19th century saw further large numbers of Germans immigrate to the United States, with around five million making the journey. Indeed, to encourage immigration, books such as The German in America were published, with German and English texts on facing pages, extolling the opportunities in the New World. The majority moved to the mid-western states, buying land when they could afford to and farming. To cater for this population, a huge number of German-language newspapers were published, with over 1,000 in circulation by the end of the century. Following the outbreak of World War I, German-Americans were faced with increasingly difficult choices as to where their chief loyalties lay, but by the time America entered the war, the vast majority of German-

Americans had opted to dedicate themselves wholly to their new nation, and German had declined rapidly as a national language.

From 1820 onwards, the pattern of emigration from Ireland to the United States also began to change. Before this, the vast majority of emigrants were Ulster and Scottish Protestants. Many Scottish Highlanders had emigrated as a result of the Highland Clearances, as they were turfed from common land, and today there are far more people of Highland descent in America than in Scotland. But later, more Irish Catholics began to make the crossing, with a huge expansion in numbers during and after the Great Famine (1845-1849), which had decimated the population of Ireland. The Irish emigration was the single largest population movement of the 19th century. Scots and Irish, whether Protestant or Catholic, shared the experience of the coffin ships, in which unscrupulous ship owners crammed as many people on board for the passage as could be held, resulting in death rates of up to 30 per cent.

While the German immigrants moved westwards, the impoverished Irish mainly settled in the east coast cities where they landed, although young men found work as labourers building the expanding railway network. With significant prejudice against Irish Catholics, the new settlers began to form tight communities, with many finding work in city public services, in particular the police. By the 1860s, half of New York's police force was Irish - as were the people they arrested.

But immigrants did not only arrive at the east coast ports. The discovery of gold in California in 1848 led to a gold rush with the 'forty-niners', as they were called, coming across the continental United States and over the Pacific. Many of these new immigrants were Chinese, and they faced the largest barriers of prejudice erected against any group apart from black Africans. Having taken loans to pay for passage across the Pacific, Chinese immigrants had to work for lower wages than their white counterparts, which made them popular with employers but aroused great resentment from the poor whites who saw them as taking their jobs. In 1850, the State of California passed a law requiring any foreign miner who was not a 'free white person' to pay $20 tax per month in order to mine. Unable to pay the tax, the Chinese moved into cities where they competed even harder for work, many helping to build the Central Pacific Railroad. But in 1882, the Chinese Exclusion Act banned all further immigration from China to the United States. The Act remained in place until 1943.

Although the Chinese were no longer welcome to enter the United States, from 1880 onwards changes in technology were making it much easier for Europeans to cross the Atlantic to the New World. Steam ships made the journey faster and cheaper, while industrialisation led to many workers losing their jobs in their homelands. America, still expanding rapidly, was a place that called to them. It is from this era that the image of the Statue of Liberty welcoming 'your tired, your poor, your huddled masses' comes, for the statue was dedicated in 1886 and the lines, from the poem The New Colossus, were engraved on the pedestal in 1903. Ellis Island, which lies just north of the Statue of Liberty, was where new immigrants were inspected and processed from 1892 until 1954. For immigrants arriving in the New World after their long and arduous journey, the flaming beacon held

"While the German immigrants moved westwards, the impoverished Irish mainly settled in the east coast cities"

The Statue of Liberty welcomed immigrants before they disembarked on Ellis Island

Immigrants disembarking at Ellis Island, where they would be asked if they had a job they were going to, among 28 other questions. Only 2 per cent were turned back

aloft by Lady Liberty must indeed have seemed a beacon of hope.

The first person recorded to have passed through Ellis Island was a 'rosy-cheeked Irish girl' named Annie Moore from County Cork. By the time it closed in 1954, over 12 million other people had followed her. During their examination, immigrants were asked 29 questions, including if they had $50 and whether they were polygamists or anarchists (answering yes to either would have seen you deported back again). The questionnaire was not very onerous - only 2 per cent of the would-be immigrants were refused entry.

This was the great period of migration from southern and eastern Europe, with nearly 25 million leaving the Old World. Poles, Hungarians, Slavs, Greeks and Russian Jews made up the bulk of this great wave of immigration, leading to the formation of ghettoes speaking the language of the respective country of origin in east coast and mid-western cities. Notable in this human influx were the Italians, with 5.3 million emigrating to the US between 1880 and 1920. The majority came from southern Italy and Sicily, where corruption and the Mafia held opportunity in a grip that excluded those without the right family connections. However, Italian immigration was unusual in that nearly half of the emigrants, having earned enough money to establish themselves in the old country, returned home. During World War I, Italy fought alongside Britain, France and, eventually, the United States against Germany, and Italian Americans enlisted in disproportionate numbers in the US Army. But World War II saw Italy declare war on America. While some Italian Americans were supporters of Mussolini, and those who had not become citizens had to carry identity cards marking them as 'resident aliens', over half a million Italian Americans proved their loyalty by enlisting in the

armed forces. During the war, 13 Italian Americans won the Congressional Medal of Honor, the nation's highest award for gallantry, including Sergeant John Basilone, whose deeds feature in the TV series *The Pacific*.

The men and women who crossed oceans to make new starts in the New World contributed immeasurably to its growth and success: from building railroads and skyscrapers, through clearing forests and fighting crime, to fighting and dying for their adopted country, the emigrants from the Old World were the people who made America into what it became.

Texas was so big and empty that the state offered land to immigrants in a bid to entice them south

The Italian lynching

On 15 October 1890, New Orleans police chief David Hennessy and his bodyguard were ambushed as the police chief was walking home, the two assailants firing sawn-off shotguns at the men. Wounded, Hennessy returned fire, but did not bring down his attackers. When asked who had shot him, Hennessy muttered, "Dagoes." The police investigation into the attack had its one and only lead.

Hennessy died the next day and the outraged city mayor, Joseph Shakespeare, told the police to "scour the whole neighbourhood. Arrest every Italian you come across." They did, rounding up 250 Italians. By the late 19th century, many Sicilians had immigrated to America but in the south they were regarded as halfway black. One newspaper article called them "a link connecting white and black races". This was not meant as a compliment. Fears had also been roused in the white community from reports of Mafia dealings and violence among the Sicilians.

Eventually, nine Italians were put on trial for Hennessy's murder. The accused were all acquitted, for the evidence against them was contradictory and weak, but the acquittal enraged the New Orleans populace. Although found not guilty, the Italians were returned to the prison, where other Italians were also imprisoned. That evening, a notice appeared in a local paper calling for a demonstration against what many locals believed to be a miscarriage of justice.

Thousands gathered on 14 March 1891 to listen to incendiary speeches by respected local dignitaries, many with strong links to Mayor Shakespeare. Roused by the speeches, the crowd marched on the prison, chanting, "We want the Dagoes." In the prison, the warden let the 19 Italians held there out of their cells, telling them to hide as best they could. Eight managed to evade the mob, but 11 of the men were seized, with two being dragged outside and hanged, and the other nine beaten to death in the prison.

Although Mayor Shakespeare failed to be re-elected next year, the city's Italians voting decisively against him, the press coverage was mostly sympathetic, suggesting that the Italians all had links to the Mafia and had got what they deserved.

The mob is urged by rabble-rousing orators to attack the prison holding the acquitted Italians

The Birth of HOLLY

How four penniless Jewish immigrant siblings changed the face of entertainment forever and wrote their own fairy tale

Jack Warner always wanted to be famous. Actually, make that adored, powerful, rich and famous. Born Jacob Warner in impoverished Canada to Jewish immigrant parents in 1892, he changed his name to something more theatrical: Jack L Warner. As a young man he grew up obsessed with images, hanging around photography studios in the hope of being used for test shots. While his brothers were recognising the potential of early film projectors, investing in a Kinetoscope projector, Jack made money singing in theatres, showing little interest in - or aptitude for - the less glamorous side of show business.

Willed on by his parents and clubbing together with his brothers - Albert, Harry and Sam - Jack toured the Northern states showing old prints of *The Great Train Robbery*, drawing enough cash to buy a series of local theatres and launch their own distribution company, the Duquesne Amusement Company. However, the brothers' ambition didn't stop at a network of provincial theatres. The Warners had their sights set on global domination.

At the turn of the century many others were also heading west to seek a new life. One of these was Harvey Wilcox, who bought 160 acres (64 hectares) of land to the west of Los Angeles in the ironic hope of founding a conservative community. On the train from Kansas, Wilcox and his wife got chatting to a woman who talked of her summer home: Hollywood.

Wilcox's vision of founding a community became a reality and in 1910 Hollywood officially

JACK WARNER
1892-1978

Brief Bio One of the original group of movie moguls who shaped the nascent Hollywood, Jack L Warner was the cofounder of Warner Bros Studios. With brothers Harry, Sam and Albert he launched Warner Brothers in 1923 and became the dominant force of the four siblings.

Equally feared and admired, Jack was the typical mogul of Hollywood's Golden Age and was known for his ruthlessness in business. Neither actors nor directors were immune from Jack. He even disposed of his own brothers when they outlived their usefulness, discarded his wife and son when he grew tired of them and was known for casual cruelty to staff.

A notorious philanderer, Jack abandoned his wife and son for another woman in 1935. Following the death of his much-loved brother Sam in 1927, Jack's frosty relationship with Harry and Albert came to a head in 1956 when the former sold the studio's rights to films made before 1950 for a paltry sum and later arranged to buy back Warner's stock that had previously been sold, installing himself as president. The brothers never spoke again and Jack refused to attend Harry's funeral in 1958. In 1969, Jack was seen as the last of a dying breed of studio heads and, after seeing his power gradually slip away, retired. Warner Brothers remains one of Hollywood's most powerful studios to this day.

became a part of Los Angeles. At the same time, a group of actors and directors - drawn to the area by the sunny climate, lack of taxes and freedom from patents issued by Thomas Edison's Motion Picture Patents Company - started shooting motion pictures in what is now the film-making capital of the world. In 1911 Hollywood got its first studio, when the Blondeau Tavern on Sunset Boulevard became the Nestor Film Company - firing the starting pistol on a gold rush that would take place over the next two decades.

A few years later, in 1917, Jack Warner had been dispatched to Los Angeles where he bought the rights to *My Four Years In Germany*, a memoir by the US ambassador to Germany who lived in that country during the First World War. In the face of threats from local theatre owners and impressive offers from distributors, the brothers held fast and premiered the movie themselves, making a small fortune in the process. Riding anti-German sentiment following the war, the film was a smash. Warner Brothers now had a place at the top table of American film producers.

In 1918, the siblings formed Warner Brothers West Coast Studios, later incorporated as the more recognisable Warner Brothers in 1923, and moved to Hollywood. Jack shared production duties with brother Sam while Harry and Albert sold distribution rights and they launched enthusiastically into a series of low-budget farces. However, the films were not a success and the company dangled on the edge of a

THE CAMERAMAN

Innovation was key in early film cameras, with devices bulky, hard to move and requiring constant hand cranking. Having to crank a camera while focusing and aiming was difficult, so shooting was often static. Smaller cameras like the Mitchell Standard were introduced in the 1920s but the advent of sound recording posed more problems – namely the issue of sound emanating from the mechanism while recording. Stylistic innovations were slow to appear in early films due to the difficulty of using equipment.

THE DIRECTOR
(HAL ROACH)

Directors were rarely used for the ability to craft sophisticated movies in the silent era – a dynamic that continued into the talkie era. Technical knowledge and the ability to work quickly were more highly prized, with many early directors sourced from producers, actors, writers or entrepreneurs. Hal Roach was an exception, with a career lasting for several decades and well into the advent of talkies.

Making movies

The main players behind the 1919 picture *Bumping into Broadway*

THE STAR
(HAROLD LLOYD)

Stars could earn a lot of money, depending on their levels of fame. Silent film stars such as Charlie Chaplin, Harold Lloyd and Buster Keaton could command film deals worth tens of millions of dollars in today's money. Most had a strong understanding of their appeal and how it should be conveyed – enjoying significant creative freedom. That would all gradually change under the studio system of the late-1920s and throughout the 1930s.

Al Jolson in *The Jazz Singer*, Warner Bros' famous first 'talkie'

Four brothers with a dream: Harry, Sam, Jack and Albert Warner

Jack Warner in 1973, shortly after he had been ousted from his own studio

financial chasm - moving to a down-at-heel neighbourhood that locals referred to as Poverty Row. Salvation was to come in the most unlikely of forms.

A German Shepherd called Rin Tin Tin proved to be the saviour of Warner Brothers. The trained dog - rescued from a battlefield by a US soldier in the First World War - became the star of a series of silent films of derring-do. The canine appeared in over 27 Hollywood films for Warner Bros, becoming famous around the world. Noting Warner Brothers' flirtation with bankruptcy, Jack called Rin Tin Tin "the mortgage lifter." The German Shepherd was so popular in Hollywood that the Academy of Motion Pictures voted the dog best actor in 1929; sadly the Academy insisted that a human actor take the Oscar. The Rin Tin Tin films were written by Darryl F Zanuck, who later became Jack Warner's executive producer and right-hand man before his dislike of the Warners drove him to what would become 20th Century Fox. Adding names such as director Ernst Lubitsch and star John Barrymore to Warner Brothers' roster boosted sales and also lent the studio some respectability.

On the back of these successes - and fearing being shut out by the established studios - the Warners expanded, purchasing theatre companies, building a laboratory to develop film and investing in new hardware. Warners led the way with a vertical model. Rather than being a cog in a larger mechanism, the studio owned it all, from production to distribution to exhibition. Most moguls came from theatre companies so already had distribution tied up (some had virtual monopolies in certain cities) while adding production allowed for the greatest return on investment. The Warners had to beg, steal and borrow to be able to take on the existing studios.

As well as Warner Brothers, four other big studios

> "Noting Warner Brothers' flirtation with bankruptcy, Jack called Rin Tin Tin 'the mortgage lifter'"

were to emerge in the 1920s, which would become Hollywood studios recognised today: Paramount was headed by Adolph Zukor and had a reputation for quality silent films; 20th Century Fox was created from a merger in 1935, headed by Warner's old colleague Darryl F Zanuck; MGM had a huge talent roster and produced many of the era's most famous pictures; RKO concentrated their efforts on films noir.

By the 1920s, most US film production occurred in or near Hollywood. By the end of the decade, there were 20 Hollywood studios averaging about 800 film releases in a year - far in excess of modern Hollywood. Films were being manufactured in modular format, aping the success of Henry Ford's production-line process. Swashbucklers, historical or biblical epics and melodramas were most popular, though Warners would blaze a trail with gangster capers and Universal became known for its horror films. Meanwhile, Charlie Chaplin, Buster Keaton, Harold Lloyd and Laurel & Hardy were popular for their comedic movies.

The studio system that emerged enforced long-term contracts for stars and rigid control of both them and directors. This system ensured strong profits and a de facto monopoly - by 1929, the 'Big Five' studios produced over 90 per cent of the fiction titles in the States. Studios also distributed their films internationally, hogging the profits at every step of film-making and distribution.

The studios didn't just control the logistics of film-making though. They would snap up promising, good-looking young actors and actresses and construct a new public image for them, often changing their names, putting them through vocal coaching - a

The moving image

By the late-19th century a number of basic methods for showing moving images existed, but none were able to show genuine sequential images filmed by one camera, usually relying on optical illusions or a bank of multiple cameras to replicate moving images. In 1888, Thomas Edison registered a patent for a device that would "do for the eye what the phonograph does for the ear" – record and reproduce objects in motion. Despite his realisation of the Kinetoscope, the invention could

only be used by one person at a time. Edison recognised that films projected for large audiences would be a lot more profitable.

The inventor backed another device, the Thomas Armat-designed Vitascope, and publicly demonstrated it on 23 April 1896, at Koster and Bial's Music Hall in New York City. The audience was treated to moving pictures of dancing, a beach, burlesque boxing match and snippets from plays – all were described gushingly as 'wonderfully real and

singularly exhilarating.'
It was the first public showing of a motion picture on a screen in the States, a feat recognised today in a plaque erected next to Macy's Department Store in New York.

The event opened up the way for motion pictures to be developed on a mass scale. Ever the businessman, Edison soon dispensed with the Vitascope, patenting his own version, the Projecting Kinetoscope, a few months later.

From silent shows to Hollywood's golden age

-1897-
MOVING PICTURE SHOWS
Thomas Edison creates and markets his own moving-picture camera and projector system, catalysing a race among theatre owners to develop their own systems to show moving pictures in the nickelodeons and theatre halls they own across the US.

-1906-
THE FIRST FILM
The Story Of The Kelly Gang, an Australian film on outlaw Ned Kelly is the world's first full-length feature film. It is first shown in Melbourne, Australia before going on tour, being shown in the UK in 1908. Dialogue is synchronised live during screenings.

-1910-
DESTINATION: HOLLYWOOD
DW Griffith, Mark Pickford and Lionel Barrymore are among a group of actors and directors who begin filming in the village of Hollywood, a suburb of Los Angeles. The results include *In Old California* and several more films.

-1919-
ARTISTS UNITED
Charlie Chaplin, Mary Pickford and Douglas Fairbanks Sr form United Artists and take a studio on Santa Monica Boulevard. The actors, along with DW Griffiths, wield enormous power and wealth as some of the biggest stars of their day.

-1920-
BIRTH OF MGM
Metro Pictures Corporation is sold to the Loew's theatre chain – paving the way for the creators of the studio system and contractors of many of the biggest stars of the day, Metro-Goldwyn-Mayer, in 1924.

-1922-
MORAL CODE
The Motion Picture Producers and Distributors of America (MPPDA) is formed in response to a number of early scandals. The body appoints Will H Hays, who will introduce infamous Hays Code.

Studio players

Adolph Zukor
Paramount Pictures
A Jewish-Hungarian immigrant, Zukor was already a successful businessman by the time he ventured into the film industry, forming a studio that evolved into Paramount Pictures. A polymath, Zukor directed and produced, and as chairman for many years oversaw the consolidation of production, distribution and exhibition within the same company – ensuring Paramount's place as one of the Big Five studios in the early days of Hollywood.

David O Selznick
RKO
RKO was ailing when the 29-year-old Selznick, following stints at MGM and Paramount, took over production at the studio, Before long, the studio had signed a young Katharine Hepburn, recruited an impressive roster of behind-the-camera talent and made one of the defining films of Hollywood's Golden Age: *King Kong*. Selznick would move back to MGM before starting his own production company and producing, among others, *Gone With The Wind*.

Louis B Mayer MGM
Another Russian immigrant, Louis B Mayer rose to power through his ownership of a raft of theatres and his own production company, later to become MGM. Under Mayer, the studio dominated the industry and had the top stars in Hollywood – a result of his determination to have 'more stars than the heavens.' Mayer was also one of the founders of Academy of Motion Picture Arts and Sciences – famous for its annual Academy Awards.

A still from 1927's *Tracked By The Police* starring the dog Rin Tin Tin

necessity for many in the emerging talkie era – and even forcing some to undergo plastic surgery. Studios would choose which films their star made, arrange their romantic lives and force them to adhere to strict moral codes. There was significant irony to this. Jack Warner was used to having his pick of the starlets, enjoying the power that came with the success of the Warner Brothers' talkies.

In 1925, buoyed by financial and moral support from United Artists - an independent founded by Douglas Fairbanks Sr, Mark Pickford and Charlie Chaplin - the Warners embarked on a set of acquisitions, appointments and impulsive purchases. Chief among them was a bunch of old machinery from a radio station, because Sam and Jack had an idea. While silent films had their appeal - they were universal due to their lack of a specific language and sound-synchronisation technology was appallingly basic - the two brothers recognised the fantastic possibilities offered by talking pictures.

Chief among the new technologies they pursued was the new Vitaphone film sound process that allowed for synchronisation of sound and moving images, with sounds played on a gramophone. By the mid-1920s it was clear to Jack, despite his initial personal doubts, that the studio that

successfully developed sound would reap immense rewards. Other studios were investing heavily in the technology so Warners couldn't afford to be left behind. While the resulting Vitaphone technology was basic, Warner Brothers quickly kitted out their theatres with new kit, cementing them as the leaders of the new media but at the cost of $3 million; it was an enormous gamble.

Championed by Sam Warner as a cheaper alternative to paying for live music in theatres, and in the face of resistance from Harry, the new technology paved the way for 1926's *Don Juan*. Although music and sound effects featured, there was no synchronised speech. Still, the reception to the film was overwhelmingly positive - it had changed the face of the industry. But while the studio enjoyed critical success, the bottom line wasn't nearly so healthy and the cost of producing the film and fitting out theatres with the new Vitaphone projectors almost wiped them out.

With the studio mortgaged up to the hilt, the brothers embarked on another ambitious plan: the next project would feature synchronised dialogue. 1927's *The Jazz Singer* was the first to include speech and was a smash hit, earning Warner Brothers millions of dollars, despite a budget that was considered exorbitant at the time, concerns

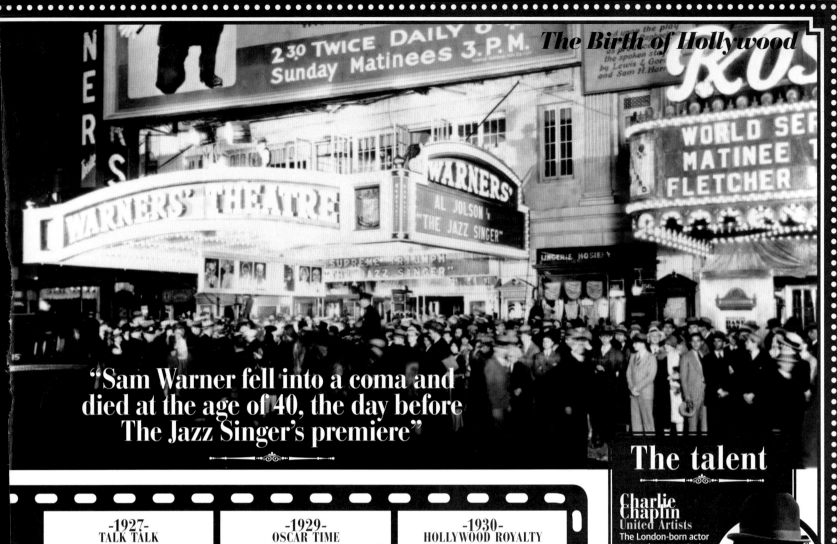

"Sam Warner fell into a coma and died at the age of 40, the day before The Jazz Singer's premiere"

The talent

-1927-
TALK TALK
The start of Hollywood's Golden Age, with the release of *The Jazz Singer*. Starring Al Jolson, it's the first to have synchronised sound, though only a few minutes of the movie had synchronised vocals, with most of the rest being a silent film.

-1929-
OSCAR TIME
The Academy of Motion Picture Arts and Sciences (AMPAS) dispenses the first Academy Awards – now known worldwide as Oscars – in May 1929. *The Jazz Singer* is given a special award, commemorating its impact on the industry.

-1930-
HOLLYWOOD ROYALTY
MGM stars Clark Gable and Joan Crawford star together in *Dance, Fools, Dance* – the first of eight features teaming them together. The pair are believed to have had an affair during their golden box-office run in the 1930s.

-1935-
LIVING COLOUR
Becky Sharp, an adaptation of *Vanity Fair*, is Hollywood's first full-length feature film in Technicolor. It paves the way for colour films in the years leading up to WWII, including *Gone With The Wind* and *The Wizard Of Oz*.

-1937-
DISNEY LANDS
Walt Disney premieres *Snow White And The Seven Dwarfs*, the first-ever feature-length animated film. With international earnings of $8m it is the highest-grossing sound film of all time for a brief period.

-1939-
KING OF HOLLYWOOD
Gone With The Wind, with a gestation period of several years and a budget of $4m, premieres. The Civic War epic confirms producer David O Selznick and star Clark Gable as leading lights of the era.

The Warner Brothers' studio lot in its early years

Charlie Chaplin
United Artists
The London-born actor enjoyed a meteoric rise as star performer and reliable, productive director within three years of moving to the US; his tramp character becoming synonymous with the silent era. Chaplin would become one of the most powerful figures in Hollywood before being denied re-entry into the US due to his alleged political views.

Douglas Fairbanks Sr
United Artists
Known for his comedies and swashbucklers, Fairbanks Sr successfully transitioned from the silent era to talkies and cemented his place as Hollywood royalty with his marriage to Mary Pickford and founding of United Artists.

Mary Pickford
Paramount/United Artists
Dubbed 'America's Sweetheart', Mary Pickford was a child actress who became arguably the most popular star of the silent films generation. In 1916, she was the first star to become a millionaire, went on to marry Douglas Fairbanks and founded United Artists studio with her husband and Charlie Chaplin.

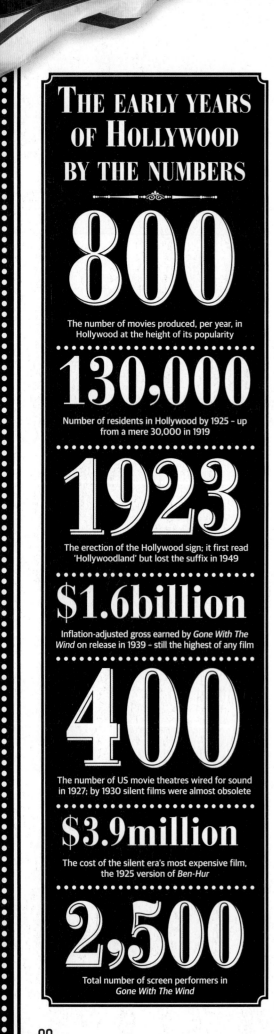

Sam Warner with his wife Lina and daughter Lita in 1925

over their star's acting abilities and the quality of the script. Realising Jolson's claim to the audience that "you ain't heard nothin' yet", Warner's stock went stratospheric; at $132 a share it was worth nearly seven times the value prior to *The Jazz Singer*. The gamble had paid off, and handsomely too - the film ensured the studio was now swimming in cash.

The celebrations would be short-lived, though. Jack had noticed that his brother Sam had been struggling with his balance and suffering from nosebleeds - the result of undiagnosed infections caused by abscessed teeth. Following months of ill health, Sam Warner fell into a coma and died at the age of 40, the day before *The Jazz Singer*'s premiere.

While he was devastated by the loss of his closest brother, this was Jack's moment. Without Sam, he became the studio's head of production, inheriting his brother's drive but combining it with a fire and no-nonsense attitude. Unlike Sam, who was generally liked, Jack gained a reputation as an uncaring boss - happy to slash costs and lay off staff for the sake of the bottom line. Under his leadership the studio gambled the astonishing sum of $100 million on the purchase of rival film studio First National. When The Wall Street Crash of 1929 - while not denting the film industry as badly as other industries - occurred it meant that, for a while, money was tight.

The studio's response was to ramp up production to a staggering 80 films a year by 1929. With no one to check his behaviour, Jack became notorious as one of the most unpleasant men in Hollywood - in a town filled with unpleasant men no mean

> ## "A classic rags-to-riches story, worthy of a script from one of Hollywood's greatest studios"

achievement. Further acquisitions and expansion would make Warner Bros one of the Big Five studios and Jack Warner one of Hollywood's most powerful players - he was, by this point, a huge success by any reasonable measure. Warner Bros had matched, then bought out and finally beaten rivals into submission, becoming the equal of the four biggest studios, MGM, 20th Century Fox, RKO and Paramount by 1930. It had taken 20 years but the Warner Brothers had done it.

The impact of Warner Bros is hard to overstate. With the release of *The Jazz Singer* the brothers revolutionised the industry - some stars were finished overnight while others saw new opportunities opening up. Silent films were dead within one or two years. Beyond that the structure of Warner Bros - with stars under contract, films made in-house at studios, owned outright and distributed to theatres owned by the studio - combined with pioneering use of new technologies and rampant acquisition of theatre chains and other studios amounted to an economic powerhouse. The four brothers were instrumental in introducing the studio system that Hollywood would soon become known for - and it was unbeatable.

From poor outsiders, immigrants, they had sweated, gambled, bartered and sacrificed to reach the apex of Hollywood. Jack Warner - who had once sung, badly, for pennies - was a powerful studio boss; the Golden Age of Hollywood arriving. For an ambitious boy who had always yearned for power, respect and adulation, it was a classic rags-to-riches story, worthy of a film script from one of Hollywood's greatest studios.

"The brothers revolutionised the industry – some stars were finished overnight, while others saw new opportunities open up"

George Cukor and Jack Warner celebrate winning Academy Awards for their 1964 production of *My Fair Lady*

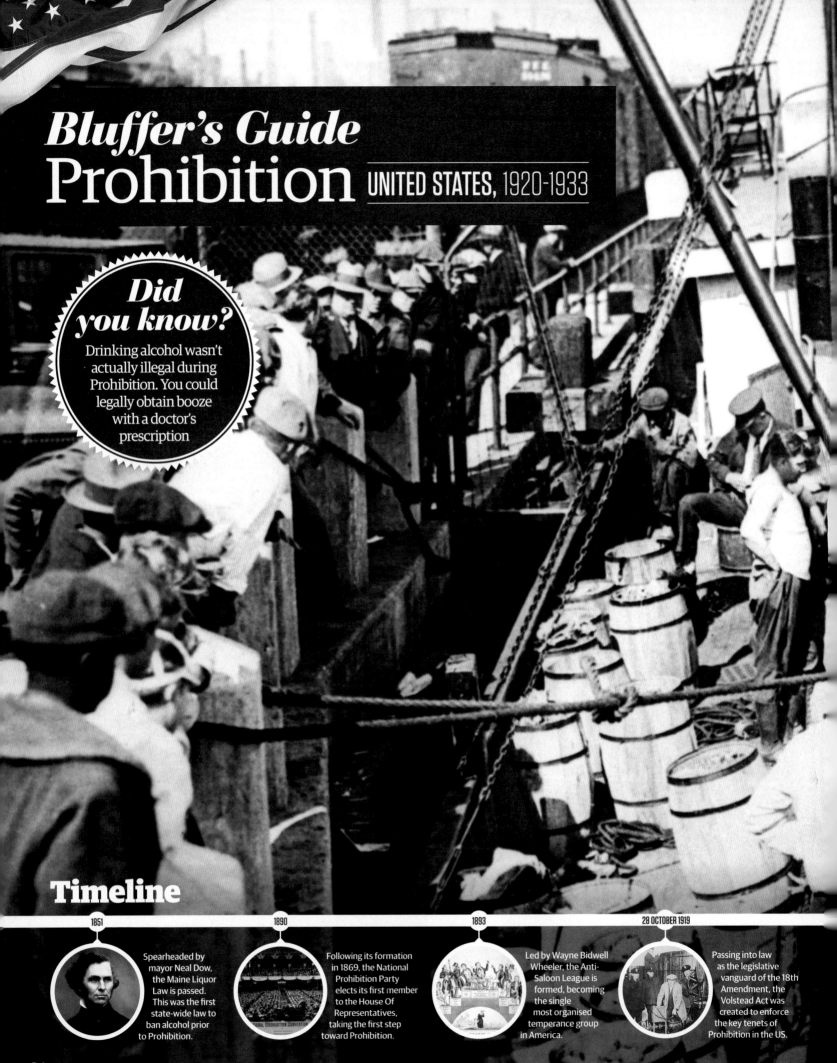

Bluffer's Guide
Prohibition

UNITED STATES, 1920-1933

Did you know?

Drinking alcohol wasn't actually illegal during Prohibition. You could legally obtain booze with a doctor's prescription

Timeline

1851
Spearheaded by mayor Neal Dow, the Maine Liquor Law is passed. This was the first state-wide law to ban alcohol prior to Prohibition.

1890
Following its formation in 1869, the National Prohibition Party elects its first member to the House Of Representatives, taking the first step toward Prohibition.

1893
Led by Wayne Bidwell Wheeler, the Anti-Saloon League is formed, becoming the single most organised temperance group in America.

28 OCTOBER 1919
Passing into law as the legislative vanguard of the 18th Amendment, the Volstead Act was created to enforce the key tenets of Prohibition in the US.

? What was it?

Almost a decade before the Great Depression brought the 'Roaring Twenties' to its knees, another movement attempted to manhandle the country into an enforced temperance before it had barely begun. Prohibition - which entered the United States constitution with the ratification of the 18th Amendment in 1920 - made the production, transportation and sale of alcohol a crime.

It transformed bars and clubs into 'speakeasies' (establishments where citizens could come and imbibe a glass illegal tipple in secret) and turned small-time gangsters and criminals into tycoons as the procurement and sale of booze became the most lucrative commodity of the underground economy.

It ran for over a decade and helped contribute to the financial irresponsibility that ultimately led to the Wall Street Crash in 1929, and the Great Depression that followed. It wouldn't be until the ratification of the 21st Amendment in December 1933 that the country would finally remove the ban and reap the benefits of reintroducing alcohol sales into a still crippled economy.

? Why did it happen?

While Prohibition would become a significant period of history for the United States in the 20th century, the origins of the movement can be found almost 100 years prior. During the 1820s and 1830s - over half a century after America's successful War for Independence - a wave of religious revivalism was sweeping the nation. Along with a growing opposition to slavery, these 'perfectionist' groups deemed alcohol a demonic influence that would ultimately lead all men to sin.

The temperance movement continued to grow, and spread along with the expansion of territory that created the Frontier. Saloons became a key staple of the Wild West and by the turn of the century, the anti-alcohol crusade turned into a nationwide attempt to forcibly prevent the sale of booze. By 1906, attacks on the sale of liquor by the Anti-Saloon League were commonplace, but it would be the support of figures of industry and certain political figures that would ultimately lead to the 18th Amendment.

? Who was involved?

Neal Dow
20 March 1804 – 2 October 1897
As the mayor of Maine (the first state to enforce anti-alcohol laws), Dow became known as the 'Napoleon of Temperance'.

Carry Nation
25 November 1846 – 9 June 1911
In the fight for Prohibition, Nation led hundreds of men and women in brutal attacks on saloons and bars.

Wayne Bidwell Wheeler
10 November 1869 – 5 September 1927
A shrewd politician and lawyer, Wheeler masterminded the Anti-Saloon League and was key in bringing Prohibition into effect.

5 OCTOBER 1931

With the trial and imprisonment of the notorious gangster, Al Capone, alcohol bootlegging sees its most prolific and high profile mobster removed from power.

5 DECEMBER 1933

Following much debate in the Senate, the 21st Amendment is passed, removing the staples of the 18th Amendment and re-established the legality of alcohol sales in the process.

The Wall Street Crash

Panic took over on Black Tuesday as stock prices sunk lower than ever before, sending shock waves through international markets and heralding the arrival of the Great Depression

Richard Whitney was a man who lived beyond his means, surrounding himself with luxury and power, swimming in the richest social circles of New York. Treasurer of the Yacht Club, vice president of the New York Stock Exchange, he was one of the most powerful men in the country. Looking down onto Wall Street through a window high up in the Exchange building at the height of summer in 1929, the rays of the sun shone brightly on the streets, giving them a golden glow. For Whitney and others the streets may as well have been paved with gold, such was the amount of money that some were making in the city that famously never sleeps. Whitney could never have guessed that the stocks he owned were going to nosedive, that he would become infamous for embezzling money, or that scenes of panic and desperation would unfold on the street beneath him. Right then, much like the rest of the US, he was convinced that the good times wouldn't stop.

The United States had been thriving throughout the Jazz Age and it seemed that nothing could stop its relentless rise to true prosperity. After a shaky start in the years immediately following the end of the Great War, the economy had bounced back on its feet while Europe remained in a slump, hard-hit and shattered from fighting across the continent. France was severely underpopulated and Germany was economically crippled due to the cost of war and the Treaty of Versailles, relying on loans from countries like the United States. But in bustling cities across the Atlantic Ocean like New York it was a different world; business was booming and driving a market bubble the likes of which the world had never seen before.

New technologies were being brought to market, better and more modern models quickly replacing the last as all sorts of wonders suddenly became available. The 1920s was a time of great innovation and for the first time people could afford to buy brand-new devices like electric blenders, toasters and vacuum cleaners for their homes. Great industrial titans like Henry Ford were making their fortunes too, with the new Model A replacing the original Model T, and Chrysler's Dodge and Plymouth cars hitting the road as the great marques made their mark on the US. In 1926, 4.3 million automobiles were produced, rising to nearly 5.4 million in 1929. It was an exciting time, the first great economic boom in recorded history, and made much more intense by the sudden frenzy of speculation that swept the nation.

The latest craze to make it into the dance clubs and cafes, the brokers' offices and even homes, was having a ticker on the wall that gave the latest stock quotes. For years speculation had been part of the arcana of powerful Wall Street bankers, investors and stock traders, people who made a fortune - and maybe lost it again - in a day's work. Above them was an elite group of individuals across New York who came together to discuss the market and agree a silver-lined nudge here, a deep investment there. These were men like Charles

Before the Wall Street Crash many Americans had been living beyond their means

Richard Whitney, vice president of the New York Stock Exchange

Many soup kitchens opened up during the Great Depression

world; you simply buy up some stock, wait for the price to rise again and sell it. The rate of return on investments - even those of the safest, most low-risk sort - continued to rise toward the end of 1928. Foreign businesses began to pour their money into New York stocks as fast as they could, as word of 12 per cent returns reached them, and so the financial boom was being shared in by the entire world. Some stocks were rising by as many as 20 points in a day during the months leading up to the crash, and on 12 June 1929 over five million shares traded hands. It seemed like nothing could stop the power of the free market.

The beginning of the end was Black Thursday, 24 October 1929, when 12.9 million shares were sold in a day. Heavy selling from the outset meant that the market immediately lost 11 per cent of its value, and the chaos was such that an emergency meeting was called among the elite bankers. Among the attendees of this meeting were Charles Mitchell, president of the National City Bank of New York, Richard Whitney, vice president of the New York Stock Exchange and Thomas Lamont, chairman of JP Morgan. Together, they decided to pool $250 million in order to support key stocks and companies that would not only protect their own interests but also bolster market confidence.

It seemed the national nerve was failing, though, that people were beginning to suspect there wouldn't always be someone available to sell to. An innocent enough thought by itself, but when magnified through a country full of people speculating on the assumption that prices are always going to keep rising, a very dangerous one indeed. Suddenly, there were no longer enough people to buy the stocks and keep everything changing hands. Owning stocks on the margin was no longer attractive - rather than make you money, they could ruin you. The bubble burst spectacularly as people began to realise quite how much financial trouble they'd be in if the music stopped and they were left without a chair to sit in.

Richard Whitney led the charge from the Wall Street elite, rallying the traders by making audacious bids. Whitney confidently strode onto the floor of the New York Stock Exchange amidst

Mitchell of National City Bank, Thomas Lamont of JP Morgan and John Rockefeller. But now, for the first time, everyday people had access to brokers' offices, since a rash of these offices had spread across the country in recent times, in which they could speculate alongside the best of Wall Street. For most people, all they knew was that they could make a heck of a lot of money betting on the stock market - nearly everyone was doing it.

These investors out for a quick buck could borrow beyond their means in order to buy stocks, and one common way of doing this was to buy on the margin. Essentially, this meant that someone could put up only a small amount of the money

required and then reap the profits on both that part and the part provided by the broker. It was possible to get up to 75 per cent on the margin, and toward the end of 1929 almost 90 per cent of stocks traded were done so on the margin. It was indicative of the times, as the 1920s was when 'buy-now-pay-later' came into the fore, with hundreds of thousands of people getting themselves into debt in order to take these new consumer goods home for nothing more than a deposit and an IOU.

Stocks were the talk of the town and newspapers were full of stories of teachers, maids and factory workers suddenly making it big in one of the offices downtown. It was the easiest thing in the

"Foreign businesses began to pour their money into New York stocks as word of 12 per cent returns reached them"

Four causes of the Great Depression

Overproduction
Technological innovation brought more consumer goods to market, and the increases in demand led to a rise in industrial output. Yet there came a point at which there was not enough purchasing power to sustain this pace and as the market saturated, firms were left with rising costs and falling sales.

Bank runs
At the beginning of the decade there were over 30,000 independent banks in America; by 1931 over 2,000 had closed, and 9,000 by the end of the decade. Small banks were susceptible to bank runs that would ruin them. People would get spooked and withdraw their cash from a bank, threatening its solvency.

No money
With the unemployment rate standing above 25 per cent at times, there was a reduction in spending throughout the economy. People were also having to pay back their buy-now-pay-later goods, pay their mortgages and then somehow pay other bills. There was a severe lack of disposable income.

Debt
Just before the crash, around 90 per cent of speculation was done on the margin. Credit was freely available in the 1920s so people took advantage of this. National debt-to-GDP ratio was at an all time high before the Great Depression, at 300 per cent. But when the debts were called in, intense deflation set in.

The spectacular rise and fall of the Dow Jones Industrial Average

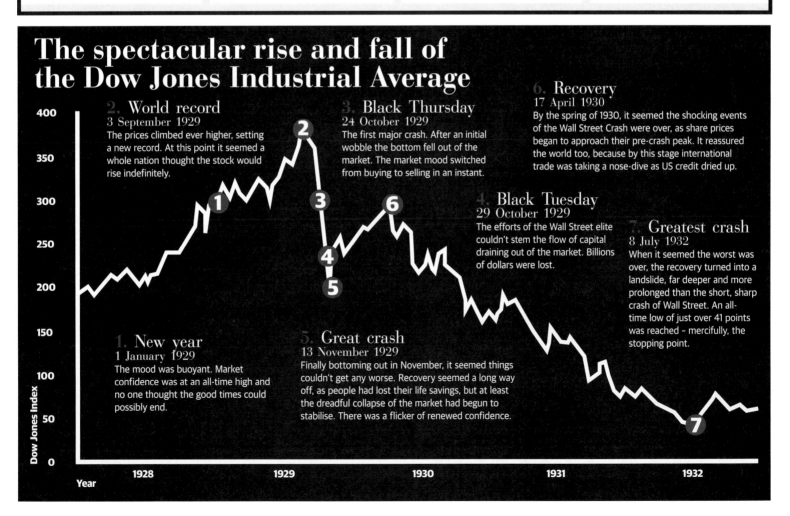

2. World record
3 September 1929
The prices climbed ever higher, setting a new record. At this point it seemed a whole nation thought the stock would rise indefinitely.

3. Black Thursday
24 October 1929
The first major crash. After an initial wobble the bottom fell out of the market. The market mood switched from buying to selling in an instant.

6. Recovery
17 April 1930
By the spring of 1930, it seemed the shocking events of the Wall Street Crash were over, as share prices began to approach their pre-crash peak. It reassured the world too, because by this stage international trade was taking a nose-dive as US credit dried up.

4. Black Tuesday
29 October 1929
The efforts of the Wall Street elite couldn't stem the flow of capital draining out of the market. Billions of dollars were lost.

7. Greatest crash
8 July 1932
When it seemed the worst was over, the recovery turned into a landslide, far deeper and more prolonged than the short, sharp crash of Wall Street. An all-time low of just over 41 points was reached – mercifully, the stopping point.

1. New year
1 January 1929
The mood was buoyant. Market confidence was at an all-time high and no one thought the good times could possibly end.

5. Great crash
13 November 1929
Finally bottoming out in November, it seemed things couldn't get any worse. Recovery seemed a long way off, as people had lost their life savings, but at least the dreadful collapse of the market had begun to stabilise. There was a flicker of renewed confidence.

the panic, bid $205 for 10,000 shares of US Steel and then went off to buy 25,000 other shares and make similar bids for a dozen other stocks. His calm demeanour and bold deployment of dollars reassured people, and for a while the general panic subsided. The scale of the fall on Black Thursday was matched by the recovery later that day and the rally led by Whitney was a testament to the skill of Wall Street's bankers.

Wall Street had already been warned at the beginning of autumn, though: "Stock prices have reached what looks like a permanently high plateau," said Irving Fisher. But although economists like Fisher had been sounding the market's death knell for months, predicting it had peaked and a crash was imminent, people could scarcely believe what had happened. Black Thursday came seemingly out of nowhere and complete disaster was only narrowly averted. A special police detail was dispatched to keep the peace on Wall Street as crowds started to gather around the Exchange on Broad Street, from which the cries of frantic traders could be heard on the street below.

The visitor's gallery in the Exchange, where Winston Churchill had been watching the desperate scene unfold, was closed at 12:30pm, though the crowds spilling outside soon continued to relay the news from the trading floor. Churchill had been taking a rail tour of Canada before he came to Wall Street, determined to make his fortune in the securities market. He was brought up to the gallery by a stranger who offered to show him what was going on as Churchill strolled along Wall Street and discovered the bedlam that had

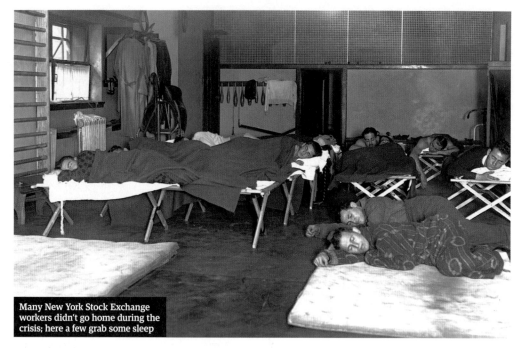
Many New York Stock Exchange workers didn't go home during the crisis; here a few grab some sleep

erupted. He'd invested in the Simmons Bedding Company among other stocks because he liked their advertisements, which he could hear on the radio, but he lost $100,000 in a day.

The weekend following Black Thursday was subdued and things more or less held together after a statement from the chairman of JP Morgan, Thomas Lamont, to reassure the press, but confidence totally ebbed once the market opened for trading again. On Black Monday, 28 October, the market fell another 13 per cent despite the continued efforts of power bankers to buy colossal

amounts of stock to prop it up. The next day, Black Tuesday, was brutal. The market fell another 11 per cent as over 16 million shares were desperately off-loaded. In total the Dow Jones Index had dropped 25 per cent over four days of trading, wiping $30 billion off the value of companies in the process - the equivalent of almost $400 billion today. Industry icon General Motors went down on Black Tuesday, as did US Steel. The Wall Street elite continued to bail hard on the flooding deck of the ship, with William Durant of General Motors, Henry Ford and members of the Rockefeller family trying to demonstrate confidence by buying huge quantities of stock despite the hordes of people fleeing a routed market. Rockefeller bought a million shares in Standard Oil alone, and yet none of these grand gestures were enough. These heavyweight companies all lost massive amounts of their value, and in the years that followed, sales and employers vanished too.

Of course, not everyone was brought low by the great crash - a few people, like Jesse Livermore, managed to turn it into an opportunity. Jesse made his first speculative bets when he was around 16 years old. He had a knack for avoiding or thriving in disaster, making a load of money

"Suddenly, there were no longer enough people to buy the stocks and keep everything changing hands"

How the value of money plummeted
What five dollars would get you in 1932

●●●
●●●
●●●
●●●
●●●
●●●
●●●●●●●●●●●●●●●●●●●
333 eggs
(Before the crash – 102 eggs)

●●
●●
●●
263 pounds of potatoes
(Before the crash – 139 pounds of potatoes)

▢▢▢▢▢▢▢▢▢▢▢▢▢▢▢▢▢▢▢▢▢▢▢▢
▢▢▢▢▢▢▢▢▢▢▢▢▢▢▢▢▢▢▢▢▢▢▢▢
▢▢▢▢▢▢▢▢▢▢▢▢▢▢▢▢▢▢▢▢▢▢▢▢
100 pounds of sugar
Before the crash – 71 pounds of sugar)

During the Crash, many people headed to Wall Street to try and find out what was going on

by selling stocks short before the San Francisco earthquake in 1906. Selling short is risky, yet somehow Livermore got away with it. He made over $1 million selling short during a stock market crash in 1907 and he claimed to have made $3 million selling wheat short in 1925. During the great crash, he capitalised on the panic selling and made more than $100 million selling short, though he was to lose it all in the hard years that followed.

The aftermath of the great crash of Wall Street was incredible. A nation's confidence was shattered and its economy left in tatters, paving the way for the world's worst financial crisis; the Great Depression. While Wall Street alone didn't cause the Great Depression, it was certainly a violent expression of the growing malaise. The boom times were bound to end, and once that moment the tide turned came - when there was a tacit acceptance that no one out there wanted to buy any more, and that you might not be able to sell to pay your debts - the lives of hundreds of thousands of Americans were brought crashing down.

Richard Whitney, Charles Mitchell, John Rockefeller, Thomas Lamont and countless other barons of business lost great swathes of their estates. Whitney would actually be imprisoned in 1936 for embezzlement and thousands of people turned up at Grand Central Station to watch him being escorted in handcuffs by armed guards onto a train bound for prison. Despite his imprisonment, Whitney still had his wealthy family and friends to lean on; most Americans weren't as lucky. Stores of all sorts closed as they struggled to find or pay for suppliers, warehouses emptied themselves of hard-working people since there were no contracts to pay their wages, the extravagant clubs couldn't find enough spenders to keep the doors open, and the butchers and barbers closed their shops for lack of customers. People lost their jobs, began eating frugally and infrequently and could no longer

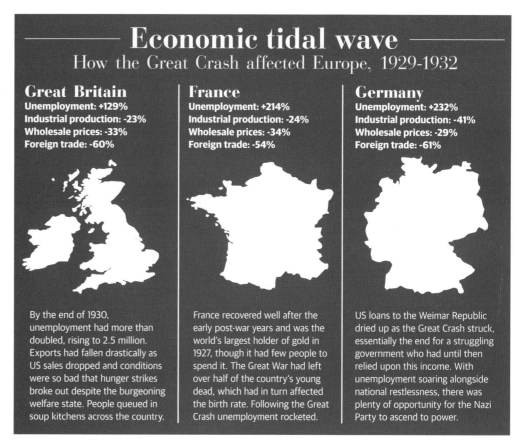

Economic tidal wave
How the Great Crash affected Europe, 1929-1932

Great Britain
Unemployment: +129%
Industrial production: -23%
Wholesale prices: -33%
Foreign trade: -60%

France
Unemployment: +214%
Industrial production: -24%
Wholesale prices: -34%
Foreign trade: -54%

Germany
Unemployment: +232%
Industrial production: -41%
Wholesale prices: -29%
Foreign trade: -61%

By the end of 1930, unemployment had more than doubled, rising to 2.5 million. Exports had fallen drastically as US sales dropped and conditions were so bad that hunger strikes broke out despite the burgeoning welfare state. People queued in soup kitchens across the country.

France recovered well after the early post-war years and was the world's largest holder of gold in 1927, though it had few people to spend it. The Great War had left over half of the country's young dead, which had in turn affected the birth rate. Following the Great Crash unemployment rocketed.

US loans to the Weimar Republic dried up as the Great Crash struck, essentially the end for a struggling government who had until then relied upon this income. With unemployment soaring alongside national restlessness, there was plenty of opportunity for the Nazi Party to ascend to power.

pay for the fuel to keep their cars running, or the electricity to keep their kitchen gadgets and bed warmers working. The ranks of the poor swelled as society slipped down a notch en masse, and as the winter winds blew through the New York streets they all grew cold together.

With unemployment, decimated purchasing power and no credit flowing through the economy, the Great Depression set in for the long haul. US exports suffered, as did its provision of loans to

Germany. The lack of trade and aid in Germany turned an impoverished state into a hotbed for extremism, giving rise to the Nazi Party, while the depression in Britain was felt even harder after the post-war struggle and lack of boom years that were enjoyed in the States. It seemed that USA's sudden loss of confidence during the great crash of Wall Street cost the world its spirit, turning a panic on the floor of the New York Stock Exchange into a prelude to disaster.

A man who has been financially wiped out by the Crash attempts to sell his expensive car

$100 WILL BUY THIS CAR MUST HAVE CASH LOST ALL ON THE STOCK MARKET

The unfortunate American who lost it all

William Durant was among the biggest losers of the Great Crash. He started out as a cigar salesman in Michigan and went on to turn a $2,000 horse-drawn carriage venture into a $2 million franchise. Durant was later a co-founder of General Motors, a titan in the automotive industry. He made a fortune through speculation, including about $8 million in securities the year prior to the crash but he lost it all in the Wall Street Crash. He started selling his stock before the end, but he still lost $40 million.

THE NAVY NEEDS **Ave** **PEARL HA**

let's go

THE BIRTH OF A SUPERPOWER

The catastrophic events of World War II changed the United States' standing on the world stage forever

SHIPS TO

© BETHLEHEM STEEL COMPANY

ENOLA GAY

82

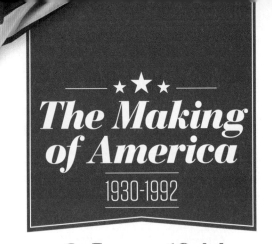

The Making of America
1930-1992

--- **6 June 1944** ---

The D-Day invasion

On Tuesday, 6 June 1944, the Allies were finally ready to bring the fight back to the Nazis in a seaborne invasion the likes of which the world had never seen. Four years of planning and preparation between the United States, Britain, the Soviet Union and its fellow Allies would lead to one of the famous invasions in history: D-Day.

By 1944, Nazi Germany had been bludgeoned by five long years of war, occupation and blockades. The German war machine had had its nose bloodied in a long and ultimately fruitless war of attrition with the Soviet Union following Hitler's fateful decision to betray Stalin and create the Eastern Front in 1941. Yet even with the drawn out loss to the Soviets, the Germans were far from defeated.

Operation Overlord - the grand plan to invade an exhausted yet fiercely determined Germany - was years in the making by the time the beaches of

Normandy were selected for the seaborne point of invasion. The Allies knew the Germans suspected such an attack would come from the French coast - and that preparations would already be underway to counteract such an act - but they also knew that Germany needed time to heal its wounds and prepare a response. So the Allies struck on the morning of 6 June 1944, striking with a flurry of airborne assaults, infantry and armour.

Over 4,000 Allied troops died on the beaches of Normandy on the first day alone as they shed blood for every grain of sand and dirt taken from the Germans. Over 133,000 men would eventually be deployed into occupied France, with 10,000 vehicles unleashed across 50 miles of coastline. Operation Neptune would ultimately prove successful for the Allies, but it would come at a price. By the end of the Normandy landings, over 425,000 men had died on both sides.

> The vast undertaking of the Normandy landings saw the Allies stage the largest seaborne invasion in history

While D-Day didn't solely lead to the downfall of the Third Reich, it did provide a tipping point that accelerated its defeat

Defining moments

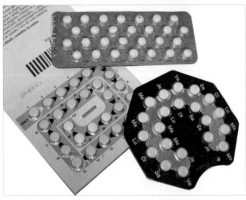

• The North Atlantic Treaty is signed
4 April 1949
Four years after the end of the World War II, the US joined with 28 other nations in forming the North Atlantic Treaty Organisation (NATO). Having been forced to intervene in catastrophic global conflicts twice in just over 30 years, the US was determined to ensure that such a calamity would never happen again.

• Alaska becomes the 49th state
3 January 1959
Alaska was first bought by the US in 1867, when it paid Russia $7.2 million for 586,000 square miles of tundra and ice. Following the creation of military bases during WWII to defend against a potential Japanese invasion, the Alaskan population grew and in 1959, President Dwight Eisenhower officially signed the country into the Union.

• The birth control pill hits America
9 May 1960
When the birth control pill was introduced to the United States in the spring of 1960, it changed American society forever. Freeing sex from its stifling union to procreation granted American women a powerful new control of their own bodies, and created a sense of equality between men and women when it came to the view of sex and contraception.

ORIGINS

Stalin calls on the US and UK to form a 'second front', June 1941

Allies agree to cross-channel invasion during Trident Conference, May 1943

Initial D-Day is postponed due to need for more ships, May 1944

LEGACY

Nazi Germany forced to fight a disastrous two-front war

Led to the liberation of Nazi-controlled European countries

Enabled the Allies to push Nazis back onto German soil

• The inaugural Super Bowl is held
15 January 1957

Super Bowl I (or *the* Super Bowl as it was then referred to) marked the first time the two biggest American football leagues in the states - the NFL and the AFL - had competed against one another. NFL champions the Green Bay Packers took on AFL superstars the Kansas City Chiefs in a thrilling grudge match that saw Green Bay rise triumphant with a 35-10 win.

• Alcatraz is occupied
20 November 1969

Six years after the closure of the infamous Alcatraz Federal Penitentiary, the abandoned island off the coast of San Francisco was quietly occupied by a group known as the Indians of All Tribes. Initially formed by 89 Native Americans that had relocated to the Bay Area, the land was claimed as rightful territory of the disaffected people. The occupation lasted 14 months and is seen as a landmark in Native American activism.

• The Gulf War erupts
2 August 1990

Codenamed Operation Desert Shield, the Gulf War saw an alliance of 35 nations take organisation military action against Iraq following its invasion and annexation of Kuwait. Led by the US, the Gulf War became the most well-documented war of its time due to the introduction of live, rolling broadcasts. While Iraqi forces were pushed out of Kuwait, Iraqi president Saddam Hussein held on to power until he was finally toppled in the 2003 Iraq War.

Bluffer's Guide
The New Deal

UNITED STATES, 1933-1939

Timeline

4 MARCH 1933

As soon as FDR enters office, he begins orchestrating a huge array or legislative reforms and programs to kick-start the economy.

9 MARCH 1933

Within a week of taking office, FDR signs the Emergency Banking Act to stabilise the American banking system and avoid further failures. It proves a great success.

5 APRIL 1933

Due to the new Civilian Conservation Corps, over 3 million unemployed Americans are brought onto a new paid program to maintain forests.

9 NOVEMBER 1933

Much like the CCC, the Civil Works Administration employs over 4 million unemployed civilians to build roads, schools and more.

? What was it?

In the wake of the Great Depression - a catastrophic economic recession triggered by the stock market collapse of 1929 - the New Deal was a series of federal reforms aimed at rebuilding the economy of the United States. It was a vast and many-headed political program that was designed to do everything from re-energising agriculture to placing safety measures on the scuttled banking system that had led to the Wall Street Crash in 1929. Masterminded and spearheaded by president Franklin D Roosevelt, the New Deal lasted for eight years of FDR's presidency and fundamentally repaired the divide between the State and the people.

Boiled down to its purest ideals, the New Deal was built upon the foundation of three key principles: relief, recovery and reform. FDR wished to provide relief to the poorest demographics of the country, instigate a recovery for industry and agriculture, and reform the banking system that had ultimately crippled the country in the first place. As its architect, FDR's 'fireside' public addresses during this period became a voice of hope to struggling Americans.

? What were the consequences?

For Herbert Hoover, who served as president from 1929 to 1933, the Wall Street Crash and the genesis of the Great Depression were merely a economical phase that would eventually pass. He believed that no real federal intervention was needed and that it was "a passing incident in our national lives." However, the economy failed to recover and a lack of reform or government-aided relief efforts saw the country slip further and further into financial mire.

Delivering on a key tenet of his campaign for the White House, Hoover's successor would start orchestrating a series of multiple reforms within days of taking office. Forming the crux of his presidency over the next eight years, what would become the New Deal was designed to rebuild America's domestic economy, help support the poorest parts of the country and stop such a calamity from every repeating itself in the future.

? Who was involved?

Franklin D Roosevelt
30 January 1882 – 12 April 1945
The architect of the New Deal, Roosevelt supported the reform through the 1930s, and World War II, before his death in 1945.

Dr Francis Townsend
13 January 1867 – 1 September 1960
The Townsend Plan was a popular pension proposal during the Great Depression that influenced the Social Security Program.

Huey P Long
30 August 1893 – 10 September 1935
Both a Louisiana governor and senator, Long was a key advocate for the redistribution of wealth during the Great Depression.

Did you know?
The New Deal didn't restart the economy as fast as FDR had hoped, so he began a more radical plan known as the Second New Deal in 1935

8 AUGUST 1934
FDR orchestrates the plan to build a canal that not only provides irrigation water across the country, but also sets the stage for hydroelectric power.

12 APRIL 1945
FDR dies from a cerebral brain haemorrhage. The legacy of the New Deal would long outlive the president who spearheaded it, and many of its reforms still exist in US law to this day.

Remember PEARL HARBOR

Inside the infamous attack that shocked the world and rallied the American public for war

I n 1941, the United States of America was not a superpower. In fact, its military strength only consisted of approximately 200,000 servicemen scattered throughout the continental US and overseas. Since its costly involvement in World War I, the USA had resisted the temptation to involve itself with global affairs, practicing instead a policy of isolationism. The 'Day of Infamy' would change all that.

On 7 December 1941, Japan launched an unprovoked attack against the US Fleet anchored at Pearl Harbor on the Hawaiian island of Oahu. This pre-emptive strike was intended to blunt US power in the Pacific and to bully the USA into staying out of Japan's business as it went about conquering its neighbours.

In the event, the United States' Pacific Fleet would be set ablaze, but Japan would fail to destroy its three aircraft carriers, all of which - Japanese intelligence had failed to reveal - were elsewhere that day. Pearl Harbor was considered a success for Japan at the time, but it would prove one the costliest miscalculations in the history of warfare. Rather than fold in the face of Japanese aggression, the American public united under a banner of patriotism, and in the supposed warning words of Japanese Admiral Yamamoto, who masterminded the attack, a sleeping giant awoke.

By the time the USA's conflict with Japan ended four years later, it was a global player in possession of the most powerful war machine the world had ever seen. By harnessing its huge industrial might, the country had built a military that boasted 8.3 million troops, jet fighters, long-range bombers and the world's first atomic weapons. 7 December 1941 was, in US President Franklin Roosevelt's words, "A date which will live in infamy." Here's how its dramatic moments unfolded.

Sunday 7 December 1941, 5am

As the sun rose over the vast blue expanse of the central Pacific Ocean, a Japanese fleet that included two battleships, three cruisers, nine destroyers and six aircraft carriers waited 370 kilometres north of Hawaii, safely out of range of US radar. Hundreds of pilots gathered on deck to say their prayers. They would shortly deliver the first blows in a terrible war against the United States that would eventually result in the reduction of two Japanese cities - Hiroshima and Nagasaki - to irradiated dust. The Japanese had trained these pilots well. For almost a year they had been secretly practising low-altitude torpedo runs against sea-borne targets, as well as high-altitude precision bombing drills, at Ariake Bay on Kyushu, the southernmost of Japan's main islands. With its narrow entrance and shallow waters, this location was a geographical ringer for the pilots' real target at Pearl Harbor in Oahu, Hawaii - the US Pacific Fleet.

> "It was a Sunday morning in a tropical paradise, the US was not at war and Outerbridge's message would be left un-decoded. In fact, it wouldn't be read until moments before the raid began"

6.10am

As unsuspecting Americans on Oahu dozed in their beds, still 370 kilometres away, Admiral Chuichi Nagumo - commander of Japan's First Fleet Air Arm - gave the order to launch the first attack wave. Hundreds of Japanese aircraft hurtled off of the aircraft carriers' decks and into the early morning sky. Among the strike force were Japanese fighters, torpedo planes and dive-bombers. They launched with split-second timing, and the entire air armada was airborne within 15 minutes. Lieutenant Commander Chigusa on the destroyer Akigumo was impressed. "We felt rather confident seeing the planes flying to their rendezvous points," he later wrote in his diary. "Our crew waved to the planes as they were flying past our upper deck, [and] I noticed that I was waving my cap vigorously and unconsciously from my position on the bridge. By and by, the first group launched and joined in a formation of 183 planes, and they soon disappeared into the southern sky." The Japanese assault had been planned to take place in three waves. The first would attack all military installations on Oahu, the second would zero in on more specific targets, while the third would smash fuel-storage tanks, dry docks, and repair facilities. The three aircraft carriers the Japanese were hoping to destroy in the raid, however, were not present.

USS Lexington was hundreds of kilometres to the east ferrying planes to the US airbase on Midway Island. USS Saratoga was in San Diego, California, having just had a refit, while USS Enterprise was on exercise 320 kilometres to the south of Oahu. Around the same time that the Japanese first wave took to the skies, 18 aircraft also left the decks bound for Ford Island in the centre of Pearl Harbor. Their estimated time of arrival was 8am.

6.30am

The destroyer USS Ward was on routine patrol around the entrance to Pearl Harbor when its crew spotted an unidentified submarine turret. Ward's commander, Captain Outerbridge, followed protocol and dropped depth charges. At 6.53am, he sent a message to the commandant of the 14th Naval District on Oahu. It read: "Have dropped depth charges upon submarine operating in defensive sea area." It should have been enough to put the whole naval base on high alert. However, it

An aerial view of Pearl Harbor with Ford Island in the centre, the navy yard beyond it and Hickam Field in the upper left

was Sunday morning in a tropical paradise, the US was not at war and Outerbridge's message would be left un-decoded. In fact, it wouldn't be read until moments before the raid began.

7.02am

On Oahu's north coast, at the remote Opana Radar station, two young US army privates Joseph Lockard and George E Elliott watched as a mysterious shimmering light filled the top of the screen they were monitoring. Concerned, they called in a warning to their unit's information centre at Fort Shaftner in Honolulu. Most of the staff were at breakfast. A new and inexperienced officer, Lieutenant Tyler, took the call, telling them not to worry: a flight of US B-17 Flying Fortress bombers was expected in from California that morning, and was probably ahead of schedule. He told the two privates to shut the station down and return to base.

7.15am

The Japanese fleet, now 340 kilometres from Oahu, received the order to launch the next wave of aircraft. Chigusa, again a witness, wrote: "The second group of 167 attack planes started their launch one by one... I saw all the planes off, earnestly wishing them 'The best of luck.' The first news came from one of our patrol planes: ➤

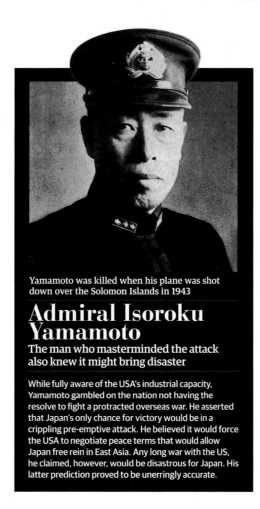

Yamamoto was killed when his plane was shot down over the Solomon Islands in 1943

Admiral Isoroku Yamamoto

The man who masterminded the attack also knew it might bring disaster

While fully aware of the USA's industrial capacity, Yamamoto gambled on the nation not having the resolve to fight a protracted overseas war. He asserted that Japan's only chance for victory would be in a crippling pre-emptive attack. He believed it would force the USA to negotiate peace terms that would allow Japan free rein in East Asia. Any long war with the US, he claimed, however, would be disastrous for Japan. His latter prediction proved to be unerringly accurate.

Roosevelt proved a great war-time leader, but died of stroke before the nation's victory

Franklin D Roosevelt

One of the USA's greatest ever presidents had known war was coming

President Roosevelt had long argued that the USA couldn't remain isolated from what was rapidly becoming a global conflict. By supplying Great Britain and other Allied countries with arms and materiel since the start of 1941, the US had already effectively picked sides. When, in July of that year, Roosevelt issued a trade embargo against Japan after its invasion of French Indo-China, he helped convince the Japanese leadership of the need to curtail American influence.

The super-dreadnought USS Pennsylvania sits behind the jumbled mass of wreckage of the destroyers Downes and Cassin

This U.S. Vought OS2U Kingfisher was destroyed on the ground at Ford Island during the attack

Japan's military rivalries

How a feud between Japan's navy and army sparked the attack on the USA

While the Imperial Japanese Navy (IJN) was launching its attack on the USA, the Imperial Japanese Army (IJA) was busy on the far side of the Pacific invading British-held colonies there. As bombs and torpedoes were ripping the US Pacific Fleet apart, more than 5,000 Japanese troops were storming beaches in the Malay Peninsular, while a further 52,000 would later seize Hong Kong.

The two attacks may appear to be tactically co-ordinated, especially as the pre-emptive strike at Pearl Harbor was a gamble, aiming to ensure the US played no part in trying to stop its colonial ambitions throughout Asia. But both stemmed from a deep-rooted rivalry between Imperial Japan's navy and its army.

The origins of this inter-service rivalry could be traced back to the Meiji Era, which between 1868 and 1912 saw Japan transformed from an isolated feudal society to a modern, Western-style country. Although both the IJA and IJN were formed around the start of this era, political jostling, competition for resources as well as snobbery (the army tended to recruit from the rural peasantry, while the navy from more sophisticated, urban sections of the population) created a tension between the two.

This began to manifest itself in geo-political terms in the early 1930s when two opposing factions emerged, both with different ideas about how Japan could achieve its imperial ambitions. These were known as Hokushin-ron and Nanshin-ron – literally 'strike north' and 'strike south'. Both groups advocated seizing territories rich in the necessary raw resources– in particular oil – that Japan needed to supercharge its economy.

The strike north faction, which favoured seizing Siberia by way of Manchuria, was understandably backed by the army, which saw in its military philosophy a chance for glory. The strike south faction, meanwhile, made the case for grabbing Indonesia's myriad islands, a scenario that would require the navy to be the dominant military force.

Initially, strike north had the upper hand, launching a successful invasion of China in 1937. However, when the IJA was defeated by the Soviet army at the Battles of Khalkhin Gol in 1939, further expansion north became impossible and the argument presented by the strike south faction gained momentum, paving the way for the war in the Pacific and the attack on Pearl Harbor.

A Mitsubishi Zero fighter aboard the IJN aircraft carrier Akagi prior to departing for the attack

➤ 'Eleven capital ships are in Pearl Harbor'." Although the Pacific Fleet's three carriers were elsewhere, there were still rich pickings to be had. Of those anchored in Pearl Harbor, USS Oklahoma was one of the finest battleships in the American fleet and home to 1,398 officers and crew. It had earlier been moved from its customary defensive mooring to the south of Battleship Row on Ford Island, as it was due to undergo an inspection. Because of this, all its exterior portholes and interior hatches had been opened to make it more comfortable for the inspecting officers. In peacetime, this was a routine practice. In wartime, however, it was potentially disastrous, and so it was to prove.

7.35am

Approaching Oahu from its craggy eastern coast, the first wave of Japanese warplanes wasn't picked up by US radar because of a dead zone caused by a mountain range. The first Japanese planes reached the island completely undetected. The element of surprise – so necessary for the success of Admiral Yamamoto's plan – had been achieved perfectly. Commander Mitso Fuschida was leading the first wave. At about 7.40am, he gave the order 'Tenkei' (Take attack position), slid back the canopy of his torpedo bomber as it roared along at 370 kilometres per hour and fired a green flare. It was the signal to attack.

7.52am

Commander Fuschida radioed the fleet with the signal "Tora! Tora! Tora!" (Tiger! Tiger! Tiger!), which was a code meaning that maximum strategic surprise had been achieved. Moments later, the first Japanese assault wave, with a mixture of bombers, torpedo planes and fighters, swept out of the skies and began hunting their targets. With orders to make multiple simultaneous attacks, the first wave struck. Explosions could be heard all across the island. Dive-bombers struck at Kaneohe Naval Air Station in the north of Oahu. More dive-bombers and fighters screeched down on Bellows Air Field in the east. Parked aircraft erupted in flames, as stunned aircrew were sent scattering amid a thunderclap of high explosives and machine-gun fire.

All over Oahu there was mass confusion on the ground. In the air, meanwhile, unchallenged Japanese fighters ran into the aircraft dispatched from USS Enterprise earlier that morning as they arrived on time and unarmed. As they desperately tried to land on Ford Island, they were caught

Rescue crews scramble to reach survivors from USS West Virginia shortly after the assault

between enemy and friendly fire when those on the ground began to fight back.

8.02am

As a torpedo tore a huge hole in the battleship Nevada's port bow, its anti-aircraft gunners opened fire on a swarm of Japanese planes. Gunners on Arizona and the vessel moored next to it, the repair ship USS Vestal, also shot back. After being hit by a torpedo on the portside, USS California began to sink. It was time for high-level bombers to begin their run on Battleship Row.

8.08am

The local radio station *KGMB* interrupted its regular music programme to announce: "All army, navy and Marine personnel are to report for duty." By this time, high-level Japanese bombers were unleashing armour-piercing, delayed-action bombs from 3,000 metres. An 800-kilogram

> "An 800-kilogram bomb plunged downward with precision accuracy towards Arizona. Moments later, the battleship's magazines erupted. The resulting explosion sent a huge fireball soaring 150 metres into the pristine blue sky"

Smoke rises from the blazing ruins of aircraft Hanger 6 on Ford island

Above: This detailed Japanese map of Pearl Harbor was found inside one of the midget submarines used in the attack

bomb released by Japanese Pilot Officer Kanai Noboru plunged downward with precision accuracy towards Arizona. Moments later, the battleship's magazines erupted. The resulting explosion sent a huge fireball soaring 150 metres into the pristine blue sky. The mighty warship twisted and shrieked as its bough broke. It sank in under nine minutes, with the loss of 1,177 lives. Two ship lengths away, USS Oklahoma was the next ship to be targeted. After being struck by several torpedoes, explosions ripped huge holes into its hull, and because its portholes and watertight hatches had been left open, seawater surged into the ship. At 8.14am, it capsized. More than 400 men trapped inside could be heard pounding against the steel hull. Desperate attempts to free the entombed sailors would continue into the night.

8.17am

As well as attacks from the air, the Japanese had earlier dispatched five two-man mini-submarines to attack the ships anchored at Ford Island from below. The first had been sunk earlier that morning by USS Ward. USS Helm, the first of several destroyers to escape Pearl Harbor, spotted another stuck on a reef at the harbour's entrance and opened fire. Over the next 20 minutes, the fate of the other mini subs was settled, as one by one they were knocked out of the fight, most dramatically when another destroyer, USS Monaghan, rammed one inside Pearl Harbor itself.

8.50am

The second wave of Japanese aircraft led by Lieutenant Commander Shigekazu Shimazaki began to arrive from the north, under orders to strike military targets right across the island with fighters, torpedo planes and bombers. Minutes later, the second attack run started as dozens of dive-bombers hit ships in Pearl Harbor, while high-level bombers hit the air stations. The fighters, meanwhile, circled over the island tightening their grip on air supremacy. Many US fighters attempting to confront them were shot up on the runways of the island's various airfields before they could take off. If the first wave of the Japanese attack had caused immediate confusion, the second one created total chaos. Americans were firing at anything in the sky. Alarmingly, some of the planes they shot down were the unarmed bombers arriving from the mainland.

9.05am

KGMB Radio issued urgent warnings for Hawaii's citizens to stay off the roads. Meanwhile, in the harbour, rescue workers - toiling amid the furnace blast of battle - began working on the capsized Oklahoma. They used blowtorches on the thick steel hull in the hopes of cutting their way through to the crewmen who were fighting for their lives on the other side.

9.25am

The island's fire-fighting capabilities were, by this time, exhausted. When USS Shaw, a destroyer in dry dock, was hit by three bombs and fires began to rage through the vessel, there were no means to extinguish them. Shortly after 9.30am, as the last Japanese aircraft disappeared over the smoke-choked horizon, those fires reached its forward magazine. The raid was brought to its cataclysmic conclusion as another giant explosion ripped through the Hawaiian sky. Yamamoto's plan, it seemed, had worked. Pearl Harbor was in flames, the US military was in chaos, and its once mighty Pacific Fleet lay in waste.

Japan attacks

How the Imperial Japanese Navy launched one of history's most devastating raids

Picked up by radar
At 7.02am, the Opana radar station picks up the first wave, however, it's mistaken for the flight of B17s.

FIRST ATTACK
49 HIGH-LEVEL BOMBERS
51 DIVE-BOMBERS
40 TORPEDO BOMBERS
43 FIGHTERS

SECOND ATTACK
54 HIGH-LEVEL BOMBERS
78 DIVE-BOMBERS
36 FIGHTERS

The second wave
At 7.20am, the Japanese launch another 167 attack aircraft. This follow-up assault is designed to hit specific military targets.

The first wave of attacking aircraft
Launched at 6.10am, it takes the 183 attack aircraft just 15 minutes to get airborne and in formation.

Opana Radar Station

Wheeler field
Japanese fighter planes target Wheeler first and, about four minutes later, attack Pearl Harbor.

Haleiwa field

Schofield barracks

Wheeler field

Haleiwa field
Nine Japanese aircraft are shot down by pilots from this airfield.

Keneohe Nas

Keneohe

USS Shaw explodes
This destroyer is in dry dock for repairs, and is bombed towards the end of the raid, causing its magazines to erupt.

Ewa field

PEARL HARBOR

Bellows field

Bellows field
Eight Zeros attack, shooting down two US fighters.

AI-256

Aichi D3A 'Val' Dive Bomber
Of the 441 aircraft in Japan's task force, 153 were 'Val' dive-bombers. Thought to be obsolete by the Allies, they were used to devastating effect at Pearl Harbor. With a 250-kilogram bomb strapped to its fuselage, the Val went on to sink more Allied warships than any other Axis aircraft during the entire conflict.

Battleship row
What vessels survived the attack?

USS Pennsylvania
Damaged

In dry dock at the time, repeated Japanese attempts to torpedo the caisson it was held in failed. Damaged by bombs, 68 of its crew were killed or wounded.

USS Arizona
Sunk

Attacked by ten Kate torpedo planes during the first wave. One torpedo hit the ship's forward magazine resulting in a gigantic explosion. Of its 1,512 crew, just 335 survived.

USS Nevada
Seriously damaged

Despite being torpedoed, Nevada was able to escape Battleship Row during the attack. It was repeatedly targeted by dive-bombers from the second wave.

USS Oklahoma
Sunk

Hit by three torpedoes early in the raid. As it capsized, a further two torpedoes smashed into its listing hull, and its crew was machine gunned while attempting to abandon ship.

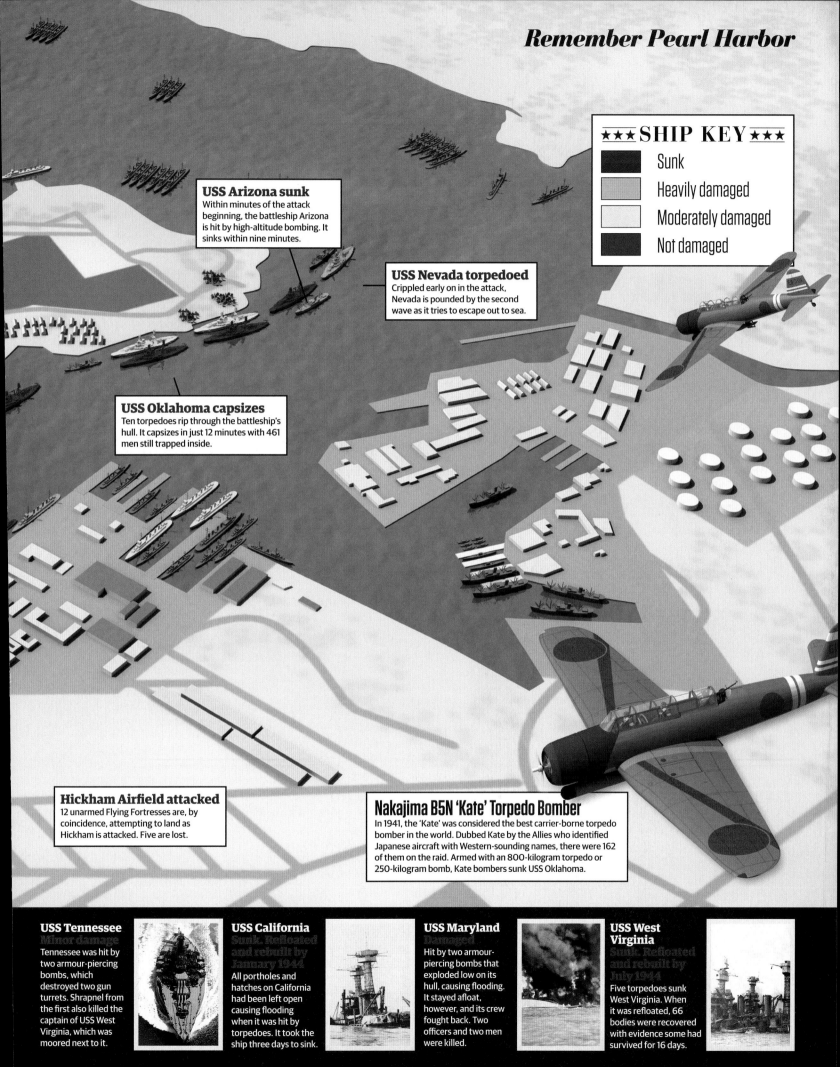

★★★ SHIP KEY ★★★
- Sunk
- Heavily damaged
- Moderately damaged
- Not damaged

USS Arizona sunk
Within minutes of the attack beginning, the battleship Arizona is hit by high-altitude bombing. It sinks within nine minutes.

USS Nevada torpedoed
Crippled early on in the attack, Nevada is pounded by the second wave as it tries to escape out to sea.

USS Oklahoma capsizes
Ten torpedoes rip through the battleship's hull. It capsizes in just 12 minutes with 461 men still trapped inside.

Hickham Airfield attacked
12 unarmed Flying Fortresses are, by coincidence, attempting to land as Hickham is attacked. Five are lost.

Nakajima B5N 'Kate' Torpedo Bomber
In 1941, the 'Kate' was considered the best carrier-borne torpedo bomber in the world. Dubbed Kate by the Allies who identified Japanese aircraft with Western-sounding names, there were 162 of them on the raid. Armed with an 800-kilogram torpedo or 250-kilogram bomb, Kate bombers sunk USS Oklahoma.

USS Tennessee
Minor damage
Tennessee was hit by two armour-piercing bombs, which destroyed two gun turrets. Shrapnel from the first also killed the captain of USS West Virginia, which was moored next to it.

USS California
Sunk. Refloated and rebuilt by January 1944
All portholes and hatches on California had been left open causing flooding when it was hit by torpedoes. It took the ship three days to sink.

USS Maryland
Damaged
Hit by two armour-piercing bombs that exploded low on its hull, causing flooding. It stayed afloat, however, and its crew fought back. Two officers and two men were killed.

USS West Virginia
Sunk. Refloated and rebuilt by July 1944
Five torpedoes sunk West Virginia. When it was refloated, 66 bodies were recovered with evidence some had survived for 16 days.

The USA's call to arms

The attack was supposed to destroy US resolve; instead it inspired vengeance on an almighty scale

Thousands of US citizens of Japanese origin were forced into internment camps after the attack

By 10am, the first Japanese aircraft began arriving back at their carriers, now lying just 300 kilometres north of Oahu, with the second wave of planes following closely behind. Despite insistent pleas from Commander Fushida - who had led the first wave - to launch the third part of the assault, Admiral Nagumo decided against it. Unsure of the location of the American aircraft carriers, he was unwilling to risk it for fear of being spotted and attacked from the air, so he withdrew. The Japanese fleet retreated back into the vast blue expanse from which it had appeared just hours earlier.

On Hawaii, however, the local population were steeling themselves for an invasion as rumours of Japanese paratroop assaults and amphibious landings spread. At 12.30pm, the Honolulu Police Department raided the Japanese Embassy in the Hawaiian capital to discover diplomats busily burning documents. Meanwhile, government agents began raiding the homes of Hawaii's sizeable Japanese community,

seizing domestic radio sets for fear that they might be used to communicate with Japanese forces in order to help co-ordinate further attacks. Later that day, after consulting with President Roosevelt over the phone, Hawaii's Governor Joseph Poindexter declared Hawaii (not then a US State) be placed under martial law, handing full control of the island over to the American military.

Oahu, meanwhile, was a chaotic mess. The wreckage of burned-out aircraft littered airstrips, buildings - both military and civilian - were left shattered and charred, while hospital staff struggled to cope with thousands of casualties. At Pearl Harbor, rescue workers toiled ceaselessly to save the lives of the 461 men trapped in the overturned Oklahoma. After hours of desperate attempts, just 32 sailors would eventually be pulled from the capsized battleship.

The following day, Roosevelt addressed a joint session of the United States Congress and delivered the following speech:

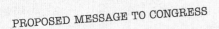

December 7th, 1941

PROPOSED MESSAGE TO CONGRESS

Yesterday, December 7th, 1941 - a date which will live in infamy - the United States of America was suddenly and deliberately attacked by naval and air forces of the Empire of Japan... The attack yesterday on the Hawaiian Islands has caused severe damage to American naval and military forces. I regret to tell you that very many American lives have been lost...

Yesterday, the Japanese government also launched an attack against Malaya. Last night, Japanese forces attacked Hong Kong. Last night, Japanese forces attacked Guam. Last night, Japanese forces attacked the Philippine Islands. Last night, the Japanese attacked Wake Island. And this morning, the Japanese attacked Midway Island.

Japan has, therefore, undertaken a surprise offensive extending throughout the Pacific area. The facts of yesterday and today speak for themselves. The people of the United States have already formed their opinions and well understand the implications to the very life and safety of our nation... I ask that the Congress declare that since the unprovoked and dastardly attack by Japan on Sunday, December 7th 1941, a state of war has existed between the United States and the Japanese Empire.

Franklin D Roosevelt

Prior to the attack, the United States of America had been a divided nation. Still recovering from the aftershocks of the 1929 Wall Street Crash and the subsequent Great Depression, it now became galvanised.

Overnight, opposition to American involvement in what was now clearly a world war evaporated as the country patriotically responded to the call to "Remember Pearl Harbor!" In fact just one member of the US House of Representatives voted against Roosevelt's appeal for Congress to declare war on Japan.

The USA's economy was switched into overdrive as it geared up to produce an overwhelming amount of arms and munitions. It was the birth of what would come to be known as the country's military-industrial complex.

Three days later, Japan's allies Germany and Italy declared war on the United States, and for the second time in less than a week, Congress again voted for war. More than two years after the start of hostilities, the United States had finally joined the fight.

IN NUMBERS

3,581
Number of US casualties at Pearl Harbor

68
Civilians were killed in the raid

347
US aircraft were destroyed or damaged during the raid

29
Japanese planes were destroyed in the attack

32
out of the 461 sailors trapped in the hull of the capsized Oklahoma were saved

1
Just one Japanese prisoner was taken

The attack lasted
90 minutes

19
US warships and auxiliary ships were destroyed or damaged during the attacks

5
Japanese mini-subs also participated in the attack. Four were destroyed and one captured

The fate of Japanese Americans

The attack provoked a reactionary response both from the US public and its government that caused thousands to suffer

Almost as soon as the raid was over, the Japanese-American population was targeted for revenge both on Hawaii and on the mainland. As well as racist assaults, innocent citizens became subject to official persecution when, 74 days after the attack, Roosevelt issued Executive Order 9066. This forced more than 110,000 Japanese Americans to leave their homes along the US's West Coast to be sent to one of ten detention camps in an isolated part of the US's vast interior. Not one was charged with a crime and about 70 per cent of those imprisoned were actually US-born citizens.

Although the government called these camps 'relocation centres', they were surrounded by barbed wire and policed by armed soldiers. Families sent to them lived in barrack blocks with no running water and little heat, sharing public bathroom facilities.

Most Japanese Americans were kept in these camps until well into 1944, although one way out was to join the US military. Japanese Americans served in segregated units, with the 100th Infantry Battalion being the most recognised. Japanese-American troops of this unit served with distinction in Europe racking up 18,413 individual awards including 21 Medals of Honor – the US military's highest award for valour. For its size and period of service, the 100th Infantry Battalion became the most decorated unit in the US Army.

The first atomic bomb

Eyewitness

DUTCH VAN KIRK

Having already served 58 missions in Africa and Europe during World War II, Dutch Van Kirk transferred to the 509th Composite Group. He was the navigator on the Enola Gay, which on 6 August 1945 dropped the first nuclear bomb on the Japanese city of Hiroshima. Here he recounts those events before his death in 2014 at the age of 93.

" I didn't feel too good about dropping the bomb – but I didn't feel too bad about dropping it either. It could have been us... "

Theodore Van Kirk, known to everyone as 'Dutch', was having trouble sleeping.

It was a common affliction among soldiers before a mission, but then again Dutch and his fellow 11 crewmates stationed on the tiny Pacific island of Tinian had more reason than most to be suffering from insomnia that night. The date was 5 August 1945 and tomorrow morning they were to drop the first-ever atomic bomb on Hiroshima.

To pass the time, some of the crew – including navigator Dutch, bombardier, Tom Ferebee, and pilot, Paul Tibbets, played poker. It was quite prophetic considering that in a matter of hours they would be gambling again – but this time with much higher stakes.

Sure, the USA had successfully detonated the first nuclear device the previous month during the Trinity test in New Mexico, and Dutch, like all the crew, had several months' intensive training at Wendover Airbase in Utah under his belt. Nevertheless the fact remained that what they were about to do had never before been attempted in warfare. Indeed, Dutch recalls, "One of the atomic scientists told us we think you'll be okay if the plane is [14.5 kilometres] nine miles away when the bomb detonates." When challenged on his use of the word *think*, he levelled with them: "We just don't know."

Dutch had been hand-picked to join the 509th Composite Group – the unit tasked with deploying nuclear weapons – by his former commander: "I flew with Paul Tibbets all the time in England. We flew General Dwight Eisenhower [later to become US president] from Hurn [on the south coast of Britain] down to Gibraltar, for example, to command the north African invasion. Then we were all separated and doing various things – I was at a navigation school, for example, teaching other navigators. Tibbets was picked to take command of the 509th group and that's when he looked up some of the people he'd worked with in the 97th [Bombardment Group]."

The history books often paint a picture that the US government and other Allied powers were hand-wringing right up until the final hour over the decision to use the A-bomb. However, although Japan was presented with an ultimatum to surrender on 26 July – which they rejected two days later – Dutch personally felt it was always a foregone conclusion: "I knew that I was going to drop the atomic bomb from February of that year [1945]. It didn't come as a surprise. We were posted to the US airbase at Tinian for about a month prior to dropping the bomb, just keeping in shape."

Around 10pm, the crew were called from the barracks to have an early breakfast before one last briefing and final checks of the Enola Gay. Dutch remembers they had pineapple fritters because he hated them, but Paul Tibbets loved them. While he might not have seen eye to eye with his commander when it came to the choice of breakfast, he has only praise for the man that piloted

Countdown to destruction

16 July 1945

5.29am
First detonation
US scientists successfully detonate the first nuclear device at the Trinity test site

28 July

Japanese government rejects surrender terms put forward in the Potsdam Declaration

5 August

2pm
Calm before storm
Having been told they have the go-ahead to drop the atomic bomb, Van Kirk and the rest of the crew try to get some sleep

3pm
The Little Boy bomb is loaded onto the Enola Gay

6pm
Struggling to sleep, Van Kirk, Ferebee, Tibbets and others play poker

10pm
The crew gets up to prepare for the flight to Hiroshima and eat breakfast

6 August

12am
Van Kirk and the crew make their way to the Enola Gay, after a final briefing

1.37am
Weather report
The three weather planes leave North Field Airbase on Tinian to confirm conditions are favourable

2.45am
The Enola Gay takes off, followed by three other B-29s taking part in Special Mission #13

5.52am
Little Boy armed
The planes fly over Iwo Jima island, where the Enola Gay's backup, Top Secret, lands. The Little Boy bomb is armed

7.30am
With the all-clear from the weather planes, the Enola Gay, The Great Artiste and #91 head for Hiroshima

8.13am
Pilot, Paul Tibbets, hands over control to the bombardier, Tom Ferebee, to make the bomb run

8.15am
Payload dropped
Little Boy is released and it detonates 43 seconds after, about 600m (1,900ft) above the city of Hiroshima. The Enola Gay experiences a shockwave moments later

3pm
Mission complete
The Enola Gay touches down on Tinian, its mission successfully completed. Paul Tibbets receives the Distinguished Service Cross

Seven of the Enola Gay's 12-man bombing crew stand before the aircraft; Dutch is third from the left, looking down, next to pilot, Paul Tibbets

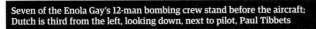

The North Field Airbase on Tinian played host to 15 modified B-29s and their crews

the specially modified B-29 to Hiroshima - and then back again.

"He was an outstanding pilot. His skill saved all of the crew's lives a number of times in Europe and Africa. When he got in an aeroplane, he [became] part of it. When you flew with Paul Tibbets you didn't have to have your shoes polished or your pants pressed - and all that sort of stuff - but when you got in the plane, you better damn well know what you were doing!"

It's hard to imagine what the mood on the Enola Gay must have been like as it took off at 2.45am, but from Dutch's perspective this mission was the same as any other. "We were going a long distance over water, using Iwo Jima as a checkpoint on the way. Now if you got lost between Iwo Jima and Japan, you really were a sorry navigator! Everybody on board was doing his own thing. Ferebee took a nap, for example, [while] our radio operator, as I recall, was reading a whodunnit about some boxer. Everybody was making sure they did what they were there to do, and that they did it right."

While the Enola Gay and Bockscar (the plane that dropped the Nagasaki A-bomb) are the two that have gone down in history, Dutch is keen to point out that the operation was a lot wider than that: indeed, seven aircraft were involved in Special Bombing Mission #13 to Hiroshima on 6 August. Three were observational planes that flew ahead to ensure conditions were right, Top Secret was a backup to the Enola Gay which landed on Iwo Jima, while the other two aircraft - The Great Artiste and Plane #91 (later named Necessary Evil) - accompanied the Enola Gay for the full operation.

"The Great Artiste had instruments that were to be dropped at the same time as we dropped the bomb. If you were to ask me the name of them, I couldn't tell you; I just always called them 'blast meters' because that's what they were measuring. The other aircraft [Plane #91] was flying about [32 kilometres] 20 miles behind with a large camera to get pictures of the explosion. Unfortunately on the day the camera didn't work. So the best pictures we got were from the handheld camera of the navigator on that plane."

The three aircraft arrived at Hiroshima without incident around 8am. The city had been chalked as the primary target for several reasons. There were a great number of military facilities and troops there, as well as a busy port with factories supplying a lot of the materials that would be used to defend Japan in the event of an invasion. Beyond these factors, Hiroshima had never been previously targeted by Allied forces, so any damage recorded later could solely be attributed to the nuclear bomb. Tragically for the citizens of Hiroshima, it also meant the Japanese authorities had very little reason to suspect an attack there - even when the tiny squadron of three B-29s was no doubt spotted approaching...

On the actual bomb run, Tibbets relinquished control of the Enola Gay to bombardier and close friend of Dutch's, Major Tom Ferebee. As the Little Boy bomb (which actually was not so little, weighing in at 4,400 kilograms/9,700 pounds) was released, the plane experienced an upward surge, but Tibbets managed to stabilise the B-29 and beat a hasty retreat.

"We made the 150-degree turn that we'd practised many times and pushed down the throttle to get away. All people were doing was holding on to something [in preparation for] the turbulence that was sure to follow. A loose person or a loose anything in the plane was going to go flying, so we all made sure we were in position and wearing our goggles." They were about 14.5 kilometres (nine miles) away when the bomb exploded, 43 seconds after it had been released. "We couldn't hear a thing over the engines, but we saw a bright flash and it was shortly after that we got the first shockwave.

"When we turned to look back, all we could see of Hiroshima was black smoke and dust"

The destruction wreaked on Hiroshima by the A-bomb was on an unprecedented scale

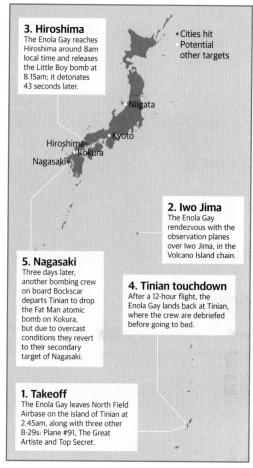

3. Hiroshima
The Enola Gay reaches Hiroshima around 8am local time and releases the Little Boy bomb at 8.15am; it detonates 43 seconds later.

• Cities hit
□ Potential other targets

Niigata

Kyoto

Hiroshima
Kokura

Nagasaki

2. Iwo Jima
The Enola Gay rendezvous with the observation planes over Iwo Jima, in the Volcano Island chain.

5. Nagasaki
Three days later, another bombing crew on board Bockscar departs Tinian to drop the Fat Man atomic bomb on Kokura, but due to overcast conditions they revert to their secondary target of Nagasaki.

4. Tinian touchdown
After a 12-hour flight, the Enola Gay lands back at Tinian, where the crew are debriefed before going to bed.

1. Takeoff
The Enola Gay leaves North Field Airbase on the island of Tinian at 2.45am, along with three other B-29s: Plane #91, The Great Artiste and Top Secret.

"When we turned to take a look back, all we could see of Hiroshima was black smoke and dust. The mushroom cloud was well above us at about [12,190 metres] 40,000 feet and still rising. You could still see that cloud [480 kilometres] 300 miles away." What the crew of the Enola Gay couldn't have known at that point was just how destructive the atomic bomb had been. Underneath all that smoke and dust nearly 70 per cent of the city's buildings had been laid to waste and 80,000 people were dead - and that figure was set to rise with the much-underestimated effects of radiation.

Unlike The Great Artiste with its faulty camera, as far as Dutch was concerned on board the Enola Gay "everything had gone exactly according to plan. The weather was perfect; I could probably see Hiroshima from [120 kilometres] 75 miles away. My navigation was only off by six seconds," he says with pride. "Tom put the bomb exactly where he expected. We got a lot of turbulence, but the plane did not break up, which it could have done, and we got home. Now, as for the second mission to Nagasaki, everything went wrong. They had a lot of luck on that mission..."

Indeed, three days later on 9 August, a different bombing crew on Bockscar almost didn't make it to Nagasaki due to a combination of bad weather and logistical errors. However, they managed to salvage the mission; the result of their success was the obliteration of another city and at least 40,000 of its inhabitants. Less than a week later Emperor Hirohito made a radio announcement, declaring Japan's surrender due to "a new and most cruel bomb, the power of which is incalculable, taking the toll of many innocent lives."

A few weeks after the bombings, Dutch Van Kirk was part of the crew transporting scientists to Nagasaki to measure the devastation of one of these 'new and most cruel bombs' first-hand. "Having picked up some

scientists in Tokyo from the Japanese atomic programme - they were also working on atomic bombs, you see - we flew down to Nagasaki; we couldn't land at Hiroshima at that time. We landed on a dirt field and the Japanese commander of the base came out, looking for someone to surrender to. We were given old cars - 1927 Chevrolet models, or similar - to drive to the city centre, but they all broke down three times before getting into Nagasaki.

"There wasn't really anything that shocked us, though there is one thing [that has stayed with me]. The Japanese military was being broken up at the time and one of the soldiers arrived on the bus looking for his home - but it had been destroyed. I remember looking at Tom Ferebee, and saying, 'You know, Tom, that could have been us if the war had gone the opposite way.' I didn't feel too good about dropping the bomb - but I didn't feel too bad about dropping it either. This was one man among many that were saved by dropping the bomb" - because it had precluded a full-scale invasion of Japan. "It was very important we saw that, and we both recognised how lucky we were."

Along with all the other Enola Gay crew, who have since passed away, Dutch Van Kirk has no regrets about dropping the atomic bomb, seeing it as the lesser of two evils. Asked whether he believes the result would have been the same - ie World War II would have been forced to end - if things 'had gone the opposite way' and Japan had dropped an atomic bomb on America first, there's a long pause, before Dutch responds, "No, I don't think so. I think we would have been more resilient."

But underneath the assured bravado of his reply, there's no getting around how long he had hesitated before he answered - or the fact that, like that atomic scientist who couldn't offer any certainties on Tinian back in 1945, he had used the word *think*.

Origins and aftermath

The US started developing the nuclear bomb following a warning from Albert Einstein and other physicists in 1939 that the Germans were close to constructing their own. Project Manhattan got underway in 1941 and by July 1945 had successfully detonated the first-ever nuclear device in the Trinity test. By this point Germany had already surrendered so the Allied forces' sights were now trained solely on the last remaining Axis power: Japan. Having refused an ultimatum to surrender in the Potsdam Declaration, the Allies felt they were left with two options: a full-scale invasion or the use of nuclear bombs. They opted for the latter. It remains one of the most controversial military decisions ever taken, yet many argue that invading Japan would have claimed many more lives in the long term.

Little Boy produced a force equivalent to around 15,000 tons of TNT

© Corbis, Alamy

Napalm bombs explode on what the US Air Force called 'Viet Cong structures', south of Saigon

The Vietnam War

Re-examining the two-decade Cold War conflict that ended in American defeat, Communist victory and the deaths of millions

From the arrival in 1950 of the first American advisors in French-controlled Vietnam to the helicopter evacuation of American embassy staff from Saigon in 1975, the Vietnam War was both a crucial arena of the Cold War struggle between Russia and the United States, and a defining struggle of postcolonial nationalism. The Americans believed that they and their South Vietnamese allies were holding back Soviet- and Chinese-sponsored communism. The North Vietnamese, armed by China and Russia and aided by the Viet Cong, the pro-Communist South Vietnamese militia, believed that they were fighting a 'Resistance War', to free their country from colonial rule. The war for Indochina took more than 3 million lives in Vietnam, and neighbouring Laos and Cambodia, and the lives of over 58,000 American servicemen. And though the US eventually triumphed in the Cold War, the domestic consequences of its involvement and defeat in Indochina – the 'Vietnam Syndrome' – continue to shape American foreign policy.

During the Second World War, President Franklin D Roosevelt's Atlantic Charter had committed the United States to dismantling the British and French empires in Asia. After 1945, however, this objective became entangled with the strategic need to combat Russian- and Chinese-sponsored communism. In Vietnam, the United States first supported Vietnam's French colonial masters, and then replaced them.

During World War II, the French colonial authorities in Vietnam had aligned themselves with both the pro-German Vichy puppet government in France, and also the brutal Japanese military occupation of Vietnam. In 1941, a communist militia, the Viet Minh, had launched guerrilla wars simultaneously against the French and Japanese administrations. The Viet Minh's leader was Ho Chi Minh (1890-1969), a French-educated magistrate's son whose travels had included periods in the US, Russia, China, the kitchens of various London hotels, and service as a pastry chef on the Newhaven to Dieppe ferry route. The United States adopted Ho and his 'men in black' as allies against French and Japanese fascism. The Viet Minh received military training and medical aid from the Office of Strategic Services, the forerunner of the CIA.

In August 1945, the defeat of the Japanese and the pro-Vichy French left a power vacuum in Vietnam. On 2 September, Ho Chin Minh declared the independence of the Democratic Republic of Vietnam, with himself as its leader. When Ho wrote to President Truman and appealed to the Atlantic Charter, he received no reply. No

> Supported by the Soviet Union and China, communist leader Ho Chin Minh sought to reunite Vietnam

government recognised Ho's state. When the French reoccupied Vietnam in 1946, Ho first allied with them, massacring non-communist nationalists, then turned against them. In 1950, Ho secured recognition for North Vietnam from Stalin, and military support from Mao Tse-Tung. By 1954, when Ho's militia defeated French paratroopers at the Battle of Dien Bien Phu, the French were beaten in Vietnam.

The United States had been sending military 'advisors' to assist the French since 1950. After 1954, the Republican administration of President Eisenhower, following the counsel of Secretary of State John Foster Dulles, cultivated the autocratic and corrupt South Vietnamese leader Ngo Dinh Diem who, as a Catholic from the central highlands of Vietnam, had a narrow base of support in the

mostly Buddhist south. Some 900 American advisors now replaced French soldiers as the trainers of the South Vietnamese army, which now faced a pro-communist insurgency in the south. In March 1959, Ho Chi Minh, encouraged by Russia, launched a new offensive, the People's War to unite Vietnam. Diem's government in Hanoi, the CIA warned, was the Unites States' only defence against the playing out of the 'Domino Theory', in which the collapse of Vietnam would presage the collapse of Asia to communism.

"Burma, Thailand, India, Japan, the Philippines, and obviously Laos and Cambodia are among those whose security would be threatened if the Red Tide of Communism overflowed into Vietnam," Democratic senator John F Kennedy had warned in 1956. In 1960, Kennedy won the presidency.

Determined to "draw a line in the sand" against Soviet and Chinese influence, Kennedy multiplied the number of 'advisors' from Eisenhower's 900 to over 16,000. But Diem's troops remained weak in the field, and although Kennedy's vice-president Lyndon Johnson had returned from a trip to Vietnam convinced that Diem was "the Winston Churchill of Asia", Diem faced revolt from his subjects.

On 3 November 1963, Diem was overthrown by his generals with American support. On 22 November 1963, President Kennedy was assassinated. With a series of unpopular and incompetent generals in charge in Hanoi, and the Viet Cong now holding most of the countryside, Kennedy's vice-president Lyndon B Johnson deepened America's commitment to the war. The

A Douglas Skyraider drops white phosphorus on a Viet Cong position in South Vietnam, 1966

Napalm bombs explode on Viet Cong structures south of Saigon, 1965

Soldiers from the Third US Marines inch towards the summit of Hill 881N during the Battle for Khe Sanh, 1968

Timeline

1954

● **The Domino Theory**
"You have a row of dominoes set up," President Eisenhower says in 1954, following the North Vietnamese victory at Dien Bien Phu. "You knock over the first one, and what will happen to the last one is that it will go over very quickly."
1954

● **The First American advisors**
In 1956, instructors from the US Military Assistance Advisor Group (MAAG) replace French instructors in the training of South Vietnamese troops.
1956

● **Birth of the Viet Cong**
In 1960, as John F Kennedy enters the White House, North Vietnamese leader Ho Chi Minh creates the National Liberation Front for South Vietnam: the Viet Cong.
1960

● **Kennedy is assassinated**
In November 1963, President Kennedy is assassinated. Though he has raised US troop levels from 900 to over 16,000, the South Vietnamese government remains unstable.
1963

● **Gulf of Tonkin Incident**
President Johnson alleges that US Navy ships have twice been attacked by North Vietnamese torpedo boats in the Gulf of Tonkin. Congress grants him war powers.
1964

● **Rolling Thunder and Arc Light**
President Johnson launches two massive three-year bombing campaigns. More than a million tons of bombs are dropped, including chemicals like napalm and Agent Orange.
1965

● **The ground war begins**
In March 1965, Johnson dispatches a defensive deployment of 3,500 soldiers amor the 9th Marine Expeditionary Brigade. By the end of 1965, there are 200,000 American soldiers in Vietnam.
1965

Protestors at the march on the Pentagon, 1967

● **Protests in New York City**
Anti-war protesters march through the city and listen to speakers including Martin Luther King and Dr Benjamin Spock. The latter will later be convicted of conspiring to counsel evasion of the draft.
1966

● **The anti-war movemen begins**
In March 1965, as US involvement mounts, anti-war students and faculty at the University of Michigan at Ann Arbor conduct the first 'teach-in' about the war.
1965

Democrats, the party of Franklin D Roosevelt, the Atlantic Charter and postcolonial liberation, now led the United States into an imperial folly costing thousands of American lives. The pretext was the Gulf of Tonkin Incident of August 1964.

Johnson's administration alleged that North Vietnamese torpedo boats had fired on two separate days in early August on American warships in the gulf. It is unclear whether the North Vietnamese fired at all in the first of these encounters, though it is confirmed that the USS Maddox fired at the boats. It is possible that the second alleged encounter never happened at all; when documents were declassified in 2005, America's National Security Agency admitted as much. Still, Johnson used the Gulf of Tonkin Incident to secure a mandate for war from

Congress, and to launch Operations Rolling Thunder and Arc Light, two massive bombing campaigns against North Vietnamese positions and villages.

Though Johnson promised not to commit "American boys to fighting a war that I think ought to be fought by the boys of Asia to help protect their own land", in March 1965 he sent 3,500 US Marines to Vietnam, to prop up the government in Hanoi. By the end of 1965, some 200,000 American soldiers were in South Vietnam. With the South Vietnamese forces unable to defeat the Viet Cong insurgency, and the American garrison losing morale, General William Westmoreland proposed a three-stage offensive plan for a ground war, with victory by the end of 1967.

Johnson agreed, but did not tell the media that American strategy had now shifted from defensive support of the South Vietnamese government to a village-by-village battle with the Viet Cong and their rural supporters. US pressure secured troops from Australia, New Zealand, South Korea, Thailand and the Philippines. Britain's prime minister Harold Wilson refused to assist. "Not even a battalion of Black Watch!" Johnson complained.

American public opinion had strongly supported Johnson's insertion of ground forces in March 1965. This support declined with the rapid increase in the scale of the American presence, the indiscriminate casualties caused by US bombers, and the first reports of American casualties. Three factors forced Vietnam to the front of domestic awareness. As the US armed forces were mostly conscripts, almost all American families were affected by 'The Draft'. Unlike the Korean War, the Vietnam War was an immediate, real-time experience for American civilians, because each episode was televised in colour on the news.

Furthermore, powerful currents of revolt against authority, some of them more sympathetic to Ho Chi Minh's communist dictatorship than American-style capitalist democracy, were brewing on US university campuses.

On 30 January 1968, the North Vietnamese Army and the Viet Cong broke the traditional Set (New Year) ceasefire and launched the largest and most important battle of the Vietnam War. In the Tet Offensive, more than 85,000 troops attacked some 100 cities. Only weeks earlier, General Westmoreland had declared that American involvement was reaching the point "where the end comes into view". Now, Viet Cong insurgents were besieging Westmoreland's headquarters and the US embassy in Hanoi. In one week of

> The Vietnam War was the first truly televised war, with events being replayed in US living rooms every evening

Crewmen from the USS Durham take aboard Vietnamese refugees in April 1975

The Tet Offensive
A wave of surprise attacks catch the US forces off their guard. The Americans turn back the North Vietnamese assault, but the US public loses confidence in the war.
1968

A B-52 Stratofortress dropping bombs on Vietnam

Operation Breakfast
Elected to extricate the US from Vietnam, Richard Nixon orders Operation Breakfast: the secret bombing of neutral Cambodia. The bombing continues for the next 14 months.
1969

'Peace is at hand'
Henry Kissinger announces that "Peace is at hand" in the Paris negotiations. But South Vietnamese president Theiru opposes the treaty. To secure the deal, Nixon steps up the bombing.
1972

The Fall of Saigon
As the North Vietnamese close in on Saigon, thousands of South Vietnamese break into the US Embassy. The US evacuates its own personnel.
1975

Kissinger, Nelson Rockefeller and President Ford discuss the evacuation of Saigon

1975

Operation Cedar Falls
In a major operation near Saigon, 16,000 US and 14,000 South Vietnamese troops discover a network of underground tunnels that serves as a Viet Cong command centre.
1967

Dr King condemns the war
Dr Martin Luther King, the leader of the American civil rights' movement, calls his government 'the greatest purveyor of violence in the world'. Shortly afterwards, he endorses draft evasion.
1967

The My Lai Massacre
A company of Marines on a 'search and destroy' mission massacre as many as 500 Vietnamese civilians in the village of My Lai. The news causes a scandal in the US.
1968

Johnson retires
Realising that Vietnam has ruined him, Johnson announces that he will not contest the 1968 election. In the following months, Martin Luther King and would-be presidential candidate Bobby Kennedy are assassinated.
1968

Kent State
When anti-war protestors at Kent State University, Ohio throw rocks at the National Guard, the guardsmen kill four and wound eight. Nixon criticises both the protestors and the guardsmen.
1970

Ceasefire
On 28 January 1973, the Paris treaty signed by Kissinger and North Vietnam's Le Duc Tho takes effect. Nixon promises "peace with honour in Vietnam and Southeast Asia".
1973

Return to war
As Nixon falls from office in the Watergate scandal, the South Vietnamese return to war. Kissinger and Tho receive the Nobel Peace Prize, but Tho, claiming that there is no peace, refuses to accept.
1974

The Tet Offensive

When the North Vietnamese launched the Tet Offensive in the early hours of 31 January 1968, they hoped to provoke a national uprising against the United States, and even to seize key cities in South Vietnam. By the next morning, more than 80,000 North Vietnamese troops were attacking more than a hundred towns and cities in South Vietnam, including the southern capital of Saigon, and 36 of the 44 provincial capitals.

American intelligence had detected signs of strategic planning and troop movements in the months beforehand, but the Americans and their South Vietnamese allies were taken by surprise. The North Vietnamese troops and the Viet Cong seized the former capital city of Hué, besieged the US Embassy at Saigon, and even attacked General Westmoreland's headquarters. The Americans and their allies recovered quickly, and inflicted a severe defeat on the North Vietnamese. Yet the Tet Offensive convinced a majority of the American public that the war could not be won.

The number of Americans who felt that sending troops to Vietnam had been a mistake had risen from 25% in 1965 to 45% by late 1967. News footage of the Tet Offensive disproved the Johnson administration's claim to be winning the war, and General Westmoreland's recent assertion that victory was in sight. Not since the Japanese attack on Pearl Harbor had the United States suffered so significant a failure of military intelligence. Regaining ground lost to the Tet Offensive cost more than a thousand American lives. The battle for Hué left most of the city in ruins.

By the spring of 1968, Johnson's approval rating had collapsed, and a majority of Americans believed that direct American involvement in Vietnam had been a strategic error. "To say that we are mired in stalemate seems the only realistic, yet unsatisfactory conclusion," argued Walter Cronkite, the influential CBS news anchor in a famous broadcast.

Another defining image from the Tet Offensive won a Pulitzer Prize in 1969. Edward T Adams's photograph of South Vietnamese police chief Nguyen Ngoc Loan publicly executing a Viet Cong officer, Nguyen Van Lem, who had been captured in civilian clothing, has been called 'the picture that lost the war'.

An American helicopter spraying defoliant over the Mekong Delta, 1969

Black smoke enshrouds Saigon and fire trucks rush to the scene during attacks by the Viet Cong in 1968

fighting, 543 American soldiers were killed and over 2,500 wounded.

The Tet Offensive revealed to many Americans the 'credibility gap' between the pronouncements of Johnson and Westmoreland and the failure of the strategy in Vietnam. The US beat back the Tet Offensive on the ground, but Johnson's administration never recovered from this loss of public trust. In March 1968, Westmoreland was kicked upstairs, and his request for an additional 200,000 troops denied. In May 1968, Johnson, while continuing the indiscriminate area bombing of North Vietnam, entered peace talks with the North Vietnamese at Paris.

By the end of 1968, a Democratic administration had sent more than 30,000 US soldiers to their deaths in Vietnam, and discredited the trustworthiness of the government. Johnson's refusal to send more troops amounted to an admission that, while the US could not lose the war if it was prepared to sacrifice its sons, neither could it win it. Anti-war protests moved from the campus to the streets. The media, which had been largely complicit with Kennedy and Johnson's slide into Vietnam, now turned on the government. Johnson announced he would not seek re-election. The 1968 Democratic Party convention in Chicago general election saw fighting between more than 10,000 anti-war protesters and the police.

> Out of 2.7 million Americans who served in the Vietnam War, 58,220 were killed and over 300,000 wounded

The Republican nominee Richard Nixon won the 1968 election with promises to restore order at home, and extract American troops from Vietnam. Under the strategy of 'Vietnamization', American forces were withdrawn in stages, and the South Vietnamese army expected to take up the defence. At the same time, Nixon and his National Security Council adviser Henry Kissinger tried to secure the global framework for withdrawal by seeking détente with Russia and rapprochement with China. These two initiatives would prove crucial in defusing the Cold War but, like the Paris negotiations, they would take time to accomplish.

By early 1971, Nixon had reduced American troop numbers in Vietnam from Johnson's legacy of 549,500 by almost half. The number of American casualties in 1970 was half that of 1969, too. The strategy of Vietnamization did not, however, placate the anti-war movement. In 1969, the American public was appalled by the revelation of war crimes committed by US troops: the murder of as many as 500 unarmed Vietnamese civilians by American soldiers at the village of My Lai in 1968, and the murder by Special Forces of a Viet Cong informant in June 1969. In 1970, when North Vietnam invaded Cambodia in support of the communist Khmer Rouge, Nixon committed American bombers to another campaign of carpet bombing. Nixon

In the Situation Room of the White House, President Johnson (second from left) studies a model of Khe Sahn, where US Marines are besieged by the Viet Cong in February 1968

"The 'Pentagon Papers' showed how successive administrations had deceived the American public over Vietnam"

Marine Private D A Crum of New Brighton, Pennsylvania is treated for wounds during Operation Hué City, 1968

insisted that this intervention was necessary in order to secure the American withdrawal from Vietnam.

In 1971, the leaking of the 'Pentagon Papers', a secret history of the Vietnam fiasco commissioned by the Department of Defense, showed how successive administrations - both Democratic and Republican - had deceived the American public over Vietnam. The failure in early 1971 of a South Vietnamese attempt to cut the Ho Chi Minh Trail, the Viet Hong's supply route from neighbouring Laos convinced the American public that Vietnamization was failing, and that the United States should leave Vietnam at all costs.

"In our opinion," Vietnam veteran and future presidential candidate John Kerry testified to a Senate committee in April 1971, "and from our experience, there is nothing in South Vietnam, nothing which could happen that could realistically threaten the United States of America." Nixon, Kerry said, was prolonging the war unnecessarily. It was the "height of criminal hypocrisy" to "justify the loss of one American life in Vietnam, Cambodia or Laos" to "the preservation of freedom".

Against the background of Nixon's campaign for re-election, the Paris negotiations produced a peace treaty in October 1972. When the South Vietnamese leader Nguyen Van Thieu demanded new terms, Nixon ordered further heavy bombing of North Vietnam, and threatened to abandon Thieu. This forced the parties back to the table in Paris, but at the cost of civilian lives in North Vietnam. The treaty was signed on 27 January 1973. The last US ground troops left in March 1973.

Without American air support, the South Vietnamese army could not hold off the communist forces. In 1974, after Nixon had resigned in disgrace after the Watergate scandal, US aid to the South shrank under President Ford. In the spring of 1975, the North Vietnamese surrounded Saigon. Television cameras reported the panic as South Vietnamese officials and civilians scrambled to escape. On 30 April 1975, US Marines evacuated the Saigon embassy by helicopter, leaving thousands of their Vietnamese employees and their families to their fate.

The suffering of the Vietnamese and their neighbours was not over. The communists sent 300,000 South Vietnamese to 're-education' camps, where they were tortured, starved and forced to do hard labour. As many as 400,000 Vietnamese drowned attempting to escape communist Vietnam. The US's withdrawal also led to the ascent to power of the Khmer Rouge in Cambodia, and the genocide that ensued.

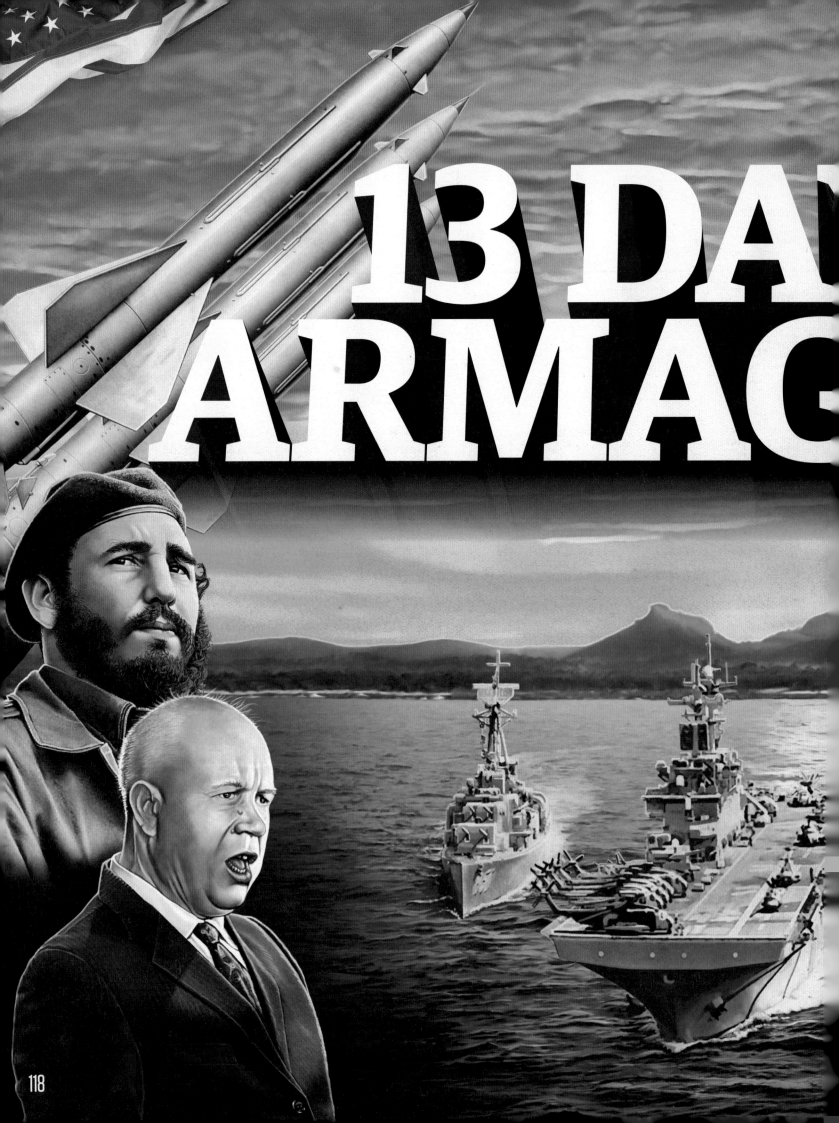

13 DA
ARMAG

YS TO
EDDON

At the height of the Cold War, Cuba became the fulcrum of a deadly face-off between the Soviet Union and the United States

n October 1962 the world almost ended. At the height of the Cold War, the United States of America and the Soviet Union found themselves in a tense standoff over Russian medium and intermediate-range ballistic missiles being stockpiled in bases in the rebellious Republic of Cuba. Over a terrifying 13 days, the two superpowers came to the brink of nuclear war, with their mutually assured destruction looking alarmingly possible. To the Russians, this dark chapter of their history is referred to as the Caribbean Crisis. To the Cubans, it's the October Crisis. But to America and much of the rest of the world, the words 'the Cuban Missile Crisis' are those that invoke that particular chill of almost unimaginable horror only narrowly averted.

By the time of the Crisis, the United States and Russia had been engaged in their Cold War for almost 20 years since the end of the Second World War – some trace it back even further to the First World War. Not a conflict in the usual sense, it had mostly been an affair played out through espionage rather than military force, although the superpowers had each involved themselves in regional wars in China, Greece and Korea. After 1945, the single-party Marxist-Leninist Soviet State found itself in complete ideological opposition to the States' 'free' capitalist society, consolidating its control over the Eastern Bloc, while the United States tried to contain it through international initiatives

KENNEDY

V

KHRUSHCHEV

POLITICAL STANCE

JFK became president in 1960 for the Democrat Party. He aimed to end racial segregation in schools and public places and liberalised immigration laws. He strengthened unemployment benefits and called on the nations of the world to band together to fight poverty, hunger and disease. He also urged Americans to be active citizens, famously saying, "Ask not what your country can do for you; ask what you can do for your country."

Khrushchev was first secretary of the Communist Party of the Soviet Union from 1958 until 1964. He was responsible for moving the Communist Party away from Stalinism, ending forced labour and closing the Gulags. He was an early backer of the Soviet Space Programme, and was behind some relatively liberal domestic policies, such as allowing more freedom to the arts and opening up the opportunity for ordinary Soviets to travel abroad.

FOREIGN POLICY

With his presidency at the height of the Cold War, Kennedy was a vehement anti-Communist. He fought Communism in developing nations and introduced the Space Race as much from a perceived necessity to beat the Russians to the Moon as for the scientific achievement. As well as the Cuban Missile Crisis, Kennedy's administration intervened in Vietnam against Communists there. After Cuba, Kennedy's US negotiated a nuclear test ban treaty with the USSR and the UK.

The Soviet premier appointed himself as head of the USSR's UN delegation in 1960, where he was accused of a double standard by claiming to oppose colonialism while at the same time attempting Communist domination of Eastern Europe and Southeast Asia and the Third World. Achieving the first manned space flight led the world to infer the USSR's nuclear weapons programme was further ahead than it was. Khrushchev was happy not to disabuse anyone of that notion.

MILITARY EXPERIENCE

He served in the US Navy from 1941 until 1945. He was working in the office of the secretary of the Navy when the attack on Pearl Harbor took place, but he subsequently saw action in Panama and the Pacific, commanding torpedo boats and achieving the rank of lieutenant. He received the Purple Heart and the WWII Victory Medal among several other decorations. He was finally released from active service due to a recurring back injury.

He served in the Red Army as a political commissar, both during the Russian Civil War (1917-1922) and WWII. The rank was roughly equal to that of a unit commander, but the commissar has the military to countermand the commander's orders when he deems it necessary. Khrushchev's primary function was as a political intermediary between troops and Moscow. He did see action at the Defence of Stalingrad in 1942, though, which he remained proud of for the rest of his life.

ADVISORS

Among Kennedy's main advisors were Vice President Lyndon B. Johnson, Secretary of State Dean Rusk, Senate Majority Leader Mike Mansfield, Secretary of Defence Robert S McNamara and Attorney General Robert F Kennedy, JFK's brother. During the Cuban Missile Crisis, Kennedy convened the special advisory committee EXCOMM, including all the above, Ambassador to the Soviet Union Llewellyn Thompson, with members of the CIA and the Defence Department.

Extraordinary as it seems, Khrushchev, after rising to power, decided Soviet policy alone, without any recourse to advisors at all. This could, of course, be viewed as a weakness since it cut his decision-making process off from others, whose input may have been valuable. But it also allowed his instincts free reign: a positive thing in regard to the Cuban Missile Crisis, where his levelheaded inclination toward peace and negotiation arguably averted a global catastrophe.

These demonstrators were part of the 'Women strike for peace' movement in 1962

A group of Cuban soldiers who helped in fighting the Bay of Pigs invasion

THE BAY OF PIGS

The failed invasion that led to the Crisis

WHY IT HAPPENED

Concern in the US over the new left-wing direction of Cuba's politics after the removal of dictator Fulgencio Batista by revolutionary Fidel Castro.

US concern over trials and executions of former Batista supporters.

Castro was an outspoken critic of the USA.

WHAT WENT WRONG?

A damning CIA report from November 1961 outlined a catalogue of points that made the attempted invasion doomed to failure. Its author, Inspector General Lyman B. Kirkpatrick, identified that there were no policies or contingency plans in place should the invasion have succeeded. Insufficient and poorly managed staff had been assigned to the project, relatively few of whom even spoke Spanish. US intelligence in Cuba had been improperly analysed. There had been little success in organising internal resistance in Cuba, or of involving exiles from the Castro regime or counter-revolutionaries. And the operation had simply been too big: jumping from covert guerrilla action to full-blown military intervention in a way that made 'plausible deniability' impossible.

TIMELINE OF EVENTS

● Prelude to invasion
16 April 1961
The US mounts diversionary activities around other Cuban locations, to disguise its true intentions. These include the 'Phony War' of 16 April, around Baracoa and Guantánamo. Cuban revolutionary military forces scramble to meet their US attackers, putting up more of a fight than the US expects.

● Day one
17 April
1,400 US troops, four transport ships and a fleet of smaller fibreglass boats enter the Bay of Pigs. Cuba responds with fighter jets and bombers. US paratroopers are dropped onto the island, but land in a swamp and lose all their equipment. Osvaldo Ramirez, leader of the Cuban resistance against Castro, is captured and summarily executed by Castro's supporters.

● Day two
18 April
Cuban troops, tanks and militia force the invaders and resistance to retreat in several areas. CIA pilots in B-26 bomber planes use bombs, napalm and rockets against Cuban targets, causing civilian casualties alongside their intended police and military victims.

● Day three
19 April
Four US airmen are killed when Cuban forces mount a spirited defence against another CIA air attack. Anti-Castro forces on the ground, with their air support lost and ammunition steadily running out, are forced to retreat in the face of a Cuban onslaught and have to be evacuated. The US withdraws from the invasion.

● The aftermath
20 April onward
US destroyer ships search for survivors along the Cuban coast while intelligence-gathering flights continue. Hundreds of executions take place in Cuba as retaliation against the opposition, and Castro gloats over his prisoners of war. He offers the US a deal to exchange them for tractors. They eventually get food and medicine instead.

---

like NATO. Having wrestled for control and influence in Latin America and the decolonising states of Africa, the Middle East and Southeast Asia in the intervening years, events between the two opponents came to a long-threatened head in Cuba.

The immediate roots of the Cuban Missile Crisis lay in Cuba's regime change of 1959: a revolution that ousted incumbent dictator Fulgencio Batista and installed the communist commander-in-chief of the Cuban Revolutionary Army, Fidel Castro, as prime minister and later president. As supporters of Batista and other Latin American dictators, the US government suddenly found itself on the receiving end of harsh criticism from Castro when he opened diplomatic relations with them. Their response was a failed attempt to assassinate Castro, after which he demanded the complete withdrawal of the US military from Guantánamo Bay. They refused and remain there; it's the only US military base in a country it doesn't officially recognise.

Castro travelled to the US in the spring of 1959 to meet with President Dwight D. Eisenhower, but was snubbed by him and met only by Vice President Richard Nixon. Their meeting did not go well, and Castro further alienated the US when he announced to the United Nations that Cuba would maintain a neutral position in the fractious relationship between the USA and the USSR. Subsequent policies redistributing Cuba's wealth were predictably unpopular with Americans, who owned land there and were seeing it removed from them at rates of compensation they were unhappy with. The CIA launched another failed assassination

> **"Assassination attempts and attacks on Havana took place, all of which the US officially denied"**

Adlai Stevenson showing photos of nuclear missiles in Cuba to the UN Security Council

Strategic Air Command personnel looking at reconnaissance photos

THE LONGEST 13 DAYS IN HISTORY

A day-by-day account of the events of the Cuban Missile Crisis

16 October
President Kennedy and his staff are briefed on reconnaissance photos of Russian missile bases under construction in Cuba. Kennedy maintains his public schedule while covertly discussing whether to launch air strikes or blockade Cuba's coasts.

17 October
Kennedy continues his official public engagements, feeling it important to keep up appearances rather than arouse concern. He has lunch with Crown Prince Hassan of Libya and visits Connecticut to support Democratic election candidates.

18 October
Soviet Foreign Minister Andrei Gromyko insists that Russia's aid to Cuba is purely in the cause of defence and presents no threat to the USA. Kennedy warns Gromyko of grave consequences should Soviet nuclear weapons be found on Cuban soil.

19 October
Kennedy heads out on the congressional campaign trail to Ohio and Illinois, as previously scheduled before the missile crisis surfaced. Debate continues to rage among his advisors as to the best course of action in Cuba as Kennedy travels.

20 October
Kennedy returns to Washington, and after an intense five hours of deliberation, the plan to blockade – or 'quarantine' - Cuba is finally decided upon. Work begins on the military and naval plans, and on drafting a speech to inform the public of the situation.

21 October
Another day of meetings and phone calls on both sides. Tactical Air Commander Walter Sweeney advises Kennedy that an air strike against Cuba could not guarantee the destruction of all the Russian missiles on the ground.

Nuclear missiles like this Jupiter rocket were placed in Turkey and Italy

A Neptune warplane flying over a Soviet transport ship in October 1962

attempt against Castro, and the US military began launching secret bombing raids against Cuban sugar facilities in October 1959, targeting one of its most lucrative exports. American attacks on Cuban oil refineries and civilian targets in Havana followed, all of which the US officially denied.

Castro signed a trade deal with Soviet Deputy Prime Minister Anastas Mikoyan in February 1960, hoping it would gain him more leverage in the US. The opposite was true, and Eisenhower, pushed to the limits of his patience with the upstart Cuba, ordered the CIA to overthrow the Republic. Soviet Premier Nikita Khrushchev publicly came out in support of Cuba; America launched yet another three failed Castro assassination attempts, one of them involving the Mafia; and by April of 1961, America had both imposed full trade and economic sanctions against Cuba and undertaken a covert attempted invasion. The newly elected president, John F. Kennedy, continued to deny any such activity, but by now the American press were on the case and the word was out. Khrushchev

warned that the Soviets would intervene against any aggression from the US toward Cuba, and the US, after the death of 200 of its soldiers and the loss of a further thousand as prisoners of war in the Bay of Pigs debacle, was forced to call off its incursion. Kennedy and his government had been thoroughly humiliated.

Beginning to see Kennedy as weak, Khrushchev and the Soviets used the lull to seize an opportunity. In August of 1962, reports began reaching the US from Cuba that Soviet trucks loaded with suspicious equipment had been seen on the island. As retaliation for the US installing its own nuclear missiles close to the USSR, Russia was doing the same in the Caribbean. A sizeable arsenal of SS-4 nuclear warheads had been installed on the island - capable of reaching the US east coast - including the political hub of Washington, DC. While initially claiming they were simply providing non-nuclear surface-to-air missiles for Cuba's defence against its hostile neighbours, Khrushchev's real agenda was to gain a stronger

> "The decision to blockade the island was [for legal reasons] sold as a 'quarantine' of Cuba"

22 October
Kennedy informs UK PM Harold MacMillan of the ongoing crisis and writes to Khrushchev. In the letter, Kennedy writes: "Not you or any other sane man would [...] deliberately plunge the world into war which no country could win." He also makes a US television address.

23 October
The US 'quarantine' ships move into place around Cuba, while Soviet submarines lurk nearby. Kennedy asks Khrushchev to prevent any Russian vessels from approaching Cuba. Robert Kennedy visits the Soviet Embassy to meet with their ambassador.

24 October
Khrushchev responds to Kennedy's letters with hostility, complaining the US is using intimidation. "You are no longer appealing to reason," says the Soviet premier. "You are threatening that if we do not give in to your demands you will use force."

25 October
Kennedy writes to Khrushchev urging a Russian withdrawal from Cuba, and rejects UN Secretary General U. Thant's proposal of a 'cooling-off period', as Soviet missiles would remain in Cuba. Heated debates between the US and the USSR take place at the UN.

26 October
Castro writes to Khrushchev urging him not to back down, even if it means making a stand with catastrophic force. But Khrushchev contacts Kennedy to suggest a solution: the USA's removal of its own nuclear weapons from Turkey and Italy in exchange for the USSR's withdrawal from Cuba.

27 October
A US U-2 plane is shot down over Cuban airspace by Soviet missiles, and the pilot is killed. Meanwhile, a Russian submarine with a nuclear warhead aboard is attacked. Robert Kennedy secretly meets with the Soviet ambassador and cautious terms are agreed.

28 October
Radio Moscow announces the USSR has agreed to leave Cuba on the understanding that the US can never again attempt an invasion, and that US WMDs will be removed from sites near Russia. Castro is furious to learn the news from public radio.

123

political foothold both against the US and its allies in Britain and Europe.

Kennedy's response was to set up EXCOMM - the Executive Committee of the National Security Council - which suggested six options. Doing nothing was obviously impossible, but diplomacy was already not working; threatening Castro generally achieved the opposite of the desired effect; and either war with or the occupation of Cuba was an enormous risk. The ultimate decision, then, was to blockade the island, although for legal reasons (it would be considered an act of war) this was sold as a 'quarantine' of Cuba.

At 7pm on 22 October 1962, Kennedy announced on US television and radio that this 'quarantine' of Cuba was in effect immediately, stopping the shipment of all offensive military equipment to Cuba. 5,000 US troops were deployed to the Guantánamo base, along with airborne and naval forces. In turn, Castro began to mobilise Cuba's forces, and Khrushchev declared the quarantine to be a hostile manoeuvre, threatening that war with the United States was becoming a very real possibility if the States didn't leave Cuba alone.

The next day, US planes ascertained that the Soviets were actually performing launch tests on their missiles, leading US ships to take up position off Cuba's coastline, barring any ships from getting any nearer to the island. By 25 October, Kennedy had written to Khrushchev promising full-scale conflict if the Soviets didn't remove their missiles from Cuban soil. Khrushchev's eventual response on 26 October was to suggest a compromise: the USSR would withdraw its nuclear arsenal in exchange for a legal assurance from the US that it would never invade Cuba again, or support any other country attempting to do so.

Kennedy was willing to use this as the basis for some serious negotiations, but Castro, caught in the middle of the standoff, remained unconvinced, distrustful of Kennedy. He wrote to Khrushchev outlining his belief that the US would eventually invade Cuba regardless of what had been agreed, and giving carte-blanche to the Soviets to remain in Cuba with their missiles, as the island's first best line of defence and deterrent. "I believe the imperialists' aggressiveness is extremely dangerous," said the Cuban prime minister in what's now known as 'The Armageddon Letter'. "If they actually carry out the brutal act of invading Cuba in violation of international law and morality, that would be the moment to eliminate such danger forever through an act of clear legitimate defence, however harsh and terrible the solution would be."

> "Castro, who had not been consulted, was furious to learn the news of the Soviet withdrawal from the radio"

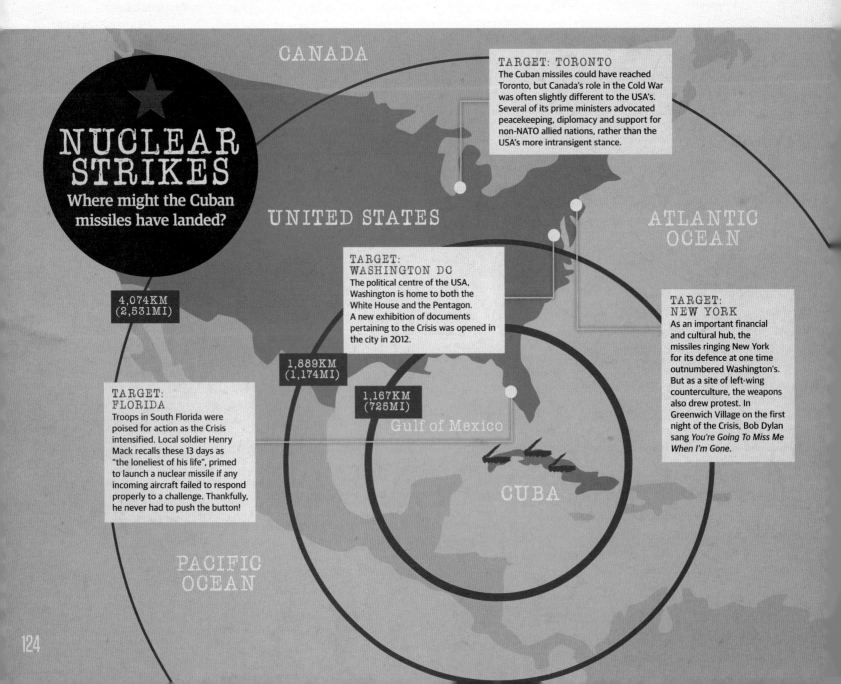

NUCLEAR STRIKES
Where might the Cuban missiles have landed?

CANADA

TARGET: TORONTO
The Cuban missiles could have reached Toronto, but Canada's role in the Cold War was often slightly different to the USA's. Several of its prime ministers advocated peacekeeping, diplomacy and support for non-NATO allied nations, rather than the USA's more intransigent stance.

UNITED STATES

ATLANTIC OCEAN

4,074KM (2,531MI)

TARGET: WASHINGTON DC
The political centre of the USA, Washington is home to both the White House and the Pentagon. A new exhibition of documents pertaining to the Crisis was opened in the city in 2012.

TARGET: NEW YORK
As an important financial and cultural hub, the missiles ringing New York for its defence at one time outnumbered Washington's. But as a site of left-wing counterculture, the weapons also drew protest. In Greenwich Village on the first night of the Crisis, Bob Dylan sang *You're Going To Miss Me When I'm Gone*.

1,889KM (1,174MI)

1,167KM (725MI)

Gulf of Mexico

TARGET: FLORIDA
Troops in South Florida were poised for action as the Crisis intensified. Local soldier Henry Mack recalls these 13 days as "the loneliest of his life", primed to launch a nuclear missile if any incoming aircraft failed to respond properly to a challenge. Thankfully, he never had to push the button!

CUBA

PACIFIC OCEAN

These Soviet missiles were
placed in Cuba in October 1962

Kennedy signing the
Cuba Quarantine
Proclamation

A Soviet nuclear missile
being displayed in the Red
Square in Moscow

On 27 October the confrontation escalated alarmingly, when US Air Force Major Rudolf Anderson was shot down and killed in his F-102 fighter when he strayed into Cuban airspace. Further US reconnaissance aircraft attempting to ascertain the lie of the land were also fired upon from the ground, while at practically the same time, dangerous events were occurring beneath the waters of the Caribbean. The US naval destroyer USS Beale had tracked down the Soviet submarine B-59 and begun dropping depth charges on it, scoring several hits. However, the Beale's crew didn't know the B-59 was carrying a 15-kiloton nuclear torpedo. Running out of air and surrounded by ships that wouldn't allow it to surface, the B-59's officers came horrendously close to desperately launching their payload before Captain Vasili Arkhipov managed to persuade his comrades to stand down and surrender. He may have saved the world in the process.

As all this was occurring, Kennedy received another letter from Khrushchev offering to withdraw his weapons from Cuba if the US would do the same in Turkey. The attacks on the US planes had not been officially sanctioned by the Russians, but had been on the orders of commanders acting independently. The USSR seemed dangerously close to losing control of its own forces, and if that happened, catastrophic consequences might have been on the cards.

Kennedy replied to Khrushchev accepting his terms: pledging the US would never again invade Cuba if the Russian warheads were removed and, in a private addendum, agreeing to remove the USA's own missiles threatening the USSR from

Turkey. Khrushchev revealed later that Kennedy also offered to remove the US's nuclear arsenal from Italy: a symbolic gesture only since the Italian weapons were obsolete.

At 9am on 28 October, a message from Khrushchev was broadcast on Radio Moscow, stating that work at the Russian weapon sites in Cuba would cease immediately, and that the arsenal would be dismantled and returned to the USSR. A relieved Kennedy responded immediately, promising to honour the agreement and calling Khrushchev's decision "an important and constructive contribution to peace." Castro, who had not been consulted by either side, was furious to learn the news from the radio.

The US 'quarantine' of Cuba didn't end immediately, with aerial reconnaissance continuing to monitor whether the Soviets were packing up as promised. These missions were thankfully uneventful, and the Russian missiles and their supporting equipment were successfully loaded onto eight ships, leaving Cuban waters between 5 and 9 November. The blockade officially ended on 20 November and the USA removed its nuclear missiles from Turkey the following April. Castro may have been angry, and Soviet-Cuban relations significantly cooled, but the fact was that his position had been thoroughly strengthened by the Crisis. The US couldn't now attack Cuba - or Castro personally - without breaking the terms of their own peace treaty and risking the full weight of Russian reprisal.

In the aftermath of the Crisis, the Moscow-Washington hotline was set up, directly connecting the two political superpowers to facilitate easier negotiation should such a dire situation ever occur

> "The B-59's officers came horrendously close to desperately launching their payload"

EXCOMM meets to discuss tactics on 26 October 1962

IN THEIR OWN WORDS The three leaders state their cases

"In our discussions and exchanges [...] the one thing that has most concerned me has been the possibility that your government would not correctly understand the will and determination of the United States in any given situation, since I have not assumed that you or any other sane man would, in this nuclear age, deliberately plunge the world into war which it is crystal clear no country could win and which could only result in catastrophic consequences to the whole world."
Kennedy to Khrushchev, 22 Oct 1962

"You, Mr President, are not declaring a quarantine, but rather are setting forth an ultimatum and threatening that if we do not give in to your demands you will use force. Consider what you are saying! And you want to persuade me to agree to this! [...] You are no longer appealing to reason, but wish to intimidate us."
Khrushchev to JFK, 24 Oct 1962

"The Soviet Union must never allow circumstances in which the imperialists could carry out a nuclear first strike against it. [If] the imperialists carry out an invasion of Cuba – a brutal act in violation of universal and moral law – then that would be the moment to eliminate this danger forever, in an act of the most legitimate self-defence. However harsh and terrible the solution, there would be no other." **Castro to Khrushchev, 26 Oct 1962**

THE HOTLINE

It's good to talk

Pictured in the popular imagination as a red telephone, the Moscow-Washington hotline has never been a phone at all. It began life as a Teletype system, and kept that form for two decades until it was replaced with fax machines. Since 2008 it's been a secure computer link for email messages. The hotline was set up immediately after the Cuban Missile Crisis in 1963, linking the Pentagon directly to the Kremlin, so that immediate communication can begin should any hostilities or 'misunderstandings' arise. During the Crisis it dangerously often took many hours for the US to translate and decode Khruschev's messages.

While it seems like a sensible idea, Kennedy was criticised by the Republican Party of the time over the hotline's implementation. The accusation was that Kennedy would alienate his "proven allies" by speaking to his "sworn enemies" first!

Kennedy meeting with Soviet Foreign Minister Andrei Gromyko on 18 October 1962

again. Major Rudolf Anderson remained the only combatant killed during the standoff (although a further 18 personnel died in crashes and accidents) and his body was returned to the States and buried in South Carolina with full military honours.

While Castro was reasonably secure, neither the US nor the USSR came out of the Crisis covered in glory. Khrushchev remained in power in the Soviet Union for two more years, but his eventual ousting was directly attributable to the embarrassment he and his country had suffered in Cuba, and the Politburo's perception of him as having managed the situation ineptly.

Meanwhile, while the US publicly attempted to sell the outcome as a victory, it was also conflicted. US Air Force General Curtis Le May for example, although his was a minority opinion, called the Cuban Missile Crisis "the greatest defeat in [US] history." Le May had stridently argued for an invasion of Cuba from the earliest moments of the crisis, and continued to do so after the Russians'

withdrawal. "We could have gotten not only the missiles out of Cuba, we could have gotten the Communists out of Cuba at that time," he was still railing 25 years later.

In the end, it was perhaps humanity itself that won the Cuban Missile Crisis, receiving in the process a desperately urgent wake-up call that the balance of international power was being juggled between two super-states who had the capacity to annihilate one another at a moment's notice, likely taking almost everyone else with them. Conservative estimates suggest casualties of a nuclear war between the US and the USSR would have numbered in the hundreds of millions.

Scarily enough, however, the famous Doomsday Clock, which provides a symbolic, visual

> "Khrushchev was seen as having backed away from circumstances he had initiated in the first place"

representation in 'minutes to midnight' of how close the world is at any given time to a politically related global catastrophe, didn't move during the Crisis, since it happened faster than the clock's board could react. Immediately before the Crisis it stood at seven minutes to midnight, and afterward it moved back to 12, the world deemed a safer place thanks to the treaty. Today, the Doomsday Clock's hands stand at five minutes to midnight, 'thanks' to the lack of global action to reduce nuclear stockpiles, the potential for regional conflict, and the effects of avoidable climate change. The idea of mutually assured destruction may in modern times feel like an anachronism belonging firmly in the past. But some sources suggest it's closer than ever.

"I have a dream"

Explore the blood, sweat and tears behind one of the most iconic speeches in American history

MARTIN LUTHER KING JR
1929-1968

Brief Bio

Born in Atlanta and allegedly named after the German religious reformer Martin Luther, King was a bright student, skipping the ninth and 12th grades and enrolling at college without formally completing high school. The son of a reverend, King was initially sceptical of religion but changed his mind and entered the seminary. He fought for civil rights, with his "I have a dream" speech arguably his most iconic moment. He was assassinated aged 39.

Martin Luther King, the pastor who believed in nonviolent protest, addressed the hundreds of thousands of people gathered in Washington, DC with these words: "I am happy to join with you today in what will go down in history as the greatest demonstration for freedom in the history of our nation." The date was 28 August 1963 and while he spoke confidently, no one really knew how significant his role and the words he was yet to speak, sharing his iconic dream, would be in bringing it to life.

The day's events - known officially as The March on Washington for Jobs and Freedom - had been in planning since December 1962. An original focus on unemployment among the black population had swiftly expanded to include the broader issue of segregation and discrimination, and soon a programme of speeches, song and prayer had been arranged, reflecting a powerful vision of racial equality. Dr Martin Luther King - the man now synonymous with the march and arguably black history itself - was last on the bill.

Proceedings started early. Word of the march had spread far and wide, and at 8am the first of 21 chartered trains arrived in the capital, followed by more than 2,000 buses and ten aeroplanes - all in addition to standard scheduled public transport. Around 1,000 people - black and white - poured into Lincoln Memorial every five minutes, including a number of well-known celebrities, which gave the march extra visibility. Charlton Heston and Burt Lancaster were among the demonstrators, as was

King gave his speech to just under a quarter of a million people

Gandhi's influence

While the two never met in person, King derived a great deal of inspiration from Mahatma Ghandi's success in nonviolent protest, and so in 1959, made the journey to Bombay (now known as Mumbai).

King and his entourage were greeted with a warm welcome: "Virtually every door was open to us", King later recorded. He noted that Indian people "love to listen to the Negro spirituals", and so his wife, Coretta, ended up singing to crowds as often as King lectured.

The trip affected King deeply. In a radio broadcast made on his last night in India, he said: "Since being in India, I am more convinced than ever before that the method of nonviolent resistance is the most potent weapon available to oppressed people in their struggle for justice and human dignity."

"King was a man who had endured death threats, bomb scares, multiple arrests and prison sentences"

Marlon Brando, brandishing an electric cattle prod - a less-than-subtle symbol of police brutality. Soon speakers were preparing to give their speeches to an audience of a quarter of a million, a far greater number than the 100,000 hoped for.

The growing crowd buzzed with hope and optimism, but undercurrents of unease also rippled through the throng. Against a backdrop of violent civil-rights protests elsewhere around the country, President Kennedy had been reluctant to allow the march to go ahead, fearing an atmosphere of unrest. Despite the organisers' promise of a peaceful protest, the Pentagon had readied thousands of troops in the suburbs and nearly 6,000 police

officers patrolled the area. Liquor sales were banned throughout the city, hospitals stockpiled blood plasma and cancelled elective surgeries, and prisoners were moved to other facilities - measures taken to prepare for the civil disobedience many thought an inevitable consequence of the largest march of its kind in US history.

Many of those attending the march feared for their own safety but turned up on that warm August day because of how important they believed it was for their country, which was being ripped apart at the seams by race. In his book, *Like a Mighty Stream*, Patrik Henry Bass reported that demonstrator John Marshall Kilimanjaro, who

The long road to civil rights in america

1619	1712	1780	1790-1810	1863	1865
First known slaves The first known instance of African slavery in the fledgling English Colonial America is recorded.	**New York Slave Revolt** A group of 23 enslaved Africans kill nine white people. More than 70 blacks are arrested and 21 subsequently executed. After the uprising, the laws governing black people are made more restrictive.	**A minor victory** Pennsylvania becomes the first state in the newly-formed United States to abolish slavery by law.	**Manumission of slaves** Slaveholders in the upper south free their slaves following the revolution, and the percentage of free blacks rises from one per cent to ten per cent.	**The Emancipation Proclamation** President Abraham Lincoln proclaims the freedom of blacks still in slavery across ten states - around 3.1 million people.	**Black Codes** Black Codes are passed across the United States - but most notoriously in the south - restricting the freedom of black people and condemning them to low-paid labour.

travelled to the march from Greensboro, North Carolina, said that many attending the march felt afraid. "We didn't know what we would meet. There was no precedent. Sitting across from me was a black preacher with a white collar. We talked. Every now and then, people on the bus sang *Oh Freedom* and *We Shall Overcome*, but for the most part there wasn't a whole bunch of singing. We were secretly praying that nothing violent happened."

Kilimanjaro travelled over 480 kilometres (300 miles) to attend the march. Many from Birmingham, Alabama - where King was a particularly prominent figure - travelled for more than 20 hours by bus, covering 1,200 kilometres (750 miles). Attendees had invested a great deal of time, money and hope in the march, and anticipation - nervous or otherwise - was high.

The headline speaker, Martin Luther King, prominent activist, revered pastor and diligent president of the Southern Christian Leadership Conference (SCLC) had yet to finalise his speech, despite retiring to bed at 4am the previous night after a long and wearied debate with his advisors. "The logistical preparations for the march were so burdensome that the speech was not a priority for us", King's confidante and speechwriter Clarence B Jones has since admitted.

It wasn't until the evening before the march that seven individuals, including Jones, gathered together with King to give their input on the final remarks. It was Jones' job to take notes and turn them into a powerful address that would captivate

One of the many trains from New York arrives at Washington's Union Station for the march

Clarence Jones, one of King's speech writers

Folk singers Joan Baez and Bob Dylan singing at the 1963 Civil Rights March on Washington

1876-1960

● **Jim Crow Laws**
The enactment of racial segregation laws create 'separate but equal' status for African Americans, whose conditions were often inferior to those provided for white Americans.

1964

● **The Civil Rights Act**
One of the most sweeping pieces of equality legislation seen in the US, the Civil Rights Act prohibited discrimination of any kind and gave federal government the power to enforce desegregation.

1991

● **A stronger act**
President George HW Bush finally signs the Civil Rights Act of 1991, which strengthens existing civil-rights law - but only after two years of debates and vetoes.

2009

The first black president ●
Barack Obama is sworn is as the 44th president of the United States - the first African American in history to become the US president.

What you need to know about the language of the speech

Dr Catherine Brown, convenor and senior lecturer in English, New College of the Humanities

• "The speech derives its power from a combination of disparate elements. On one hand, it is addressed to a particular time and place, and emphasises this fact: the situation is urgent; now is the time change must happen. On the other, the speech is dense with allusions to the *Bible* and foundational American documents and speeches.

• King is explicitly saying that the Emancipation Proclamation is a 'bad check' that has yet to be honoured in regard to 'the Negro people', and the speech calls on that cheque to be honoured.

• The other texts he refers to were not written by black people, but by using their phrases and rhythms he is asserting his place - and the black person's place - in the cultural, intellectual, and political tradition that they're part of. In his very words, he is not allowing himself to be 'separate but equal.'

• Behind the rhetoric of all these American texts is that of the King James translation of the *Bible*, and the rhetoric of Ancient Greek and Roman orators. Both empires, and the authors of the *Bible*, are multi-ethnic; white supremacy would have been foreign to them."

"In a heartbeat, King had done away with his formal address and began to preach from his heart his vision"

the hearts and minds of the nation - no mean feat as everyone at the meeting had a significant stake in the speech and wanted their voice to be heard. "I tried to summarise the various points made by all of his supporters", wrote Jones in his book, *Behind the Dream*. "It was not easy; voices from every compass point were ringing in my head." According to Jones, King soon became frustrated, telling his advisors: "I am now going upstairs to my room to counsel with my Lord. I will see you tomorrow."

No doubt the magnitude of the task at hand weighed heavily on King's mind that night as he tried to rest. By this point, King was a well-known political figure, but few outside the black church and activism circles had heard him speak publicly at length. With the relatively newfangled television networks preparing to project his image into the homes of millions, King knew that he must seize the unprecedented platform for civil rights.

When he was finally called to the podium, it was clear King's placement on the bill had put him at an immediate disadvantage. An oppressively hot

day was quickly draining the crowd's enthusiasm and many had already left the march in order to make their long journeys home. A state-of-the-art sound system had been brought in for the day, but an act of sabotage before the event meant that even with help from the US Army Signal Corps in fixing it, some of the crowd struggled to hear the speakers. But King was a man who had endured death threats, bomb scares, multiple arrests, prison sentences and constant intimidation in his pursuit for equality; he would not be undone by unfortunate circumstance.

Placing his typed yet scrawl-covered notes on the lectern, King began to speak, deftly and passionately, invoking the Declaration of Independence, the Emancipation Proclamation and the US Constitution. Early on, he gave a nod toward Abraham Lincoln's Gettysburg Address ("Five score years ago..."), an equally iconic speech that, 100 years previously, set down the then-president's vision for human equality. King used rhythmic language, religious metaphor and the repetition

Many of the leaders of the protest are held back before the March on Washington

In the papers

Newspapers around the country brandished mixed headlines following King's speech. While many reported on the march's orderly and peaceful nature, several complained of the event's effects on traffic and transport in the area. Others, perhaps deliberately, gave the march only a few column inches, referring to it as a 'racial march' rather than a call for equality.

This front page from the *Eugene Register Guard* reflects the apprehension felt by many at the time. "Massive Negro Demonstration 'Only a Beginning'" is somewhat scare mongering, implying the US should be fearful of the black population. The strapline "No Evidence of any Effect on Congress", meanwhile, seems to purposely undermine the efforts of those involved in the march.

of a phrase at the beginning of each sentence: "One hundred years later..." he cries, highlighting Lincoln's failed dream. "We cannot be satisfied..." he announces, boldly declaring that "America has given the Negro people a bad check."

Jones, watching King captivate the crowd, breathed a sigh of relief. "A pleasant shock came over me as I realised that he seemed to be essentially reciting those suggested opening paragraphs I had scrawled down the night before in my hotel room", he reveals in *Behind the Dream*.

Then something unscripted happened. During a brief pause, gospel singer Mahalia Jackson, who had performed earlier in the day, shouted "Tell 'em about the dream, Martin!" King pushed his notes to one side and stood tall in front of his audience. Jones, sensing what was about to happen, told the person next to him, "These people out there today don't know it yet, but they're about to go to church."

In a heartbeat, King had done away with his formal address and began to preach from his heart his vision, his dream, which came to represent a

King's Speech: by the numbers

11 TIMES KING SAYS THE WORD 'DREAM'

17 MINUTES – THE LENGTH OF THE SPEECH

20 HOURS SPENT ON A BUS BY MANY TRAVELLING TO THE MARCH

100 BUSES ARRIVING PER HOUR BY 8AM

5,900 POLICE OFFICERS ON DUTY

250,000 PEOPLE AT THE MARCH

Civil-rights leaders of the March on Washington meet with John F Kennedy in the Oval Office, 28 August 1963

"King was targeted as a major enemy of the US and subjected to extensive surveillance and wiretapping by the FBI"

legacy that would change civil rights forever. "I have a dream", he said, in one of the speech's most famous lines, "that my four little children will one day live in a nation where they will not be judged by the colour of their skin but by the content of their character."

"Aw, sh**", remarked Walker Wyatt, another of King's advisors. "He's using the dream." Wyatt had previously advised King to stay away from his dream rhetoric. "It's trite, it's cliché. You've used it too many times already", he warned. Indeed, King had used the refrain on several occasions before at fundraisers and rallies but, crucially, in the days before mass media it had not been publicised. To the millions watching on TV and in person, the speech was as original as they come.

When King had talked about his 'dream' before, it had been generally well received, but certainly hadn't been groundbreaking. This time, however, it was different: thousands upon thousands of listening voices cried out in approval and unity, and King's final line: "Free at last, free at last, thank God Almighty - we are free at last!" was met with a rapturous standing ovation from the enormous crowd.

King's speech was a defining moment in black history and the fight for civil rights. "Though he was extremely well known before he stepped up to the lectern," Jones wrote, "he had stepped down on the other side of history." Even President Kennedy, no mean orator himself, reportedly turned to an aide and remarked: "He's damned good."

However, the clout of King's address was not entirely positive. The Federal Bureau of Intelligence (FBI) was wary of King's activities, and its director J Edgar Hoover considered King to be a dangerous radical. Two days after the march, FBI agent William C Sullivan wrote a memo about King's increasing sway: "In the light of King's powerful demagogic speech yesterday he stands head and shoulders above all other Negro leaders put together when it comes to influencing great masses of Negroes. We must mark him now, if we have not done so before, as the most dangerous Negro [...] in this nation from the standpoint of communism, the Negro and national security."

From this point on, King was targeted as a major enemy of the US and subjected to extensive surveillance and wiretapping by the FBI. According to Marshall Frady in his biography, *Martin Luther*

Kennedy and King

King never publicly endorsed any political candidate, but did reveal in 1960 he "felt that Kennedy would make the best president".

Many claim Kennedy owed his presidency to King after securing his release from prison following a protest in Atlanta, Georgia - a gesture that helped gain a large proportion of the black vote. But when the pair discussed the possibility of a second Emancipation Proclamation, Kennedy was slow to act.

Kennedy was caught between opposing forces: on one side, his belief in equality, and on the other, a preoccupation with foreign threats such as communism.

King delivers his iconic speech from the Lincoln Memorial

The March was attended by around 250,000 supporters

The speech's legacy

Despite the success of King's speech, his address was largely forgotten afterwards, due to the speed of subsequent events, and to King's increasing disillusionment with his dream. He said that it had "turned into a nightmare." According to William P Jones, author of *The March On Washington*, in the mid-1960s "most people would not have said it was the most powerful speech ever."

King's assassination led the nation to rediscover his speech, yet remarkably the full speech did not appear in writing until 15 years later, when a transcript was published in the *Washington Post*.

The original copy of the speech is currently owned by George Raveling. The then-26-year-old basketball player had volunteered at the last minute as a bodyguard during the march, and after King's speech asked him if he could have his notes. Raveling has been offered as much as £1.8 million ($3 million) for the original copy, but he says he has no intention of selling it.

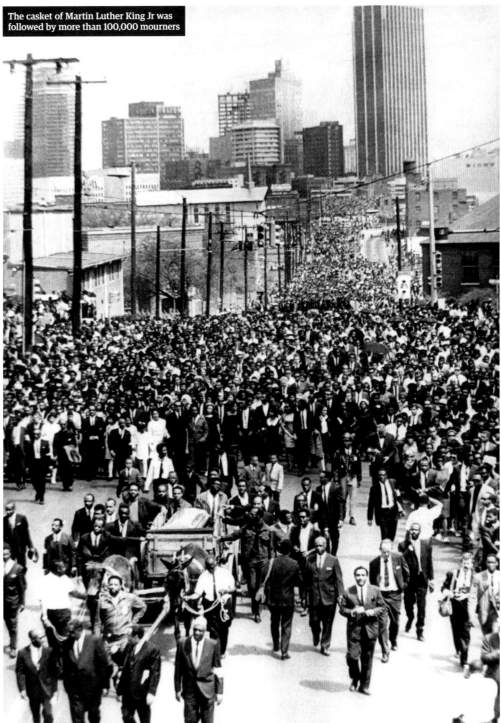

The casket of Martin Luther King Jr was followed by more than 100,000 mourners

King Jr: A Life, the FBI even sent King intercepted recordings of his extramarital affairs in a thinly-veiled attempt, King believed, to intimidate and drive him to suicide.

It seems incredible to believe, but contemporary criticism not only came from the establishment, but from King's peers. Civil-rights activist and author Anne Moody made the trip to Washington DC from Mississippi for the march and recalls: "I sat on the grass and listened to the speakers, to discover we had 'dreamers' instead of leaders leading us. Just about every one of them stood up there dreaming. Martin Luther King went on and on talking about his dream. I sat there thinking that in Canton we never had time to sleep, much less dream."

Human-rights activist Malcolm X also famously condemned the march, as well as Dr King's speech itself. Allegedly dubbing the event "the farce on Washington", he later wrote in his autobiography: "Who ever heard of angry revolutionaries swinging their bare feet together with their oppressor in lily pad pools, with gospels and guitars and 'I have a dream' speeches?"

Whatever some of the critics might have said, though, there was no doubt that King's speech singled him out as a leader. His oration has been lauded as one of the greatest of the 20th century, earned him the title of 'Man of the Year' by *Time Magazine*, and subsequently led to him receiving the Nobel Peace Prize. At the time, he was the youngest person to have been awarded the honour.

Most importantly, though, both the march and King's speech initiated debate and paved the way for genuine and tangible civil-rights reforms, putting racial equality at the top of the agenda. The Civil Rights Act of 1964 - landmark legislation that outlawed discrimination based on race, colour, religion, sex or national origin - was enacted less than a year after King shared his dream.

Halfway through the speech, before doing away with his notes, Martin Luther King Jr declared to his thousands of brothers and sisters in the crowd: "We cannot walk alone." That he spoke from his heart in such a poetic and unrepentant way ensured that, in the coming years, nobody did.

The Saturn V launch vehicle was crucial in a propelling the Apollo spacecraft to the Moon

Sputnik 1 remains a symbol of national pride for Russians, even today

on 3 November 1957. Weighing more than 450 kilograms, it carried a live female dog called Laika into orbit and had a packed payload including radio transmitters, a telemetry system, scientific instruments and a temperature control panel.

To make matters worse, the USA's launch attempt of Vanguard TV3 on 6 December 1957 saw the rocket lift just over one metre before falling back down and exploding, leading to humiliating headlines such as "Kaputnik" and "Flopnik". It eventually launched its own satellite, Explorer 1, on 31 January 1958, and while it followed it in March with the first solar-powered satellite, Vanguard 1, the USA was seen to be lagging behind their Soviet rivals.

In an attempt to catch up, NASA was formed in October of that year, with a remit to expand human knowledge of phenomena in the atmosphere and space and to preserve the role of the USA as a leader in aeronautical and space science and technology. Significantly, it was set apart from the US military with the message being that scientific exploration of space would be for

peaceful applications. And yet the Russians were already on the next page: manned spaceflight.

Korolev and his team had started designing a manned space capsule in 1955 and they began selecting volunteers for vigorous training in 1959. 20 Soviets had come forward and they were being put through their paces. At the same time, NASA had chosen seven astronauts of its own, which it dubbed the Mercury Seven. The Americans put their Mercury spacecraft through strenuous tests to ensure that it was safe enough for human travel. Yet it took slightly too long.

The USSR had whittled its volunteers down to six by June 1960 and eventually chose 27-year-old cosmonaut Yuri Gagarin to be the pilot for its manned mission. On 12 April 1961, he made history on board Vostok 1 becoming the first human in space when he orbited Earth once during a 108-minute-long flight. It proved to be yet another blow for the USA, who would send their own candidate – Alan B Shepard – into space just three weeks later on 5 May.

The space race became highly pressurised with Korolev and von Braun's teams urged to come up with the next big, jaw-dropping moment. The USSR and the USA were locked in a battle to prove they were technologically more advanced and it was a deep psychological test for both sides. The Russians had already proved they were not the backward people the Americans had made them out to be. There was also a feeling that conquering space could give the victor control of Earth. So it was that US President John F Kennedy lay down a challenge. He said the USA would send a man to the Moon by the end of the decade.

In 1961, NASA launched Project Gemini, which was a series of spacecraft created to test Moon-bound technology. In 1962, a second group of astronauts was selected and a third was picked in 1963. NASA was achieving some great feats, benefiting from a 500 per cent boost in funds. Walter Schirra orbited Earth six times and Mariner 2 performed a fly-by of Venus, returning data on its atmosphere, magnetic field, charged particle environment and mass. Gemini examined the long-term effects of space travel on astronauts and allowed for ten manned missions.

Timeline

1944

Germany launches its V-2 rocket
The V-2 long-range guided ballistic missile was developed by Dr Wernher von Braun and his team in Nazi Germany. A vertical launch crosses the boundary of space. **1944**

Rush to discover V-2 tech
The Allies capture the V-2 rocket complex although USSR experts including Sergei Korolev attempt to recover the secrets of V-2 technology for themselves. Braun begins working for the USA. **1945**

USSR plans to launch satellite
Korolev is the lead Soviet rocket engineer working on the development of ballistic missiles. The R-7 is the world's first intercontinental ballistic missile and Korolev says it could be used to launch a satellite into space. The seeds of space exploration are cast. **1953**

The Space Race begins
The USSR launches Sputnik 1. The United States – which had spoken of launching its own satellite only two years earlier – is worried Russia will use the satellites to attack. **1957**

Sputnik 2 is launched
A month later, the USSR launches its second satellite, this time carrying a dog called Laika – one of the first live animals to be sent into space. It is understood Laika dies within hours of take off. **1957**

US satellite Explorer 1 launches
The USA launches its first satellite, which carries a scientific payload and discovers the Van Allen radiation belt. Explorer 2 later launches, but does not reach orbit. **1958**

NASA is formed
The first solar-powered satellite, Vanguard 1, is launched by the US in March, followed two months later by the USSR's Sputnik 3. In order to better advance the US' efforts, President Eisenhower establishes the National Aeronautics and Space Administration (NASA). **1958**

First man in space
Russian cosmonaut Yuri Gagarin becomes the first human to go into outer space, completing a single orbit of Earth. Alan B Shepard will become the first American in space on 5 May. **1961**

Sergei Korolev spearheaded the USSR's space programme as the lead rocket engineer and spacecraft designer

Yet Korolev was working on the USSR's manned spacecraft Soyuz, and in 1965, Russian cosmonaut Alexei Leonov spent 12 minutes on the first spacewalk. Here, the Soviets had indulged in a spot of mischief: it knew NASA was planning a spacewalk with astronaut Ed White (which took place three months later) so Korolev's team added an airlock to the second Voskhod launch. He had then turned his attention to developing the potentially powerful N1 rocket.

The race to the Moon was well and truly on. Although the Soviets were uncertain a lunar-landing programme was necessary, it nevertheless sought to beat the Americans and claim another victory. But it suffered a major blow. Korolev, who was excited by the prospect of putting a man on the moon, had suffered six years of ill health. He died of complications during routine colon surgery on 14 January 1966. Pravda printed his obituary, finally letting the Soviet public and the world know who was behind the USSR's space programme.

Korolev's death meant that he never saw the fruits of his team's labour on the N1 rocket although perhaps that is just as well given that none of the four launches got off the ground. The

Soviet space programme had also become a mess with internal designers competing rather than working together. Korolev had been given overall control in 1964 but, now that he was gone, disarray ruled once more. In April 1967, cosmonaut Vladimir Komarov died during re-entry on Soyuz 1.

Not that NASA didn't have setbacks too - a fire in the Apollo 1 capsule during a launch pad test killed US astronauts Gus Grissom, Ed White and Roger Chafee - but it was far better organised. On 20 July 1969, Neil Armstrong and Buzz Aldrin became the first men to walk on the Moon. The USA had achieved the long-awaited and promised dream.

It firmly put the USA in pole position but it also heralded a new direction. Interest in manned lunar missions faded and instead the USSR looked to launch the first human-crewed space station, Salyut 1, while the US looked at missions to Mars. The Moon mission was the beginning of the end of space-related hostilities, though. In 1975, the joint Apollo-Soyuz mission saw three US astronauts launched aboard an Apollo spacecraft that docked with a USSR Soyuz vehicle. When the two commanders met, they greeted each other. The space race was over.

The failed Soviet mission to the moon

When JFK told the USA in 1961, "I believe that this nation should commit itself to achieving the goal, before this decade is out, of landing a man on the Moon and returning him safely to the Earth," it opened a new front in the fledgling space race. But Moscow had been secretly working on its enormous two-man N1 rocket since 1959. Powered by 30 engines, it was thought to be an equal to the USA's Saturn V booster. The first failed launch of this great hulk was attempted on 21 February 1969. The second, on 3 July 1969, was catastrophic. At 11.18pm Moscow time, the rocket lifted but a loose bolt was sucked into a fuel pump, causing the rocket to stall. As it leaned and fell back to Earth, the on-board propellent ignited and the rocket exploded with the force of a small nuclear bomb. US spy satellites picked up on the devastation, which affected buildings as far as 40 kilometres away, destroyed the launch pad and killed dozens. It took the Soviets about 18 months to rebuild the launch pad but two further explosions saw them scrap their plans to send a cosmonaut to the Moon. Such was the secrecy in the USSR that official confirmation of the second launch disaster only emerged in 1989.

● **NASA announces the Gemini programme**
Project Gemini will run for five years, developing space travel techniques to land astronauts on the Moon. It looks at orbital docking, re-entry methods and the feasibility and safety of long-duration missions. **1961**

● **First woman in space**
Soviet cosmonaut Valentina Tereshkova is chosen from 400 applicants to become the first woman to fly in space. The photos she takes will be used to identify aerosol layers within the atmosphere. **1963**

● **First close-up Moon images**
Gordon Cooper spends 34 hours in space from 15 May while Ranger 7 becomes the first US spacecraft to transmit close-up images of the lunar surface to Earth before it hits the Moon. **1964**

● **The first spacewalk**
Russia's Alexei Leonov embarks on a 12-minute spacewalk during the Voskhod 2 mission, which nearly ends in disaster as he struggles to re-enter the craft. Ed White would perform the USA's first spacewalk on 3 June. **1965**

● **Luna 9 lands on Moon**
Russia's Luna 2 had impacted the Moon on 13 September 1959, which was a first, but Luna 9 soft-lands. On 3 April, Luna 10 becomes the first satellite to orbit the Moon. **1966**

● **First man on the Moon**
The USA manages this gigantic leap when Neil Armstrong and Buzz Aldrin set foot on Earth's natural satellite. With a TV audience of half-a-billion viewers, they plant the American flag into the dusty lunar landscape, hailing a major victory in the Space Race. **1969**

● **First human-crewed space station**
The USSR launches Salyut 1 as attention shifts to orbiting space stations. But relations between the two nations will eventually thaw: a joint Soviet-US crew will dock an Apollo Command/Service Module with Soyuz 19 in July 1975. **1971**

Nixon's scandal: Watergate

Inside the events that brought down a US president and changed the political lexicon forever

With beads of sweat forming at his brow, the president of the United States of America looks straight down the lens of a television camera and says defiantly: "I'm not a crook." The president, Richard Nixon, is in the middle of an hour-long televised question-and-answer session with over 400 journalists. That the leader of the world's foremost superpower is forced to make such an astonishing statement shows the scale of a scandal that has spread like wildfire through the White House. It will lead to the first and only resignation of an incumbent president to date and become the defining political misdemeanour of the 20th century.

So seismic is Watergate that the last syllable will be added as a suffix to any public series of events deemed scandalous, yet the origins are seemingly small-fry in comparison to many political controversies - a burglary at the Watergate Hotel, the site of the Democratic National Committee.

At the time Richard Nixon delivers the quote, late in 1973, the walls are beginning to close around him, yet it will take almost another year for the president to tender his resignation following a 'death by a thousand cuts' that sees allies and aides resigning or cast ruthlessly aside. Days before Nixon resigns, beleaguered and facing impeachment, he consults an old colleague, Henry Kissinger, on his options. Seeing a broken man in torment at the prospect of only the second presidential impeachment and a potential criminal trial, Kissinger tries to console Nixon and even accedes to his request that the pair of them get down on their knees and pray. That it has come to this is an indication of the devastating nature of the revelations over a dirty-tricks campaign that struck at the heart of the White House.

18 months earlier, on 17 June 1972, five men had been arrested by police on the sixth floor of the Watergate Hotel building in Washington, DC. Noticing that a number of doors have been taped open to prevent them from locking,

a security guard called the police. All five were arrested and found to have connections with the CIA and a group that raised funds for the re-election of Richard Nixon, the Committee for the Re-Election of the President (CRP), often satirically abbreviated to CREEP.

Nixon is a familiar face, having been a vice president to Dwight Eisenhower between 1952 and 1960 and previously unsuccessfully fighting John F Kennedy for the White House. During a debate, the future president falls foul of a relatively new medium in political campaigning - while voters listening on the radio believe that Nixon has triumphed, television viewers are won over by JFK's good looks and charm; they are equally dismayed by Nixon's hunched shoulders, jowly appearance and sweaty brow. But, having narrowly won the presidency in 1968, Nixon wins by a landslide in 1972 and enjoys approval ratings of more than 70 per cent - almost unheard of for a president in his second term.

However, Nixon deploys an array of dubious techniques to smear opponents. The CRP becomes a de facto intelligence organisation engaged in dirty campaigns against potential rivals: bugging offices, seeking material that could be used against opponents and attempting to prevent leaks to the media. While the CRP is technically and officially a private fundraising group, its existence and true nature is known to several federal government employees and Nixon himself - while he is aware that the CRP gathers intelligence on his rivals and administration's enemies, conversations reveal that he is either unaware of the scale of their activities or simply chooses not to know.

The five men arrested at the Watergate were likely there either to recover bugs that had been left on the telephone of senior Democrats or install new surveillance equipment but originally little significance is ascribed to the break-in. When the *Washington Post*'s rookie reporter Bob Woodward is sent to a local courthouse to cover the story, he discovers that the

While Woodward and Bernstein are busy uncovering the paper trail to the White House, another revelation will prove just as disastrous for Nixon. James McCord sends a letter to Judge Sirica in March 1973, explaining that he has perjured himself, alleging orders from high up in the White House. Also in March, Nixon gets a lengthy rundown from John Dean on the scale of the dirty-tricks campaign and how the Watergate burglary came to happen. Nixon listens, appalled, as Dean recounts the web of deceit in which many of his staff are now trapped - Dean's prognosis is grim: "We have a cancer, close to the Presidency, that's growing. It's growing daily. It's compounding, it grows geometrically now because it compounds itself."

An exasperated Nixon sighs his way through Dean's prognosis, which reveals illegal activities, blackmail and perjury on a grand scale. It is clear the chain is only as strong as its weakest link - and those are cropping up everywhere as the net tightens. Asked about his personal feelings on the matter, Dean replies he is not confident the administration can ride it out. Even Dean himself is starting to feel the pressure and can't shake the impression that he is being set up as a scapegoat. He is probably correct: Nixon fires Dean, who turns star witness for the prosecution, and the president rolls the dice and gambles by disposing of some of his most trusted lieutenants, asking for the resignation of both Haldeman and Ehrlichman. Richard Kleindienst also resigns.

Coincidentally, at around this time, confirmation hearings begin for installing L Patrick Gray as permanent director of the FBI. During the hearings, Gray reveals that he has provided daily updates on the Watergate investigation to the White House and alleges that John Dean has "probably lied" to FBI investigators, enraging the White House. It is subsequently revealed that Gray has disposed of some of the contents of a safe belonging to Hunt - drawing the FBI into a web of deceit along with the CIA, the federal government and the Republican Party - forcing his resignation in April 1973. In just a few turbulent weeks Nixon had lost his three most trusted lieutenants, his attorney general and the head of the FBI. By May, more people disapprove than approve of Richard Nixon's presidency and a month later the Watergate hearings are being televised; viewers see John Dean tell investigators that he had discussed the cover-up with Nixon at least 35 times. Although Nixon can plausibly deny knowledge of the CRP campaigns and protect himself by firing staff, things are about to get much worse for the president.

Nixon is a suspicious individual who has few real friends and sees conspiracies against him everywhere. Given to brooding behaviour and capable of vulgar outbursts and ruthless behaviour, the president will later acknowledge that the American people knew little of his real personality. This side of his personality was to be his undoing. Known only to a few individuals, Nixon has had secret recording equipment installed in the Oval Office, Cabinet Room and his private office in the White House. The resulting tapes are vital in proving his knowledge of - and active participation in - the Watergate cover-up and wider culpability in allowing his aides to commit behaviour both immoral and illegal.

"Upon hearing of the arrests the next day, Nixon hurls an ashtray at the wall in fury"

Nixon's web of lies

The complex web of deception and conspiracy that brought a president to his knees

Attorney general
Richard Kleindienst
Kleindienst became aware of Watergate when G Gordon Liddy told him while playing golf that the break-in had originated within the CRP and that he should arrange for the burglars' release. He resigned the same day John Dean was fired and Haldeman and Ehrlichman quit.

Whistleblower
Mark Felt
The identity of 'Deep Throat' was one of the greatest political mysteries – until 2005, when Felt announced that he was journalist Bob Woodward's source. Felt had been the FBI's associate director in 1973 and was repeatedly passed over for the job of director by Nixon.

Government agent
Bernard Barker
A Cuban emigrant who had served in the US armed forces and probably worked for both the FBI and CIA at various times, Barker was an early recruit to the White House Plumbers and served one year in jail for his part in the Watergate break-in.

CRP Security
James McCord
A former CIA agent who acted as the security coordinator for the CRP. He was arrested at the Watergate complex and later informed Judge John Sirica that he had perjured himself at the trial and that he had been ordered to carry out the break-in by senior White House figures.

Attorney general
John Mitchell
Mitchell was a personal friend and partisan colleague of Nixon's who was rewarded with the job of attorney general in 1969. A great believer in law and order, Mitchell was heavily involved in the so-called White House Horrors – a term he coined – of Nixon's presidency, okayed the Watergate burglary and had form in threatening journalists. Mitchell was found guilty of conspiracy, obstruction of justice and perjury and served a 19-month sentence.

Vice president
Gerald Ford
Ford had found himself surprisingly promoted following the resignation of Spiro Agnew in 1973. Within a year he had become president. One of his first acts was to pardon Nixon. He lost to Jimmy Carter in the 1977 presidential elections.

White House liaison
Gordon Liddy
Liddy was instrumental in forming the White House Plumbers and was responsible for many dirty-trick schemes. Liddy supervised the break-ins at the Watergate and acted as the chief liaison to the White House. He received a stiff 20-year sentence for his role but served only four and a half.

Government agent
Frank Sturgis
Supposedly implicated in the assassination of JFK and the Cuban Revolution, Sturgis had long known E Howard Hunt. He was one of the five men arrested while burgling the Watergate. Sturgis was jailed for his part in the break-in and later made lurid allegations Kennedy's assassination.

Journalist

Bob Woodward
Woodward covered the trial of the five Watergate burglars, initially unaware of the significance. With coaxing from his editor and help from Carl Bernstein he was able to piece together a paper trail that was instrumental in exposing the White House's campaign of dirty tricks.

Solicitor general

Robert Bork
Bork was solicitor general when both the attorney general and deputy attorney general resigned over a refusal to sack Watergate Special Prosecutor Cox. Bork later claimed that Nixon promised him a Supreme Court position if he carried out this order. He complied but Nixon didn't fulfil his part of the deal.

White House aide

HR Haldeman
Haldeman was a tough White House aide who acted to block access to the president and protect his interests. Alongside Ehrlichman, he formed an impassable shield: as a result the pair became known as the 'Berlin Wall' – a reference to their activities and Germanic names.

Lawyer

Charles Colson
A lawyer who worked for Nixon, one of the Watergate Seven found guilty of obstruction of justice and who sentenced to seven months in prison. Following his release Colson found God, donating all his subsequent fees to charity.

Judge

John Sirica
John Sirica's presided over the trial of the Watergate burglars – handing out tough sentences in order to coerce admissions from them that they acted in concert with others. He later ordered Nixon to hand over tapes of White House conversations to Archibald Cox.

Deputy assistant to the president

Alexander Butterfield
Butterfield was responsible for the operation of the secret taping system, which Nixon had installed in the White House. His deposition was crucial in establishing the existence of the system – and the tapes that sealed Nixon's fate.

White House counsel

John Dean
Dean was referred to as the 'master manipulator of the cover-up' by the FBI. He turned on Nixon and became the star witness for the prosecution at the Senate Watergate Committee hearings and pleaded guilty to a single felony count after suspecting that he was being set up as a scapegoat. Dean had destroyed evidence following the Watergate burglary arrests and received a prison sentence, despite his co-operation. In later life he became a critic of the Republican Party.

CIA agent

Howard Hunt
Hunt had been drafted into Nixon's unofficial investigations unit – the White House Plumbers – charged with fixing 'leaks' to the media. He was involved in the planning of the Watergate burglaries and sentenced to over 30 months in prison.

FBI director

Patrick Gray
Gray was nominated to succeed Hoover as head of the FBI but resigned after less than a year on the job. Underestimating its significance, Gray had destroyed evidence from a safe belonging to E Howard Hunt. When the scale of the conspiracy became clear to him he resigned and spent years trying to clear his name.

Chief domestic advisor

John Ehrlichman
Ehrlichman ensured that Nixon was protected from unnecessary attention and worked as White House counsel before moving to a role as chief domestic advisor. From this position Ehrlichman launched vicious assaults on the president's enemies and created the White House Plumbers. He had worked with Nixon for over a decade – initially on his unsuccessful 1960 presidential bid – and never forgave Nixon for the lack of a presidential pardon. He served 18 months in prison and died in 1999.

Director of CRP

Jeb Magruder
Magruder served as a special assistant to the president until the spring of 1971, when he left to manage the CRP. He was heavily involved in Watergate and alleged that Nixon had prior knowledge of the affair. He served seven months in prison.

CRP chairman

Maurice Stans
Stans was allegedly responsible for raising large amounts of cash in donations that Nixon kept in a White House safe. Stans denied any knowledge of Watergate and, though indicted for perjury and obstruction of justice, he was acquitted the following year.

Archibald Cox
A respected lawman, Cox was appointed as the first special prosecutor in the Watergate case. Learning of the existence of secret tapes recorded at the White House, Cox pressed for their release. Cox was eventually fired but left with his reputation enhanced.

Watergate prosecutor

Hugh Sloan
Sloan was unwittingly responsible for endorsing cheques that went to pay the White House Plumbers. Once Sloan discovered the activities of the plumbers he resigned and became a source for Woodward and Bernstein.

CRP treasurer

Nixon met by an angry crowd while campaigning during the height of the Watergate scandal, 1974

Nixon has been at the sharp end of American politics for decades. He has made powerful friends and enemies alike and learned how to play dirty, even ordering tax investigations on Kennedy and 1972's Democratic presidential candidate, Hubert Humphrey. On the tapes, Nixon is heard to remark: "I can only hope that we are, frankly, doing a little persecuting. Right?"

In the run-up to the presidential election of 1972, when it looks like Ted Kennedy - brother of JFK - will be a potential opponent for the 1976 election, Nixon and his aides attempt to use the Secret Service and Inland Revenue Service to spy on the Democrat senator in the hope of discovering material they can use to smear him. Such operations have been learned over 25 years in politics - Nixon smears his first political opponents as communists or communist sympathisers during his 1946 and 1950 Congress election runs. His nickname, Tricky Dicky, is devised during 1950 and he finds it hard to shake. Nixon also uses the shooting of presidential hopeful George McGovern in 1972 as an opportunity to place a loyal man within a security protection detail on Ted Kennedy. The spy, Robert Newbrand, is to pass information back to the White House. "[W]e just might get lucky and catch this son of a bitch and ruin him for '76", says Nixon of Kennedy.

In light of what the president knows to be on the tapes, July 1973 brings a bombshell that Nixon instantly recognises as disastrous. The aide responsible for the president's schedule and day-to-day archiving testifies that Nixon has had recording equipment secretly installed throughout White House offices. The ramifications are obvious, with the tapes laying bare just how widespread the use of dirty tricks are and how the orders frequently come direct from the president.

Archibald Cox, leading the hearings, instantly subpoenas the tapes. Realising the gravity of the situation, Nixon refuses the request, citing executive privilege and - for the next few months - begins a high-stakes game of bureaucratic cat and mouse in an effort to keep the tapes in his possession. In October, just days after losing his vice president, Spiro Agnew, to an investigation into past corruption, Nixon astonishes his advisors by ordering Cox's firing - something only Elliot Richardson, the attorney general, could legally do.

The president, furious at Cox's intransigence over refusing to accede to an offer to appoint a Democrat senator to listen to the tapes, rather than hand them over, makes it clear that he will accept the resignation of Richardson and Deputy Attorney General William Ruckelshaus if they do not sack Cox. On a night in October, dubbed the Saturday Night Massacre, Richardson refuses the order and promptly resigns. Having been given the same order by Nixon, Ruckelshaus also refuses and resigns, leaving Solicitor General Robert Bork to reluctantly carry out the order.

Public opinion quickly turns against Nixon, with protests greeting the president's public appearances. In November, he goes on the offensive, delivering a televised question-and-answer session where he delivers the famous "I'm not a crook" speech. He claims the tapes will exonerate him, but knows that this is not the case and that his political manoeuvrings are merely buying time: his presidency is a busted flush. Nixon had earlier recognised the danger the tapes posed and asked Haldeman to dispose of them: "Most of it is worth destroying", says the president. "Would you like - would you do that?" Haldeman replies in the affirmative but crucially is not as good as his word, perhaps believing that if he is seen to be responsible for destroying the tapes he would make the president bulletproof and seal his own fate.

In July 1974, having exhausted various means of preventing their release, including releasing transcripts and heavily redacted tapes, Nixon is ordered to give up the tapes to investigators and Congress moves to impeach the president. Any possibility that Nixon might hang on disappears in August, when a previously unheard tape is released. The evidence is known as the Smoking Gun tape. On the tape Nixon is heard advising Haldeman to advise the CIA to stop the FBI from investigating the Watergate break-in: "When you

"Public opinion turns against Nixon, with protests greeting the president's public appearances"

President Nixon's resignation created a media storm

get in these people, when you... get these people in, say: 'Look, the problem is that this will open the whole, the whole Bay of Pigs thing' [...] they should call the FBI in and say that we wish for the country, don't go any further into this case, period!"

Opinion is divided as to what 'the Bay of Pigs thing' refers to, though the implication to the CIA is obvious - if they do not assist in the Watergate cover-up, sensitive information regarding the agency's role in the aborted CIA-backed invasion of Cuba in 1961 will be released by the White House. The tape constitutes authentic evidence that the president was involved in the Watergate cover-up and attempted to pressure federal agencies into participating.

Senior Republicans gather to tell Nixon that he has no support in Congress. Ever the political survivor and having claimed that he would never resign, even Nixon realises that he has exhausted his options. The president promptly resigns, knowing that he will be impeached if he remains in office. His resignation speech is broadcast from the White House the night before he leaves for his home in California. Typically, his speech wrongfoots many, with allusions to the difficulties of office and oblique mentions of wrongdoing, notions of duty and vague expressions of regret.

Nixon also includes a lengthy summation of what he sees as his achievements in office, preferring them to discussions of Watergate - a trope that would become familiar in years to come. Nixon never escapes the taint of Watergate but he becomes a respected statesman on the American and global stages and wins acclaim for his domestic and foreign accomplishments. He is almost immediately pardoned by his successor, Gerald Ford, in a move that many decry.

Nixon avoids jail but the scale of wrongdoing - and the depth of the unpleasantness that modern US politics constitute - takes voters by surprise and reveals those at the top of government as venal, vulgar, deceitful and greedy. Most of all, it shows US presidents to be flawed and long after his resignation Nixon still inspires fascination.

Upon leaving the White House, Nixon spends most of his time at his house in California - driving to a small outhouse on his golf buggy every day to work on his memoirs. In 1977, short of cash and keen to rehabilitate his reputation, he agrees to the now-famous series of interviews with journalist David Frost. The trained lawyer and long-serving politician initially runs rings around the under-prepared Frost, but on the final day of interview the disgraced president finally opens up on the Watergate scandal: "I let down the country. I brought myself down. I gave them a sword and they stuck it in. And they twisted it with relish."

The former president may have admitted some culpability but he never shakes off his ardent belief that the ends justified the means. Nixon had relied on a range of dirty tricks - many illegal - to claim power, and then affect change as he saw it. The apparently insignificant burglary that brought down the 37th president of the United States was just one of the ways that he bent the law - it's just that this time, he got caught.

An emotional Nixon gives his farewell speech at the White House, August 1, 1974

The aftermath

Following his resignation Nixon cut a sorry figure. Inconsolable at losing the job he had coveted so deeply, wounded by the thought he had betrayed the American people and lost with little to do at his home in California, he quickly became ill and almost died. However, he worked to rehabilitate himself and by the time of his death was a respected political elder; sought after for his advice by sitting presidents and even former opponents like Hillary Clinton. When he died it was revealed that he had requested not to have a state funeral, as is the usual custom for deceased US presidents.

In his resignation speech, Nixon made much of the advances he thought had been made in foreign policy - where many US presidents believe their legacy will be judged. Opinions vary on his efforts here and Vietnam will always tarnish the reputation of Nixon and his predecessor, Lyndon B Johnson. However, Nixon's work at home is perhaps more impressive. He forged ahead with the desegregation of the South, created numerous environmental acts to protect the US ecology

and steered a course that avoided the ideological impulses of following Republican presidents.

Nixon strikes a strange figure among US presidents - oddly awkward and self-aware, yet driven by a conviction that the president could not be wrong and that the interests of the ruling administration and United States were indivisible. He displayed the brooding character of someone bearing a great burden; his own self-image was laid bare in a quote from his resignation speech: "Sometimes I have succeeded and sometimes I have failed, but always I have taken heart from what Theodore Roosevelt once said about the man in the arena, 'whose face is marred by dust and sweat and blood, who strives valiantly, who errs and comes short again and again because there is not effort without error and shortcoming, but who does actually strive to do the deed, who knows the great enthusiasms, the great devotions, who spends himself in a worthy cause, who at the best knows in the end the triumphs of high achievements and who at the worst, if he fails, at least fails while daring greatly.'"

Bluffer's Guide
WEST GERMANY, 12 JUNE 1987
Reagan's Berlin Wall speech

Did you know?

The speech itself only received worldwide celebration following the fall of the Berlin Wall, two years after it was made

Timeline

20 JANUARY 1981

Following a landslide victory against incumbent president Jimmy Carter, Reagan is inaugurated as the 40th president of the United States.

11 JUNE 1982

Reagan makes one of his first visits to the currently divided nation of Germany. His arrival in West Berlin is greeted by mass protests from radical left groups.

11 AUGUST 1984

During a radio sound check, Reagan jokes with engineers: "...I've signed legislation that will outlaw Russia forever. We begin bombing in five minutes."

19 NOVEMBER 1985

Reagan and the USSR leader Gorbachev meet in Geneva to discuss nuclear arms. The two agree to meet again to discuss the 50% reduction of these weapons.

? What was it?

Two years before the eventual reunification of East and West Germany and the symbolic destruction of the wall that had divided the city of Berlin since 1961, the 40th president of the United States travelled to West Berlin to give a speech that would help usher in the eventual end of the Cold War. Standing on a podium with the infamous dividing wall behind him, Reagan uttered the famous phrase, "Tear down this wall!".

At 2pm, and protected by sheets of bulletproof glass (50,000 people had demonstrated against the US president's visit the day before, so tensions were high), Reagan stated that "the advance of human liberty can only strengthen the cause of world peace," and that there was only one true way for the USSR to show their commitment to it: by tearing down the Berlin wall. Addressing the Soviet leader directly, Reagan went on to say: "General Secretary Gorbachev, if you seek peace, if you seek prosperity for the Soviet Union and Eastern Europe, if you seek liberalisation, come here to this gate. Mr Gorbachev, open this gate. Mr Gorbachev, tear down this wall!"

? Why did it happen?

His speech in West Berlin wasn't the first time Reagan had raised his concerns about the existence of the Berlin Wall. In fact, as early as 1982 - during another state visit to West Germany - Reagan remarked, "Why is the wall there?" when asked what one question he would ask the leaders of the Soviet government. In the years that followed, Reagan and Soviet leader Mikhail Gorbachev seemingly formed a close public relationship; however, eight months prior to the speech, that union had grown cold as both parties continued to argue over the subject of nuclear weapons.

Reagan's speech in June 1987 was, when taken in context, a means of publicly calling on Gorbachev and the USSR to progress these negotiations beyond mere talk and rhetoric. Nuclear disarmament was the crux festering at the heart of the Cold War, and Reagan wanted to offer both an olive branch and a stark reminder of civic duty.

? Who was involved?

Ronald Reagan
6 February 1911 – 5 June 2004
The 40th president of the United States used his podium to urge the USSR to make good on its promise to end the Cold War stalemate.

Mikhail Gorbachev
2 March 1931 – Present
The eighth and final leader of the USSR, Gorbachev's progressive policies helped to bring an end to hostilities with the West.

Peter Robinson
18 April 1957 – Present
Robinson was one of many speech-writers who contributed to the speech given by Ronald Reagan in front of the Berlin Wall.

8 DECEMBER 1987

Reagan signs the Intermediate-Range Nuclear Forces treaty with USSR President Mikhail Gorbachev, both sides agreeing to dismantle thousands of missiles.

9 NOVEMBER 1989

A day after George H W Bush is elected president to succeed the retiring Reagan, the latter's dream of tearing down the Berlin Wall finally becomes a reality, leading to German reunification.

A NEW ERA

Faced with new challenges, both at home and abroad,
little is certain for the United States going forward

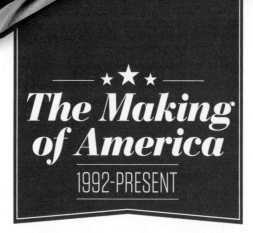

The Making of America
1992-PRESENT

19 March 2003

The Iraq War begins

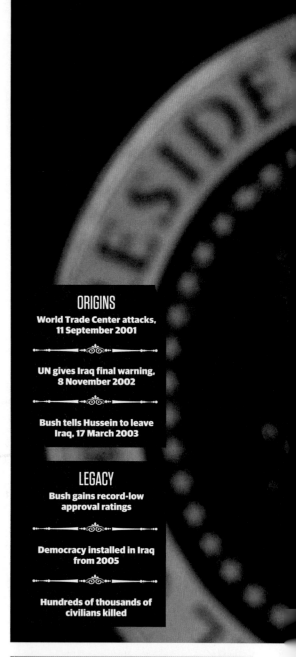

For decades, Iraqi leader Saddam Hussein had become the boogeyman of the Middle East. Behind his carefully curated public image lay a man who carried out unspeakable atrocities against his own people, sponsored multiple terrorist groups and invaded his neighbours with a constant irreverence. Such actions had forced the West's hand once already, with his invasion and annexation of Kuwait in 1991 leading to the first Iraq War.

However, by 2003, the West now had a far different view of the Middle East and nations who sponsored terrorism in any form. Post 9/11, President George W Bush was already waging the 'War on Terror' and with Osama Bin Laden seemingly vanishing into thin air, Saddam's provocative actions on Iraqi soil had realigned America's crosshairs. There was also a great deal of bipartisan support for the invasion from Congress thanks to the swift success of the war in Afghanistan in 2001. Even America's

allies, including the UK led by Prime Minister Tony Blair, were in favour of military action.

Then there was the issue of Weapons of Mass Destruction. The phantom that helped sway public opinion, and gain the support of the United Nations, WMDs were touted as the greatest threat to Western safety since the nuclear fears of the Cold War. The intelligence reports that brought WMDs into the conversation painted Hussein's arsenal as a stockpile of devastating power that wasn't just being built, but prepared for imminent launch.

Another factor was driving Bush to make that declaration of war on Iraq in 2003: oil. While the US had no outward intention to take control of Iraq's oil fields, leaving them in the hands of Hussein was a far greater danger. So by standing before those cameras and announcing his intention to invade, Bush and his allies could stop the despot from using petrodollar influence to rock foreign economies from afar.

> Over a decade on from the Gulf War, the fear of WMDs led America into another Middle East conflict

ORIGINS
World Trade Center attacks, 11 September 2001

UN gives Iraq final warning, 8 November 2002

Bush tells Hussein to leave Iraq, 17 March 2003

LEGACY
Bush gains record-low approval ratings

Democracy installed in Iraq from 2005

Hundreds of thousands of civilians killed

Defining moments

• The Republicans take the 1994 midterm elections
8 November 1994

Taking place in the middle of president Bill Clinton's first term in office, the 1994 United States elections became known as the year of the 'Republican Revolution' due to the overwhelmingly large number of members the GOP had elected to both the House of Representatives and the Senate. As a result, it challenged the iron grip the Democrats had on American policy at the time.

• Clinton impeached for the Monica Lewinsky scandal
19 December 1998

In one of the most unusual developments in US politics, 42nd president Bill Clinton was impeached by the House of Representatives on two charges: perjury and obstruction of justice. These charges rose from a sexual harassment lawsuit from an Arkansas state employee, as well as a long-running affair between the 49-year-old president and Monica Lewinsky, a 22-year-old White House intern.

• The Space Shuttle Challenger disintegrates
1 February 2003

While the Space Shuttle Challenger was preparing to launch on 16 January 2003, a piece of foam broke away and damaged one of the orbiter's left wings. Two weeks later, when the shuttle attempted re-entry, the damaged wing caused a chain reaction that destroyed the shuttle, killing all seven astronauts on board. It was Challenger's 28th and final mission.

The Iraq War lasted for almost nine years and would eventually turn public opinion against Bush and his decision to occupy the country for so long

• Hurricane Katrina hits America
26 August 2005

Having formed just three days before over the Bahamas, the terrible power of the tropical cyclone known as Hurricane Katrina hit the Gulf of America with full force on 26 August. Over the next week it would take the lives of 1,833 people, with the city of New Orleans alone suffering incredible devastation. It ranks as one of the five most deadly hurricanes in US history.

• The Great Recession
December, 2007

Following the bursting of the housing bubble inflated by irresponsible sub-prime mortgage lending, the Great Recession (as it soon came to be known) hit the United States hard in the years that followed. From February 2008 to February 2010, the national economy shed a staggering 8.7 million jobs, with unemployment rising to 10% and a retraction of US GDP to 5.1% (the lowest it had been since the Great Depression).

• The Deepwater Horizon disaster
20 April 2010

When an explosion rocked Deepwater Horizon, an offshore oil rig operating in the Gulf of Mexico, it would end up taking the lives of 11 of its operators. However, the damage of the blowout would stretch even further. The disaster caused 4.9 million barrels of oil to seep into the surrounding waters, creating the largest accidental oil spill in the world.

The War on Terror

The United States pursued terrorism from the ruins of Manhattan to the mountains of Afghanistan – but was it successful?

"Our war on terror begins with al-Qaeda," President George W Bush told a joint session of Congress on 20 September 2001, "but it does not end there. It will not end until every terrorist group of global reach has been found, stopped, and defeated."

Nine days earlier, on 11 September 2001, four teams of al-Qaeda hijackers had used civilian aircraft as weapons against the symbols of America's financial and military power. Two planes struck the 'twin towers' of the World Trade Center in New York City, and a third hit the Pentagon in Washington, DC. A fourth plane, whose target is believed to have been the US Capitol or even the White House, crashed in Pennsylvania after its passengers, aware of what had happened to the other planes, overthrew their hijackers.

The '9/11' attacks killed 2,977 Americans, and transformed the USA's relationship with the rest of the world. For the first time in American history, its cities experienced the distinctive form of modern war that is terrorism. No less distinctively, the enemy might lodge in conventional states, but was not identical with their governments. Like the ambitions of the Islamists, the War on Terror spanned the globe.

In September 2001, al-Qaeda was hosted by the Taliban government in Afghanistan, but in the 1990s al-Qaeda had been hosted by the Islamist government of Sudan. Al-Qaeda's ideological roots lay in Egypt, in the Muslim Brotherhood founded by Hassan al-Banna in the 1920s, but the group had formed from mujahideen (Islamist volunteers) who had fought the Soviet invasion of Afghanistan in the 1980s. Meanwhile, al-Qaeda's leaders, Osama bin Laden and Ayman al-Zawahiri were Saudi and Egyptian respectively, and 14 of the 19 hijackers involved in 9/11 were Saudi Arabian.

The immediate American response to 9/11 was to give the Taliban an ultimatum to surrender al-Qaeda or face war. The Taliban refused. In October 2001, The USA and Britain invaded Afghanistan and overthrew the Taliban. Al-Qaeda retreated to Afghanistan's mountainous east. In December 2001, the Western allies attacked al-Qaeda at the mountain of Tora Bora, but Bin Laden escaped, probably to Pakistan. While the Americans attempted to build a democratic, pro-Western Afghanistan nation around the corrupt Hamid Karzai, the Taliban, with deep roots in sectors of Afghan society, revived. The occupation of Afghanistan quickly turned into an expensive and bloody war without end.

The objectives of the War on Terror were both comprehensive and amorphous: the ending of terrorism, and the ending of the circumstances which fostered it. The Bush administration made rapid strides in ending state support for terrorism by Sunni Arab states. Previously, Middle Eastern dictators and US allies like Pakistan and Saudi

> Three hijacked planes found their targets on 9/11. One – United Airlines Flight 93 – was brought down after a passenger revolt

An armoured Stryker vehicle lies on its side after being hit by a buried IED near Sheikh Hamid, Iraq in 2007

155

Expeditionary Strike Group Two deploys in the Atlantic as part of the War on Terror

Soldiers from the 101st Airborne Division and their Afghan interpreters talk and drink tea with village elders near Narizah, Afghanistan in 2002

April 2007: Canadian artillery at a forward base in Helmand Province, Afghanistan

Arabia had sponsored terrorists as a cheap way of projecting power, diverting popular dissatisfaction, and gaining credibility. Now, such behaviour invited invasion. Even Libya's Colonel Gaddafi, a lifelong exporter of terrorism, allied with the US.

Yet there was no consensus on what caused Islamist violence. If it was poverty, why did so many prominent leaders come, like Bin Laden, from wealthy and educated backgrounds? If it was a lack of democratic freedom and economic opportunity, could democracy and the market economy be imposed? And would Western interests be advanced if the people then voted for the Islamists? If it was a crisis within Islam, was it born of historic defeat at the hands of the 'Crusaders', or frustration at the repressive social codes of Muslim societies – and how exactly could this be alleviated by further exposure to the military power and permissive morals of the West?

All of these complexities became eclipsed by the War on Terror's next phase. The Iraqi dictator Saddam Hussein had previously invaded his neighbours, sponsored terrorism and worked to acquire nuclear weapons. The US intelligence services believed that Saddam was still developing weapons of mass destruction (WMDs), as well as buying uranium and supporting al-Qaeda. American officials also hoped that once this anti-Western tyrant had been toppled, Iraq could become a liberal democracy.

Encouraged by Britain's Tony Blair, Bush tried to win international sanction for an invasion at the United Nations, but was rebuffed. In the run-up to war, Israel's prime minister Ariel Sharon, no friend to Saddam Hussein, sent a deputation to

"They were caught in the middle of a religious and national civil war"

Washington, advising the Bush administration of its imminent folly. In March 2003, the Americans and British invaded regardless. On 1 May 2003, President Bush announced, 'Mission accomplished' from the deck of the USS Abraham Lincoln. Yet, as in Afghanistan, a quick victory on the battlefield led to the collapse of the enemy state and endless 'asymmetric warfare'.

Nor did democratisation work as planned. The Iraqi elections of 2005 brought Iraq's long-repressed Shia majority to power. Theocratic and allied with the mullahs of Iran – far greater sponsors of terrorism than Saddam Hussein had ever been – the Shias used their new powers against the Sunni and Kurdish minorities.

The Americans and British found themselves caught in the middle of a religious and national civil war, and losing casualties to suicide bombings, many carried out by Sunnis from neighbouring countries, or 'improvised explosive devices' (IEDs), many of whose improvisers had been trained in Iran.

As Iraq unravelled and international monitors failed to find convincing evidence for Saddam's WMD program, President Bush's approval rating collapsed. He won the 2004 election, but revelations of torture by American interrogators at Iraq's Abu Ghraib prison further damaged America's faltering credibility in the region and among its allies. So did a series of revelations

> 4,486 Americans died in Iraq, and 2,345 in Afghanistan. The wounded are estimated to number over a million

about strategies ill befitting the USA's claim to be sponsoring liberal democracy: the casting of terrorist prisoners into the military prison at Guantanamo Bay, a US naval base on Cuba; the use of secret interrogation programmes in which the CIA kidnapped Islamist suspects and flew them for 'rendition' (interrogation by torture) in friendly countries; and the assassination of terrorist suspects by drone strikes.

In his second term, Bush's administration retrenched its commitment to expanding democracy in Muslim-majority states. Now, the focus was on avoiding defeat in Afghanistan and Iraq. Massive 'surges' of troops saved the US dispensation in these states. Yet no sacrifice of blood and treasure was enough to produce peace, let alone stability.

In June 2007, while Shia and Sunni militias conducted ethnic cleansing in the suburbs of Baghdad, the pro-Iranian majority in the Iraqi parliament voted that the United States should leave Iraq. Tony Blair, Bush's stalwart ally, had already announced that the small British occupation force at Basra would be leaving. In December 2008, the US and Iraqi governments signed a Status of Forces Agreement, under which all American troops would leave Iraq by the end of 2011.

The crisis of the US economy in the Bush administration's last weeks was the final blow for the War on Terror. Bush left office with the lowest approval rating in the history of electoral surveys. Bush's successor, Barack Obama, campaigned on a promise to extract the USA from foreign

An Iraqi man awaits interrogation after a raid on the village of Qarah Cham by Iraqi Police and American troops in 2007

adventures, and concentrate on 'nation building at home'. The new Democratic administration abandoned controversial phrases like 'War on Terror' and 'Islamic extremism', preferring instead to speak of targeting specific 'networks' of 'criminals'.

Yet the Obama administration stepped up the use of targeted assassination by drones. It overthrew Colonel Gaddafi, yet failed to create a stable Libya in the aftermath. It even sent American troops back to Iraq to combat the rise of ISIS, a direct offshoot from al-Qaeda. Was the War on Terror really over, or had it become a new reality, which Americans preferred not to think about? And could a global war against an idea and small groups of individuals, not a state or an army, ever be over?

In 2013, a Brown University study reported that the total cost of the Iraq War was $1.7 trillion. Another study, allowing for long-term care of veterans and economic damage and interest rates, arrived at a cost of $6 trillion by 2053. 4,486 Americans died in Iraq, and 2,345 in Afghanistan. More than a million Americans were wounded, many severely. The damage to the USA's standing in the world is incalculable.

So too is the damage caused by the war's knock-on effects. The Arab Spring of 2011 marked the end of the old dictatorships, some of them, like Hosni Mubarak of Egypt, pro-American. But Egypt's free elections brought to power the Muslim Brotherhood, the very organisation that had inspired al-Qaeda. Meanwhile, Iran continued to subvert its Sunni neighbours, and Syria collapsed into civil war. The War on Terror's legacy of human and strategic disaster continues.

Operation Enduring Freedom – Horn of Africa

In 2002, the global War on Terror turned to Islamic extremism in the Horn of Africa, and piracy on its seas

The US-led invasion of Afghanistan was code-named Operation Enduring Freedom (OEF), but the global anti-Islamic extremist strategy also included several other campaigns, like OEF-Philippines and OEF-Trans Sahara. Launched in 2002, OEF-Horn of Africa is focused on Somalia and the waters of the Red Sea. Like many other War on Terror operations, it continues today, despite the Obama administration's declarations of 2009 that the War on Terror was over.

Piracy is endemic to the Somali coast. The motives of the pirates are less religious than economic. When Somalia collapsed into civil war in 1991, the country turned into a failed state ruled by tribal militias. The civil war has never fully stopped. Millions of Somalis have lost their lives and homes. Islamist groups have exploited this vacuum, and also the sympathies of many tribal leaders.

Somalia abuts the Red Sea, and the approach to the Suez Canal. This makes Somalia's instability a problem for global trade and communications. Furthermore, the presence of Islamist militias like al-Shabab is a danger to neighbouring states like Kenya, which has frequently suffered raids by Somali-based militias and terrorist attacks planned in Somalia.

While the US-led wars in Afghanistan and Iraq dominated the news in the early 2000s, the anti-terror war in the Horn of Africa received less attention. Instead, Somalia's sufferings have been fictionalised by Hollywood

as the backdrop to American travails in dramas like *Blackhawk Down* (2001), in which a pre-War on Terror raid by Special Forces goes wrong; and *Captain Phillips* (2013), with Tom Hanks as the captain of a hijacked freighter.

The reality of OEF-Horn of Africa is less dramatic: an endless process of intelligence gathering, collaboration with local forces, raids and interrogations – and regular use of drone strikes. Since 2002, 21 countries have contributed personnel to OEF-Horn of Africa operations, including forces from the African Union. Twelve hundred pirates have been captured, and more than 500 al-Shabab members and 31 American soldiers have been killed.

Barack Obama

America's first black president was tasked with restoring the country's shattered reputation abroad and resurrecting it from the doldrums of the Great Recession

On 20 January 2009, downtown Washington DC was swamped with millions of supporters, generating the largest inauguration crowds since Lyndon Johnson's re-election in 1965. The man they had come to see: President Barack Obama. Elected to the nation's highest office at the tender age of 47, his only political experience consisting of one term in the Senate, Obama was a sensation.

Obama's upbringing was atypical, yet emblematic of the American dream that came to underscore his political story. Born in Honolulu to a mother from Kansas and a father from Kenya, he lived in Indonesia and Hawaii, splitting time between his mother and grandparents. He was unsettled

as a teen, and admitted to smoking marijuana and experimenting with cocaine to fit in. He was rigorously home-schooled for much of his childhood by his mother, and he credited this occasionally stern upbringing with instilling in him the values that would allow him to succeed. He gained national attention in 1991 when he was elected the first black president of the Harvard Law Review. He also began writing a book on race relations that would become his bestselling memoir, *Dreams From My Father*. Obama began teaching at the University of Chicago Law School, lecturing on constitutional law, and working as a community organiser. During his political career, he would often return to the measured, patient tones that he honed teaching law.

Later political opponents mocked Obama's days as a community organiser and point to his associations with unsavoury characters that he cultivated, but his work with black churches in Chicago helped bolster his image as a man of the people, rather than an elite and disconnected Ivy League scholar.

During his candidacy for the Illinois Senate, Obama gained notoriety with his bitter opposition to Bush's invasion of Iraq. At the 2004 Democratic National Convention, he electrified his party with the keynote speech, rising from obscurity to a genuine party leader. Despite a fruitful first term as Senator, Obama was a political neophyte, so few expected him to pose a serious challenge to Hillary Clinton in the lead up to the 2008 presidential election. However, Obama's accessible, tech-savvy campaign harnessed an engaged new cadre of young voters and small fundraisers. He was an excellent orator, charismatic, and rode a wave of adulation and excitement to the White House, defeating John McCain in a landslide victory.

The country was in a bad state, suffering from the wounds inflicted by a runaway Wall Street, and dealing with the worst recession since the Great Depression. Obama embraced a radical spending plan, rejecting the austerity that many European nations opted for. His stimulus plan was his most lasting and resounding success, as the country recovered quickly from the recession and unemployment decreased steadily over his two terms.

When Obama was inaugurated, the US was also embroiled in two unpopular wars in Iraq and Afghanistan. He had promised to end both wars, and when he was re-elected in 2012, he campaigned on his successes in the Middle East, having ostensibly ended the Iraq War in 2011. However, as tensions boiled over in Syria and Iraq, Obama sent troops back in — and he never did withdraw troops from Afghanistan altogether.

His presidency was characterised throughout by battles with a stubborn Congress — the Democrats had a majority in both Houses in his first term, but that didn't last. He failed to follow through on his campaign pledge to close the notorious Guantanamo Bay detention facility when Congress refused to cooperate, but supporters will wonder if he could have done more. His lingering achievement was

his Affordable Care Act, dubbed ObamaCare, which, although neutered somewhat in Congress, was a genuine and lasting effort to make basic healthcare available to all Americans. His efforts at working with Republicans on landmark legislation foundered, and he repeatedly faced the threat of government shutdowns from an increasingly fractious Republican House critical of his excessive spending. In the wake of the Sandy Hook school shooting, Obama reiterated his desire to pass gun-control legislation, but was again thwarted.

Obama will be remembered for his deep commitment to progressive ideals. He repealed the 'Don't ask, don't tell' policy, allowing openly gay men and women to serve in the military. And in 2015, a Supreme Court featuring two of his appointed justices made same-sex marriage federally legal. He considered himself an arbitrator of racial disputes, and often intervened in police matters (notably issuing statements on the killings of Michael Brown and Trayvon Martin), yet towards the end of his second term it became clear that racial tensions in the US were worse than ever before.

Obama's two terms featured notable foreign policy successes, the highlights being the rapprochement with Cuba, the killing of Osama Bin Laden, and the successful negotiations with Iran over its nuclear program. However, those were overshadowed by his failure to deal with ISIS, his sluggish action in Syria, an inability to control the security environment in Iraq, a bombing campaign in Libya that left it a failed state, frosty relations with Israel, the debacle in Benghazi, backtracking on a warning to Bashar al-Assad over chemical weapons use, and repeated humiliation at the hands of Vladimir Putin and Russia. Critics will find similarities in the foreign policy of Obama and his predecessor, as he continued Bush's extra-judicial drone strikes in dozens of countries, and stepped up a mass surveillance plan through the National Security Agency. Obama swept in on a platform of hope, and to his credit delivered on many domestic items, salvaged the economy, and did much to restore the United States' reputation abroad, yet he failed to realise many of his promises and was widely seen as indecisive when it mattered most.

> Obama worked in Baskin Robbins as a teenager and as a result can't stand ice cream

Obama won a Grammy in 2006 for the audiobook reading of his memoir

Life in the time of Barack Obama

The Great Recession
A sub-prime mortgage crisis, a shady default swaps market, and the bundling of exotic financial instruments combined with deregulation of Wall Street in the 1990s and 2000s led to a total collapse of the financial system and the housing market in 2007. Obama creditably resurrected the car industry, regulated the banks, and restored the economy over his two terms.

The Iraq War 'ends'
In early 2009, Obama announced that he would end the Iraq War within 18 months. The US public was upset with the fraudulent entry into the war and the subsequent failure of nation-building. Obama kept his word. However, when the Islamic State shrugged off the American-trained and American-supported Iraqi army, captured Mosul and carried out ethnic cleansing campaigns in 2014, thousands of US troops re-entered Iraq.

Osama meets his watery grave
In May 2011, CIA intelligence revealed that Osama Bin Laden was living in Abbottabad, Pakistan. Obama rejected a plan to bomb the compound, opting instead for a raid by Navy Seals. The raid was successful, and Bin Laden was shot and buried at sea. Though he was no longer actively involved in Al-Qaeda, the raid was considered a strategic and moral victory for the US and bolstered Obama's popularity.

Spying among friends
When Edward Snowden revealed the NSA's overreach in collecting data, the US faced a stern backlash abroad. German Chancellor Angela Merkel was particularly enraged that US intelligence was listening to her mobile phone calls. The NSA agreed to stop the overeager collection of data but Obama's popularity dipped.

A thin red line
When Syrian dictator Bashar al-Assad used sarin gas, a chemical weapon outlawed by the Geneva Convention, to murder thousands of innocent civilians in Damascus, Obama faced a conundrum. He had called the use of such weapons a red line not to be crossed, at the threat of immediate military reprisal. Yet Obama backed down from his threat and Putin mediated the situation instead, humiliating him.

The Affordable Care Act
Obama's most lasting achievement was healthcare reform, which he pushed through in 2010 with the Patient Protection and Affordable Care Acts. Despite serious opposition from the right-wing Tea Party movement and virtually every Republican in Congress, the act carried and was reaffirmed by the Supreme Court in 2012. Despite a slow roll-out of government-sponsored healthcare plans, and subsequent opposition by state governors, the Act has made affordable healthcare available to working-class Americans, and granted the consumer protection from predatory insurance company practices. Whether it will last following the rise of Donald Trump remains to be seen.

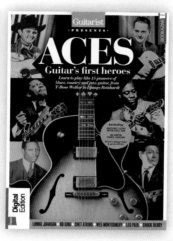
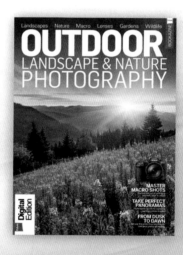

DISCOVER THE STORY OF THE AFRICAN AMERICAN FIGHT FOR EQUALITY

Take a fascinating journey back through the defining moments of the Civil Rights Movement and meet some of the movement's key figures, from Dr Martin Luther King Jr and Rosa Parks to Malcolm X

NEW

ALL ABOUT HISTORY

BOOKAZINE

CIVIL RIGHTS MOVEMENT

The story of the African American fight for freedom and equality

ON SALE NOW

ISBN 978-1-78546-983-1

9 781785 469831

★ ICONIC LEADERS ★ KEY MOMENTS ★ THE NEW MOVEMENT